IAN
ROBERTSON

Rugby: Talking a Good Game

IAN ROBERTSON

Rugby: Talking a Good Game

47 years of fun with the BBC

With Chris Hewett

HODDER

First published in Great Britain in 2018 by Hodder & Stoughton
An Hachette UK company

This paperback edition published in 2019

Copyright © Ian Rankin 2018

Paperback ISBN 9781473694675
eBook ISBN 9781473694668

Typeset in Adobe Caslon Pro by
Palimpsest Book Production Ltd, Falkirk, Stirlingshire

Printed and bound in Great Britain by Clays Ltd, Elcograf S.p.A.

Hodder & Stoughton policy is to use papers that are natural, renewable
and recyclable products and made from wood grown in sustainable forests.
The logging and manufacturing processes are expected to conform
to the environmental regulations of the country of origin.

Hodder & Stoughton Ltd
Carmelite House
50 Victoria Embankment
London EC4Y 0DZ

www.hodder.co.uk

To my children Duncan and Clare
And my long suffering P.A. Joanna

CONTENTS

THE FULL-TIME WHISTLE

IT is the back end of February 2018 and I'm heading north on the most familiar journey in a lifetime of ramblings and roamings across the landscape of rugby union: from London to Edinburgh. Or to put it in a more personal way, I'm travelling from the place where I made my home long ago to the place I still regard as home, especially when the annual Calcutta Cup match is dominating the back pages of the newspapers and eating into the broadcast schedules on both television and radio. The two cities are 350 miles apart, give or take, so there is ample time for reflection. And on this day, of all days, two thoughts occur to me. Firstly, I'm thinking that if England play well – really, really well – at Murrayfield come the weekend, they might finish within 20 points of Scotland. I'm not completely sure of my ground on this one, admittedly, but as the Scots have lost all but five of their last 30 fixtures against the great imperial power from across the border, I have good reason to have faith in our cunning ploy of lulling the opposition into a false sense of security. I've had dealings with dozens of England players down the years and feel sure they'll fall for it. They won't see through us on this occasion.

As for the second thing going through my mind, this has nothing to do with hope or expectation and it certainly doesn't involve any clutching at straws. The fact of the matter – the cold reality of the situation – is that this will be my final Calcutta Cup commentary for the BBC. Or for anyone else. As I cast my mind back over Scotland–England contests of the recent past, not to mention those played in an age so dim and distant and thoroughly antiquated that we are barely talking about the same sport, I cannot say for sure when I was first handed the microphone and told to get on with painting a word picture for all the millions of poor unfortunates without a ticket. I am, however, absolutely certain that this will be a poignant few days. There will still be a few matches left to me as I move towards retirement after almost half a century of broadcasting, but none remotely like this one. This has the potential for tears, and I'd far rather they be tears of joy at a great Scottish triumph than tears of any other description.

News of my decision to call time on my career has been in the public domain for some weeks and there has been quite a reaction, one way or another. Matt Dawson, a World Cup-winning scrum-half with England and a close BBC colleague for well over a decade, talked to me for an hour, live on the wireless, about my favourite memories: one of which, I took considerable pleasure in pointing out, was of him leading his country to a crushing 19–13 defeat at Murrayfield in 2000, the turn-of-the-century tournament that marked the beginning of the Six Nations era. Even before the airing of that programme, I had received more kind words and best wishes than I could ever begin to count. In the days since, the response has been astonishing. I cannot help thinking back to the very start of my career, when dear Bill McLaren – the finest rugby broadcaster of them all, be it past, present or (I'm willing to bet my last penny) future – suggested I might try my hand at commentary and lit up the way ahead for me. If I'm the subject of this much attention, I wonder, what must it have been like for a true great like Bill?

It is one of the sadder truths of my trade that Bill's final commentary had taken place somewhere other than his beloved Murrayfield. While he ended his long spell behind the mic with a Scotland match, it was against Wales in Cardiff in 2002. 'It's one of the things I got wrong, son,' he once confessed to me with characteristic humility, even though he'd had the satisfaction of watching blue just about prevail over red on the day of his goodbye. I tried to persuade him to join me and the rest of the BBC radio team at the 2003 World Cup, as he had done at previous tournaments between 1991 and 1999. Sharing those commentaries with him had been among the highlights of my career. But he decided it wasn't for him – 'I've thought about it, son, and I'm nae doin' it' – and concentrated instead on writing his excellent book, *Rugby's Great Heroes and Entertainers*. In light of all that, I'm counting my blessings as match day approaches. A farewell to the glories of Calcutta Cup rugby at Murrayfield. How wonderful. Especially as Scotland, to my feverishly patriotic mind at least, are a team of world-beaters in the making!

Unlike Bill, to whom I owe so much, I am going under my own steam, at a time completely of my own choosing. For almost 45 years, my discussions with the BBC's head of sport had been conducted on a two-year cycle, to cover World Cups and Lions tours. Since 1974, when I made my first Lions trip to South Africa and watched Willie John McBride's great team rip through Springbok country like wildfire and complete their 22-match itinerary undefeated, I had covered virtually everything worth covering in every corner of the world. Never had it registered with me that I might not fancy another long-haul flight to Auckland or Sydney or Johannesburg. But now it dawned on me, slowly but surely, that the 2019 World Cup in Japan might be a World Cup too far, especially for a man in his mid-70s, and when asked, I found myself saying: 'No, I don't think so. 2018 I can do, but that's my lot.'

A World Cup is a very demanding business for a BBC correspondent, because he's the focal point – the person who has to be on top of the tournament as a whole, not just England's part in it. And maintaining an accurate overview of 48 matches, the majority of which he'll be following from some distant media centre or hotel room, is just a little more difficult than falling off a log. In English-speaking countries, you at least have an even-money chance of surviving intact: when everything is being conducted in your own language, it's undeniably easier to operate at top level – to get to the people you need to see, to arrange visits to training so you can familiarise yourself with players, study their movements and give yourself the best chance of recognising them in the twinkling of an eye when a big match is being contested. Even when France hosted the event in 2007, a number of important fixtures were played in Scotland and Wales, which made it possible for me to base myself in familiar surroundings for decent periods of time. But seven whole weeks in Japan? With one team playing in Higashiosaka, another in Kamaishi and a third in God knows where? With no guarantee of me understanding so much as a syllable of the local television coverage? In theory, it would be a rather romantic thing to bow out over a plate of Sandai Wagyu and a glass of saki. In practice? That's a different thing entirely.

Once I'd made the decision to stick with my eight World Cups and leave the ninth to someone else, I did not think for a second about revisiting it. It did, however, ensure that the 2018 Six Nations and the Calcutta Cup date at Murrayfield would have an added emotional charge.

THOSE PRECIOUS RUPEES

IT is not my intention to make John Jeffrey and Dean Richards feel worse now than they did at the time, or to reopen the case in an effort to put them behind bars. I raise it because there is a reason the original Calcutta Cup is kept under lock and key these days, well out of reach of those players who spend one afternoon a year wrestling each other to the ground in pursuit of it. The oldest prize in rugby is fragile, if not quite as fragile as it was in the early hours of 6 March 1988, after the Scotland flanker JJ and the England No.8 Deano had kissed and made up following a fractious game at Murrayfield by restarting the match in the dark streets of Edinburgh, using the ancient trophy as a replacement ball. It was one thing, back in the time of Queen Victoria and the British Raj, to melt down 270 silver rupees in the casting of the prize – rupees worth scores of thousands of pounds in today's money. It was quite another to subject it to a panel-beating so severe that by the time the two forwards had finished, it could have been slipped under the hotel room door of the Scottish Rugby Union president and his good lady wife.

6

A quarter of a century after that rather notorious incident, the *Daily Telegraph* marked the anniversary by running an amusing resume in which both players offered their considered thoughts on events, as did a variety of characters more tangentially involved. Dean thought the bottle of whisky on each table at the after-match banquet amounted to 'a recipe for disaster'. For his part, JJ acknowledged that the dinner was a 'fairly boisterous' affair. As for Geoff Cooke, the victorious England manager (assuming the V-word is appropriate in connection with a desperately poor game that would not have yielded a try had it lasted a month) – well, he had an interesting take. Geoff didn't pin the blame on the lavish supply of single malt. Instead, he suggested that the England players had been taken unawares by the haggis and neeps served up by the caterers. Intoxication by sheep's innards and root vegetables? There's a radical explanation for you. The manager also pointed out, perhaps with greater justification, that as neither Dean nor JJ were 'the greatest ball-handlers even when they were sober', the cup was always going to be at risk once they started passing it, one to the other, as they made their way across a night-shrouded Waverley Bridge.

Unlike the two back-rowers, I never found a way of getting myself banned from the game. (Dean was given a one-match stand-down by the Rugby Football Union, if memory serves; JJ was suspended for six months. Justice moves in mysterious ways, its wonders to perform.) There again, I spent rather less time with my hands on the Calcutta Cup than either of the convicted. I made three appearances in the annual fixture, losing twice before winning at the final attempt. I like to think that I had the last laugh, given that the points aggregate over the trilogy was 23–21 to Scotland, but the frustrating truth of the matter is that we could have won each of the games. Had we done so I'd have spent the last half a century sleeping more easily in my bed, because for a Scottish sportsman, there is no feeling quite as sweet as prevailing over the English.

The sense of rivalry between the two nations was a part of my upbringing in central Edinburgh, where the family home in Great King Street was comfortably close enough to the thronging match-day thoroughfare of Princes Street – and, indeed, to the old Murrayfield, with its towering main stand and mighty banks of terracing – to soak up something of the atmosphere of a big international weekend. My father John, also known as 'Jock' unusually enough, was a two-handicap golfer who thoroughly enjoyed his rugby, but when it came to team sport he was more of a football man when you boiled it down. He was a decent centre-forward who made up for his lack of height by packing a powerful shot. In fact, he could shoot off both feet, and his prowess in this department caught the attention of Inverness, a forerunner of Inverness Caledonian Thistle, and he played there as a pure amateur for four years.

When I was growing up in the 1950s, Scotland's record of success against England in football was every bit as dire as that of our rugby team in the same decade. But my father was a very happy man when the dam finally burst and results started going the right way in the early '60s. A year after suffering defeat by the small margin of 9–3, when the England footballers proved themselves capable of scoring goals in greater quantity than their rugby men scored points, the likes of Jim Baxter, Billy McNeill, Denis Law and Ian St John turned things around, embarking on a brief but memorable winning streak that put the broadest of smiles on the face of the Robertson house.

As well as following the fortunes of the national team, he also had a great love for Aberdeen FC and positively revelled in their success under an imported Glaswegian by the name of Alex Ferguson, who managed the team to three league championships, four Scottish cups and a European Cup Winners title in the space of seven seasons. As far as Dad was concerned, Sir Alex, as he is now, was made of different stuff to mere mortals, and I have to say that following a few dealings of my own with him, I've arrived at the same conclusion.

I first came across Alex at a charity golf day on the banks of Loch Lomond in support of the Macmillan nurses, who do such a fantastic job in providing specialist care to cancer sufferers. For one reason or another, he was not best disposed to the BBC at that time, so when he appeared in the bar of the Cameron House hotel for a pre-dinner drink, I was hiding behind a pillar. From my place of concealment, I heard one of the organisers say: 'Alex, you've very kindly agreed to say a few words to the guests. Are you still happy to do so?' 'Yes, I'll give it five minutes.' 'Could we press you for 10 minutes, or even 15? We could do it as an interview, if that would make it easier.' 'Oh yes, I'd much prefer to be interviewed. Who do you have?' 'Well, we have from the BBC . . .' There ensued what sounded like a small explosion. '*No!*' There followed some further detonations. '*No! No! No! Not* the BBC.' The whole room was shaking. 'Can I just mention,' persisted the organiser, brave beyond the call of duty, 'that it's the rugby correspondent, Ian Rob . . . ' 'Och, no problem,' said Alex, suddenly calling off the heavy weaponry as I ventured meekly into view. 'Never met him, but I'm sure he's a top man. Come here, son.' He gave me the biggest of hugs and then sat down for the interview.

Later on, I set the auction in motion by offering, just a little cheekily, something that didn't exist: namely, a wholly mythical three-year deal with Cristiano Ronaldo, who at that point was about to leave Manchester United. 'I think £10,000 would be a reasonable starting point,' I said. '£10,000, anyone?' Alex immediately raised his hand. 'Could we go to £20,000?' I asked. 'No,' he responded, decisively. 'Going once, going twice . . . ' There and then, he sealed the deal for £10,000. I felt obliged to tell him, for the avoidance of doubt, that I'd been joking about Ronaldo. 'I worked that out, son,' he replied. Subsequently, I asked Alex if he could help a lad from the Make-A-Wish charity – a 12-year-old from Belfast, terminally ill. The height of his ambition was to see Manchester United play, just once. Might that be at all possible? 'Nothing's impossible, son,' Alex said. 'How about this weekend? I'll sort the hotel and make sure there's a car at the airport.' And on the day, the manager went to the airport himself, took the lad to the game, made sure he met the players afterwards and sent him off with some famous jerseys as part of a whole bag of souvenirs. Amazing.

Dad was a busy man. After serving as an RAF squadron leader in India during the war he went into banking and worked in London for a while before accepting a job with the Clydesdale Bank and returning to Scotland. He had a wonderful time of it in Edinburgh before, quite late in life, being promoted to manager and relocating to Thurso, which is so far north it might as well be in Scandinavia.

Meanwhile, my mother Alice contented herself with regular games of tennis – she was a good player, if not quite the female forerunner of Andy Murray – and also indulged her passion for the piano. While she was not a trained musician, she could play wonderfully by ear. I once asked her if it might not be easier to use her fingers, but she didn't think it a particularly funny joke. Right to the end of her life, she could find her way around a keyboard. Mum spent her final two years in a nursing home in the Golders Green area of North London and one Christmas, spent at my cousin's house, she decided to go back to her residence immediately after the turkey. 'No, no,' we said. 'There's pudding to come. And besides, you haven't provided us with our musical entertainment.' She told us not to be ridiculous, claiming that she hadn't touched a piano in 20 years, but she finally relented and served up 'Land of Hope and Glory'. It was note perfect. When my daughter Clare suggested a follow-up number from the top of what I still call the hit parade – needless to say, I didn't recognise the title, or anything else in its connection – my mother looked bemused. 'Tell me how it goes,' she said. Within a few seconds of Clare humming the tune, she'd worked out how the verse would unfold and made a very good stab at predicting the chorus as well. What a gift. If I could have a wish now, I would love to be blessed with just a little of mum's innate musical ability. Failing that, I'd settle for being something other than completely tone deaf. Sadly, it's probably too much to ask.

What I could do, as far back as I can remember, was run with a ball, kick a ball and pass a ball. The ball in question was not always oval-shaped; indeed, I must have been eight or nine before I had any serious brush with rugby. As a very young boy, football was the thing: partly because of my father's love of it, partly because it was the simplest of games for kids to play whenever they found a patch of grass to themselves. At the grand old age of four and a half I joined the ranks of the infants at George Watson's School, where there was the occasional opportunity to throw a rugby ball around on a minimal-contact basis. Touch rugby, they call it now, and at this point I should acknowledge that there are those in

Scotland – my first Test captain Jim Telfer, His Royal Gruffness, being the most prominent among them – who continue to argue with great passion that I never played anything but touch rugby, even in an international shirt. The only time I succeeded in confusing Jim on this subject was during a game against Argentina in Buenos Aires when, in attempting to minimise contact with the ferocious and unusually substantial Puma centre Alejandro Travaglini, I somehow stumbled into him and brought him crashing to earth just short of our line. Jim, pounding across the field towards us, looked down and shouted: 'Grrreeeaaatt tackle! Bugger me . . . it's *you*, Robertson!!!'

Entry to the senior school at 11 signalled the start of rugby proper and from there on, it was my preferred sport, with cricket a distant second. Yet even then, the playground was a football arena rather than a rugby one, and if any of us were hanging around after classes had ended for the day, the round ball remained king. My first coach – or at least, the first coach I encountered whose understanding of rugby extended beyond the ability to count to 15 and a vague notion that all in brawls were meant to be the exception rather than the rule – was Donald Scott. He ran the school's representative teams in age groups from the mid-teens upwards. More importantly to us budding enthusiasts, he played top-level club rugby for Langholm, an age-old club situated in what is now Dumfries and Galloway, and, most thrillingly of all, won caps for Scotland as both a wing and a centre. Langholm compete in the East Regional League structure these days, but they were a genuine force in the land in the 1950s and Donald was one of the men who drove them forward at that time. When I recall him now, I see him as a Jeremy Guscott-style glider who could beat people hands down with a barely perceptible sway of the hips and a light touch on the accelerator. It was certainly exciting to be in his orbit.

Donald made two Calcutta Cup appearances in the side led by Peter Kininmonth, one of the more accomplished No.8s in our rugby history – a back-rower deemed good enough to have featured in three of the four Tests in the hard fought Lions Test series in New Zealand in 1950. Donald played on the wing against England at Murrayfield that year, winning his second cap and helping us to win 13–11. The following year at Twickenham, when he moved to the centre, there was no such glorious outcome, although we went very close on a day of drenching rain before losing 5–3 (one try apiece, with a conversion by the Gloucester full-back Bill Hook deciding the issue).

I was too young to have watched Donald perform in the national shirt, but he was an inspirational figure to me. Apart from anything else, his status as a Calcutta Cup winner put him in a very special category of sporting hero. Yes, the fixture meant that much to us, even in our sporting infancy – and when, as I grew a little older, I was taken to Murrayfield with my schoolmates and was given a seat on the touchline among crowds of 75,000 and upwards, there was no better experience in the world. I didn't go to every international with the school – we had to take it in turns, for tickets were relatively scarce despite the vast numbers who managed to find their way into the stadium – but by the time we were 16, we were able to go under our own steam and feast our eyes on the mighty deeds of some true greats of the game: the full-back Ken Scotland from the Warriston corner of Edinburgh, whose passing was a thing of beauty; the wing Arthur Smith from Castle Douglas, who was one of the sport's supreme natural talents; and the Borders prop Hugh McLeod, who always liked to address his colleagues as 'my wee disciples', not that his broad accent was easily understood by the posher university types who frequently appeared in the back division. Every match was something to relish, partly because there were so few of them: during my 14 years at George Watson's there were only five home matches against full international touring sides (starting with the seminal Springboks of 1951, who just about sneaked past us 44–0) and one abroad, against the South Africans in Port Elizabeth in 1960.

If the Five Nations, as it was then, was beyond question the thing that really mattered, easily the most vital bit of it was the annual meeting with England. It was the defining event of our rugby year and probably still is – as it was, and probably still is, for Ireland and Wales. I'm not sure if it was quite as massive for the English, with their assumption of supremacy and their general air of entitlement, but if you asked any of the Scots I played alongside who they would like to beat if only one victory could be guaranteed, the reply would be unhesitating. The same went, and I rather think continues to go, for the supporters. One or two might, with a gun to the head, wonder if a win over the All Blacks might be marginally preferable, on the grounds that the Irish beat them in Chicago a couple of years ago, leaving us as the only one of the sport's eight foundation unions still waiting for a first triumph over the silver fern. But it would be one or two only. When you talk to the multitudes, they want the Calcutta Cup in their possession. In my days in the navy blue shirt, you didn't have to be a Sassenach basher like Jim Telfer to feel this way, although Jim had an unerring knack of putting everyone in touch with their inner William Wallaces when he delivered his team talks in the late 1960s. I'm convinced that we all felt the same, deep down. Even those of us whose nationalist instincts were only a tiny part of our make-up.

When I rummage through my small rugby library for history books that give a flavour of Scotland–England matches in the early days, I never fail to be amused at the thought of matches being played in parts of Edinburgh long lost to big-time sporting contests. The inaugural international in 1871 – the first of its type to be played anywhere in the world – went ahead at Raeburn Place, a patch of land adjacent to the main road running through the Stockbridge area of the city and acquired by the Edinburgh Academicals club as long ago as 1853. It now has a tiny capacity and is currently the subject of a fractious argument over development plans, yet it was Scotland's preferred rugby venue for a quarter of a century. Then there was Powderhall in the Broughton area of town, renowned as the place where the Olympic sprinter Eric Liddell – *Chariots of Fire* and all that – did his training. It was turned into a greyhound track in the 1920s and is now a housing estate. As for Inverleith, which hosted 10 Calcutta Cup games either side of the Great War, the very name conjures images of grandeur. The land for the pitches was purchased by the Scottish Rugby Union at the very end of the 19th century and it was only after the opening of Murrayfield that its status as an international venue diminished. Both Stewart's Melville College and the Edinburgh Academy own parts of the site, but the area is best known for offering some of more expensive property-buying opportunities in the country.

My own international career started in 1968 – in a Calcutta Cup match, of course – and ended some two and a half years later, when a herd of elephantine forwards landed on me during a Scotland trial match and gave both of my knees an orthopaedic examination of the most painful kind. One knee survived it, but not the other: medial ligaments could be sorted in those days, but cruciate ligaments were beyond repair. Over the course of my eight caps, seven of which were won as a fly-half, my scrum-half partners tended to chop and change: sometimes it was Gordon Connell of Trinity Academicals, a fantastic player; sometimes it was Duncan Paterson of Gala, another outstanding performer; once it was

Graham Young, my club partner at Watsonians, who joined me at the hub of things against Wales in Cardiff. Things might have been different had the selectors, bless them, not been funereally slow to conclude that the problem was not at No.9 at all, but at No.10! They're not always the quickest between the ears, committee types, but I was more than happy to leave them to their misapprehensions.

At the time of my selection, I was engaged in a year's post-graduate study at Cambridge University, having achieved a blindingly half-decent second-class degree in English and History from Aberdeen University. I was also turning out for London Scottish, because after the Varsity Match – the only thing that counted for much rugby-wise as far as the Light Blues were concerned – the student fixture list was full of what might now be described as 'Mickey Mouse games'. I thought I might be in with a shot at being picked because I had a pal on the selection panel – a fellow Watsonian by the name of George Thomson. Yet I knew the big calls were made by the chairman Charlie Drummond, who may not have been a natural ally, hailing as he did from the Borders. So when the letter of confirmation was delivered to my college, it was a moment to savour. It read as follows: 'We would like to congratulate you on your selection against England at Murrayfield on March 16th. We meet on Wednesday night at 8pm at the Braid Hills Hotel. Please bring with you one pair of rugby boots. We will present you with your stockings and jersey, which must last the whole season. Should you wish to swap your jersey with a member of the opposition, you will be able to buy a replacement for 15 shillings. If you are arriving by train at Waverley, you can catch either the 23 or the 27 bus. Your fare will be refunded in full.'

As welcome messages went, it was some way short of exuberant. However, it was positively gushing in comparison with Jim Telfer's address as captain. 'If you're not going to bloody well tackle people,' he told me, leaving me in no doubt that he'd watched my recent performances with intense interest, 'it would help if you at least tried to slow them down.' Decades later, in his memoirs, I was relieved at the conciliatory tone he used in describing my contribution, calling me simply 'not the most courageous defender' he'd ever played alongside. I subsequently met him at a rugby dinner and thanked him for his generosity. 'I know,' he said, putting on his long face and shaking his head mournfully. 'The editor said it might be libellous if I called you a wimp.' He has a way with him, does Jim.

The 1968 game was a disappointment, even though I was thrilled to be a part of it. Scotland had won their two previous Calcutta Cup fixtures at Murrayfield and there had been an indescribably mesmerising 3–3 draw before that, so we felt we had more than a chance, especially when we reached the turnaround 6–0 up, with Stewart Wilson kicking a penalty on his final appearance and Gordon Connell contributing one of the more unusual drop goals I'd ever seen, hooking the ball over the bar from a distance of six feet maximum while bending backwards like a contortionist caught in a hurricane. I could understand Gordon's reasoning: his only alternative was to pass to me. Unfortunately, we didn't see the ball after the interval and things slipped away from us. There wasn't a great deal of know-how in either side: seven of the Scottish side were in single figures when it came to caps; almost all the English were in the same boat. But my opposite number was Mike Weston, the captain, and he'd been around a good deal longer than every other back on the field. He exerted some control on events and when Mike Coulman, a tight-head prop from Moseley, broke free from a line-out and ran in from the unimaginable distance of 30 yards, our half-time advantage was wiped out. It stayed wiped when Jock Turner, our centre, missed a last-minute penalty shot from no great distance. Oh well.

By the time we reached Twickenham the following year, both line-ups had changed dramatically. England had a huge pack, full of forwards who would make proper names for themselves: John Pullin, a hooker with a high level of technique to go with his farmer's strength, was a hell of a front-rower; Peter Larter and Nigel Horton were four stones heavier than our two locks, even though Alastair McHarg and Peter Brown were nobody's idea of midgets; and the renowned Budge Rogers was back on the flank, having been absent from the championship in '68. They also had a bunch of relatively inexperienced but dangerous threequarters: Keith Fielding and Rodney Webb on the wings, David Duckham and John Spencer at centre. They had spanked the French in their previous game and their form was slightly ominous.

As for the Scotland team, none of the back division had won more than seven caps and leaving aside Jim and our hooker, Frank Laidlaw, we weren't exactly full of international iron up front, either. And me? I was chosen at inside centre – a role I had never performed before and would never perform again. I considered myself to be a fly-half for one very good reason: I *was* a fly-half. I'd been a fly-half at school, at university and at club level. Every now and again, perhaps on six or seven occasions, I'd turned out at full-back for Watsonians, the team I'd joined after the Cambridge–London Scottish days ended. It seemed okay to me and I was happy to have a go, on the basis that it was such a lovely position from which to attack. There was no better feeling than timing a run into the line, hitting a pass at speed and cruising into the distance without some stupid opposition forward lumbering around with decapitation as his default option. What wasn't lovely, of course, was that full-backs also had to defend – and defence really wasn't my thing, as Jim had detected without wasting too much time on a formal investigatory process. Whenever the ball went high, one of my fellow Watsonians would shout 'Your ball, Robbo,' more in hope than expectation. 'Don't think so,' I would shout back, decisively. 'Bye.'

Given that the centre positions are significantly more physical still, I was fairly alarmed when, having been selected at No.10, things changed the moment we gathered for training. Chris Rea, who would be a Lions tourist in New Zealand in 1971 and go on to be a fellow journalist of repute, was crocked on arrival; Jock Turner went down almost the moment we took to the practice field. 'Look, Jock's not going to make it and we've no one else,' I was told by some committee man or other. 'It'll have to be you.' As Colin Telfer of Hawick was available to cover for me, I couldn't even pretend that we'd be leaving a hole at No.10. So there I found myself, up against Duckham, who wasn't the worst player ever to set foot on a rugby field. I cannot claim, much as I would love to, that I marked him completely out of the game: there were only two tries in the match and he scored both of them, so I'd struggle to get away with it. I dimly remember making a half-break at some point during the contest, but as the emphasis was on the 'half' rather than the 'break', our only points in an 8–3 defeat came from Peter Brown's boot. Oh well, once again.

As a betting man, supplementing my meagre income as a schoolteacher at Fettes College with regular visits to the bookmaking emporiums of Auld Reekie (as Edinburgh had long been lovingly described by its inhabitants, although I was lucky enough to spend virtually all of my time in one of the city's more fragrant corners), I probably wouldn't have risked my entire week's wages on us winning in 1970 either, even though the game would be played at home. Yes, we'd beaten the touring Springboks in the final days of '69, but that had been a strange affair all round: a stadium under siege from anti-apartheid demonstrators; almost as many police officers as spectators; deserted banks of terracing; the eeriest of atmospheres. They were well enough equipped in the personnel department – no side fielding backs as powerful as Syd Nomis and Gert Muller, or half-backs as gifted as Piet Visagie and Dawie de Villiers, could ever be a pushover, and they also had Hannes Marais at prop, the extraordinary Frik du Preez at lock and one of the great back-rows in the annals of the game, with Jan Ellis and Piet Greyling flanking the highly intelligent Tommy Bedford at No.8. But they were under all sorts of pressure off the field and it showed. If we found Murrayfield a weird place to be that day, think how they felt.

Much more pertinent to the England game was our performance level over the first three rounds of the Five Nations tournament, which left a considerable amount to be desired. In our first game, against France at Murrayfield, we'd fielded a very decent team, particularly up front: Ian 'Mighty Mouse' McLauchlan, Frank Laidlaw and Sandy Carmichael were the front-rowers; Gordon Brown and Peter Stagg were in the boilerhouse; Wilson Lauder, Rodger Arneil and dear old Jim T made up the breakaway unit. The French, meanwhile, were rather less studded with Tricolore magicians than they had been when winning titles in '67 and '68. They may have travelled to us with Pierre Villepreux at full-back, Jean-Pierre Lux in midfield and a fistful (I use the word advisedly) of scary forwards, Jean Iracabal, Jean-Pierre Bastiat and the great Benoît Dauga among them, but taken as a whole, it was something less than a stellar line-up. We lost 11–9 even so and carried on in the same vein, finishing second to Wales in Cardiff and to Ireland in Dublin.

Given the circumstances, the Calcutta Cup match was what would now be called a 'must win' game for us, not that any of us would have used such terminology – or even have heard it on the lips of anyone else – in those far-off days. We'd suffered our share of championship whitewashes in the post-war era, not least during the early 1950s when we couldn't win a game for love nor money, but the sense of personal failure is never diminished by the knowledge that your fore-runners experienced a similar form of misery. As it turned out, we won 14–5.

As my role in the victory was unusually prominent, it was also the highlight of my playing career. I find a clear recollection of events to be somewhat elusive: I have footage of seven of my eight international games but never watch them now, largely because they are stored on VHS tapes, which my more technologically aware acquaintances (everyone I know, basically) tell me is a little out of date. But I remember bits and pieces, including leaning in to fool my opposite number, Roger Shackleton of Harrogate, into shooting out of position and fracturing the English defensive line. Through the hole I went to create Alastair Biggar's try. Most of the finer detail must be garnered from contemporary reports.

Apparently, John Spencer, the England centre, ran 70 yards to touch down and drag his side back into the contest. To which I can say only that it must have taken him a very long time. It is also recorded that the England players fell out among themselves as the game slipped away from them and bottom place in the table loomed. There would be a more famous public falling-out amongst the white shirted types on Grand Slam day two decades later. The more things change . . .

In all three of my Calcutta Cup appearances, the England full-back was Bob Hiller of Harlequins. Bob had a very decent career in top-level rugby: he toured South Africa with the Lions in 1968 and made the cut again for the glorious trip to New Zealand three years later; he led England on seven occasions and accumulated 138 points in 19 games for his country – a record at the time. But the memory I most cherish is not his highly successful toe-end kicking style, but his heartfelt complaint about the title sequence of the BBC's long-running *Rugby Special* programme, on which I found myself working soon after retiring from the game. 'Do you think you might find a new opening for your show?' he asked me one day, completely out of the blue. 'I love the music – absolutely love it – but maybe you could take a peek in the archives and come up with some different footage.' When I asked him why, he continued: 'Well, we're four months into the new season and there have been 16 episodes. While the music is playing, there's a clip of me dropping a high ball against Wales and giving Gareth Edwards a try; there's a kick to win a game that I hook so badly, it ends up in touch; there's my tackle on that Bastiat chap where I don't even manage to slow him down – I just jack-knife backwards while he lumbers upfield without altering his pace; and then Tom Kiernan runs round me in the Ireland match, even though he's slower than I am. We have 60 seconds of music, during which every clip is of me looking absolutely shite.' I had no idea that we'd picked on him so relentlessly. In fact, the only person who'd noticed was Bob. I felt bad for him, but not bad enough to let him off. 'I think we're keeping that sequence for the whole season,' I told him before hurrying off at top speed.

During my early years as a BBC commentator, Scotland had their share of Calcutta Cup success, particularly at Murrayfield. They won heavily in 1972 – we scored five tries, which was five more than England managed – and again, more narrowly but equally blissfully, in '74 and '76. But the games that stand out in my mind came later: 1984, 1986, 1990. The first of them was not, in the end, the highlight of a season in which we finally achieved our hearts' desire, a first Grand Slam in almost 60 years. Indeed, the England match was on the opening weekend of the Five Nations, and it was not until the final round of matches, in which we hosted France, that the job was completed. But to beat the English as comfortably as we did was satisfying in the extreme, not least because our visitors came to Edinburgh fresh from beating the All Blacks and were expected by everyone, including themselves, to douse our fires by dishing out a hiding up front.

In the event, it was the Scottish eight who prevailed, in most if not all facets of forward play, and looking back on the make-up of that pack, it is not hard to see why. Jim Aitken, almost as resourceful at holding things together as a loose-head prop as he would later be at making money, had two completely dependable colleagues at the sharp end in Colin Deans, a magnificent hooker, and Iain Milne, a bear-like presence on the tight-head side of the scrum. The locks were Bill Cuthbertson and Alan Tomes; the back row featured contrasting and wholly compatible talents in Jim Calder, David Leslie and Iain Paxton. David Johnston, one of my favourite Scottish centres, scored the opening try and I revelled in the sight of it. David had all the footballing skills in the world – he'd had a trial with Hearts and could certainly have made a living as a professional soccer player – and sure enough, he dribbled the ball to the English line before claiming the four points. He was also a fellow Watsonian, as was the other try-scorer, his midfield partner Euan Kennedy. If ever there was a day for our sort to feel a cut above the rest, that was it.

Two years later came a record victory: 33–6, with 21 points for Gavin Hastings, whom I'd coached during his time at Cambridge University. Gavin put that barely surmountable disadvantage behind him by breaking into the Scotland side, succeeding Peter Dods at full-back, and he showed obvious signs of a great career in the making by landing eight kicks against England. We scored three tries and could easily have had half a dozen more in a gloriously one-sided encounter. In fact, I was almost (but not quite) bored by the sight of us scoring. And for those of a pugilistic persuasion who like their rugby red in tooth and claw, there was rich entertainment in the shape of an early dust-up between John Beattie, a fiery No.8 from Glasgow, and the Blackpool policeman and weekend enforcer Wade Dooley, who rather revelled in his 'hammer of the Scots' image. The story goes that John, who had been on the spectacularly unsuccessful Lions trip to New Zealand the previous year and unnerved some of the English tourists with his fearless physicality, had been instructed to give the opposition lock Maurice Colclough a bit of a hurry-up at the first line-out, but managed to thump Dooley instead, thereby putting the hardest man in English rugby in something of a strop. How John managed this, no one has ever been able to fathom: Dooley had dark hair and wore a good deal of bandaging around his head; Colclough was blond and notably bandage-free. Clearly, the military men are right when they say that no strategy survives first contact with the enemy.

Those middle years of the 1980s were highly rewarding – between the two Murrayfield victories, Scotland came within a hair's breadth of winning at Twickenham and would surely have done so had not the powerful Paxton been stripped of the ball by the less than gargantuan Rory Underwood in the final seconds – but if my feet were being held to the fire, I'd have to nominate the 1990 match in Edinburgh as my favourite Calcutta Cup game of all (leaving aside 1970, naturally, on the grounds that playing rugby is more fun than watching it, or commentating on it, or writing about it). For the first time in the history of the tournament, the Grand Slam would be contested by two British teams with three straight victories behind them. Not for the first time, England headed north as favourites. The reasons why were perfectly understandable: their closest game of the championship had been in Paris, where they had won by 19 points. Neither Ireland nor Wales had threatened them in the least, losing 23–0 and 34–6 respectively. They were formidable up front, particularly at set-piece; they were tough-minded and organised at half-back, with Richard Hill and Rob Andrew in the form of their lives; and their threequarter line was lethal, with Will Carling and Jeremy Guscott finding scoring almost as easy as the predatory Underwood. Scotland had punished France almost as ruthlessly as England, partly because the French really weren't very good and partly because their flanker, Alain Carminati, left them a man short by getting himself sent off. (Carminati had been spotted stamping on the head of John Jeffrey, which must have left him suffering from a badly bruised foot to go with his chronic sense of guilt.) For all that, though, our games against Ireland and Wales had been close-run things.

Each and every pundit – including me, I admit – felt that of the two contenders, England were the ones who looked like a Grand Slam side.

They didn't look like one by close of play in the Scottish capital, that's for sure. I don't think I've ever seen a high-class team – a side good enough to reach the World Cup final the following year – look more discombobulated, unless you count the All Blacks who fell victim to a joyously riotous French performance in the semi-final of the global tournament in 1999. The uprising began with the 'slow march' into battle, which captured the imagination at the time and is now as firmly rooted in our rugby folklore as the clean sweeps of 1925 and 1984; the epic parsimony of the Scottish Rugby Union; Peter Stagg's version of fishnet stockings; and one or two of Gordon Brown's dodgy after-dinner jokes. (Politically incorrect example: 'They breed some tough girls in Glasgow. I was sitting in front of one in the cinema the other night and heard her say: "Hey, get your hand out of my knickers. Not you. *You*."')

Sadly from the journalistic point of view, I knew nothing of the 'slow march' plan in advance. I'd been covering rugby for the best part of two decades when these events occurred and I'd reached the stage where I could count on a little privileged information before a big game. But there was no talk of anything off-the-wall being planned for this one, so when the Scotland captain David Sole led out the team at walking pace – a pace that sent out the clearest of signals that the home side were deadly serious and had no intention of being messed around by anyone – the noise in the old stadium reached unprecedented levels. I had been in South Africa with the Lions in 1974 and seen the Springboks, two down with two to play, race onto the field at Port Elizabeth at breakneck speed in an attempt to startle Willie John McBride and company with the ferocity of their intent. A fat lot of good it did them, as the 26–9 defeat proved. This was a far better way of getting under the opposition's skin and making them question whatever assumptions of supremacy they might be harbouring. This was inspired.

We know now that David – as up to date in his thinking about the game as he was in his broadening of the loose-head prop's job description – decided on this tactic at the very last minute. It certainly set the right tone. Even though England looked like a million dollars, they had a few noughts knocked off that valuation in the course of a passionate contest. If I don't remember much about my own Calcutta Cup win in 1970, I have total recall of the try that won the day for my country two decades on: Mike Teague's fumble at the base of the English scrum to concede the put-in; John Jeffrey's more accomplished pick-up and pass to Gary Armstrong at scrum-half; Gary's little dummy-dart routine before throwing the ball to Gavin Hastings; Gavin's juggling one-handed take and inch-perfect chip over the onrushing England full-back Simon Hodgkinson; Tony Stanger's successful pursuit of the bouncing ball, which he grounded under the nose of the desperate Underwood. It was quite something. Everything about that day was quite something.

Even in this age of the video analyst and the consequent loss of individuality and mystique, rugby-playing nations have their own dynamic, their own motivational force. The Calcutta Cup is definitely central to Scottish rugby's sense of itself. In my day, the character of the side came to the fore whenever England were in town, and as we were a mobile rucking side rather than a pedestrian mauling one, the message from the senior players was never less than clear. 'Kick 'em out of the way,' they would say. 'Every last one of 'em.' I didn't do much kicking myself: I made it my business not to put myself in kicking range, because I really didn't fancy being kicked back. But there was a feeling of common purpose in the dressing room and even though a large proportion of the squad tended to come from the Borders, I was never made to feel like a gatecrasher. I was great mates with at least 80 per cent of my countrymen – yes, even the front-rowers, despite not being able to understand the first thing about them. Ian McLauchlan was a brilliant comrade, far wittier and funnier than me. Frank Laidlaw was a good, decent man – fundamentally honest. As for Sandy Carmichael . . . what a star. He was a great forward of few words and I enjoyed teasing him: at mealtimes, I would present him with a menu of my own design – a picture of a cow on one side, a fish on the other – and ask him to keep things simple by pointing towards his preference. He never took umbrage, even though he could have snapped me in two. All he would say was: 'Aye, Robertson. Bloody funny, aren't you?'

They were wonderful days. And the most wonderful of all were the ones when the Calcutta Cup was up for grabs. Especially when we won.

HIGH JINKS AND
HIGH TABLES

IT did not always occur to us in the days leading up to a meeting with England, but there was a big wide rugby world out there beyond the British Isles and France. I would not visit too much of it until my playing days were over, but I did see Argentina and Australia – wonderful trips in many ways, if not wholly successful on the field of play. I look on the visit to South America in 1969 as a particular highlight: partly because I played quite well; partly because of the sheer scale of the culture shock, from the raw violence of the rugby and the formidable strength of the local red wines to a first sighting of tanks on the streets; and partly (this is important!) because I finally found a way of bringing Jim Telfer, our attack dog of a captain, to heel. My triumph in this regard did not last long, but it was beautiful while it lasted.

These were the days before analysis – to all intents and purposes, they were still the days before coaching – so there was a feeling amongst the tour party of venturing into the great unknown. The Argentines knew what it was to welcome decent opposition to their shores, from combined Oxford and

Cambridge University teams to the Junior Springboks, but virtually all of their serious international-standard rugby had been against the French. However, a Wales XV had paid them a visit the previous year for a couple of non-cap 'Tests' and a handful of provincial fixtures, and had struggled like hell, losing the first of their big games and drawing the second. As that Welsh group included players as good as JPR Williams, John Dawes, Phil Bennett, Dai Morris and John Lloyd, their trials and tribulations were instructive. The Scottish selectors decided we should travel at strength, so the vast majority of our Five Nations team set out on the long journey to Buenos Aires. I was chosen as Jim's vice-captain, so there was an even greater onus on me to take things seriously. Which I did. Almost.

Our opening match, at what was then called the Gimnasia y Esgrima stadium in the capital's Palermo district, was against the Argentines' third-string team and we won handsomely, scoring five tries. As I was responsible for one of them – I remember it quite clearly because it wasn't an experience I enjoyed with any regularity – I felt a reasonable celebration was in order. What none of my countrymen knew was that, thanks to a very useful contact in the horse racing business, I'd just backed the winner of the St Leger at Doncaster. At 66–1! Suddenly, I had money to burn.

This added to my high good humour, to the extent that at the after-match banquet, I downed a bottle of red wine before noticing, through my rapidly deteriorating vision, that the massive Argentine prop sitting opposite me was diluting his own drink with unusual quantities of water. 'Ten parts water to one part wine,' he said, almost as though he were talking about a glass of Ribena. 'Do this, and the full glory of the wine will be apparent.' Good advice, but a trifle late in delivery. I'd already consumed plenty of this glory, and the glory was now consuming me. I was in a terrible state: unable to stand, speak or even think, let alone walk to the team bus. That night, I was nursed by one of our wings, Mike Smith, who was in the midst of his medical training at St Thomas' Hospital in London. Chris Rea, another saving grace from the Scotland threequarter line, also saw it as his business to help me make it through the night. Between them, they managed to reassure me that things would turn out alright. We had a training-free day ahead of us, so my recovery would be uninterrupted.

Unfortunately, Jim had other ideas. He organised an unscheduled practice session on the outskirts of the city, especially for me. Most of it involved sprinting. By the end, I was a sorry mess – sweating and retching and crawling around on all fours, with Jim glowering over me and throwing words like 'idiot' and 'disgrace' in my general direction like verbal darts. Mike and Chris, my trusty support network, helped me change out of my training gear (which was not in a pretty condition) and into a fresh set of clothes, ready for the bus trip back to the hotel – a fair distance away, far more easily measured in miles than in yards. The moment

I'd climbed up the steps leading into the vehicle, Jim ordered me back down again. 'You can bloody well walk back to the hotel,' he barked, reminding me again that I was a 'disgrace'. At which point, my senses cleared. Here was an opportunity to get my own back. 'There's no reason why you should know this, Jim,' I said, 'but there's a very good racehorse back home by the name of Intermezzo, he's just romped home in the St Leger, and I had plenty on him at 66–1. I've been on a bit of a spending spree as a result and one of my new possessions is this bus. If anyone's walking back to the hotel, it'll be you. And when you get there, you'll find I've bought the hotel too. You can pack your bags as soon as you like.' Gordon Brown, my great pal from the engine room of the scrum, then placed himself and one or two fellow forwards between Jim and me, thereby guaranteeing my safety. It was 1–0 to Robertson and Jim knew it. So too did my teammates, who were in tears of laughter. Jim didn't say a word in response. He simply sat in the front seat by the driver and smouldered.

It was a tough tour, physically speaking. All but one of the half-dozen games was staged in Buenos Aires, where rugby was more or less the exclusive preserve of the go-ahead middle classes and the players were well brought-up and well-to-do, rather than poncho-wearing primitives from the pampas. Did this genteel country-club atmosphere translate to events on the pitch? Not exactly. Jim, hardly one of life's shrinking violets, later described it as the hardest tour he ever experienced – and he played Test rugby for the Lions against the

All Blacks and the Springboks. Ian McLauchlan, even more garlanded by the Lions, unhesitatingly put it in the 'absolutely brutal' category. We weren't even being rewarded with caps for risking life and limb. Looking back, they should have given us medals. With forwards as handy as Jim, Ian and Sandy Carmichael in our side, we should have been fine. Instead, the Argentine players, some of whom were extremely good as well as frightening, simply pelted into us and made our lives a misery.

The first 'Test' was a proper eye-opener (and, for those on the wrong end of the many bunches of fives, an eye-closer). We lost 20–3, at least it seemed to us because the local referee – no neutral officials in those days – was a total desperado by the name of Ricardo Colombo. This eventually led to one of my more predictable jokes, along the lines of: 'You may have watched a TV detective series by the name of *Columbo*. Believe me, this ref had nothing like the sense of justice and fairness we associate with Peter Falk.' Everything we tried to do resulted in two things, the first being a chorus of boos from the crowd and the second a penalty decision from you know who. None of those decisions went our way. I still thank the good Lord for Carlos Tozzi, who controlled the second 'Test'. Talk about chalk and cheese. He was scrupulously even-handed – by comparison, his was the greatest refereeing performance in rugby history – and we won 6–3, courtesy of a try by Carmichael and a conversion from Colin Blaikie, our full-back. Carlos went on to occupy high office with the

International Rugby Board. As far as I'm concerned, he should have been secretary general of the United Nations.

As if events in the capital were not lively enough, our visit to Rosario, about 180 miles to the north west, put the tin hat on it. Almost literally. When we arrived, it was clear that the city was in the throes of some local difficulty of the political variety. We didn't know if it was a major outbreak of civil unrest or a mere squabble, but it was being played out on the streets and there were tanks on most of the corners. Lex Govan, a Scottish Rugby Union committee man, was on our management team, and he had a strategy. 'Right,' he said to us, 'this is serious. The Rosario union is laying on a reception for us, it'll be free food and free drink all night and that being the case, it would be rude of us not to attend. There is, however, gunfire out there – not to mention the possibility of bands of guerrilla fighters roaming between here and the venue – and there are no cars on the streets because it's too dangerous. Therefore, we will proceed as follows: we'll walk to the function two by two and I want each back to pair up with a forward. On no account should two scrum-halves venture out together. If one scrum-half gets himself shot, we can still field a side for the match. If two get killed, we'll have to call it off.' So that's what we did. We walked to the event, ate like kings, had too much to drink, and walked back to our hotel. After a head count the following morning, it was found that we still had a team. We went on to win 20–6 and all was right with the world.

Jim had been bang in the thick of the mayhem all tour and when he reflected on events later, he decided that the second 'Test' victory was as good a Scottish performance as he experienced in all his time as a player. I find it difficult to make such a judgement but it's certainly true to say that the following year, an Ireland party boasting the likes of Tom Kiernan, Tom Grace, Sean Lynch and Willie John McBride – two of them already big-name Lions, the other two Lions in waiting – went to Argentina and lost both of the games that mattered. The Pumas then squared a series with the South African Gazelles and by the end of the 1970s, they were beating both the French and the Australians in full internationals, complete with caps. You could see the way things were heading when we were there in '69 and when I next made the trip, as a journalist reporting on the fortunes of a very powerful England team under Bill Beaumont's captaincy, there was nothing in it. Maybe Jim was right.

My only other long-haul trip as a Scotland player, to Australia in 1970, was nowhere near as eventful. We had plenty of fun, as touring sides of that era tended to do, but we were well off the pace on the field, struggling in the provincial games and losing the one-off Test by a hatful. That match was played at the Sydney Cricket Ground and there was precious little comfort for us in the thought that this was not the first time a bunch of sporting visitors had been left to ponder the figures 23–3. The Wallabies had some very good players – John Hipwell at scrum-half, Peter Johnson at hooker, Greg Davis on the flank – and they ran in six tries to our none. Wilson Lauder, a back-rower from Fife who played his club rugby in Wales, was the man responsible for our points tally. He booted over a penalty in the first half – yet more proof of my status as a non-kicking No.10. Poor old Frank Laidlaw was our captain on that tour, with the recently retired Jim shouldering such coaching duties as there were, and he took it to heart. Frank was as intense about his rugby as anyone I ever played alongside: Norman Mair, who had a longer and more successful career as a newspaperman than he did as one of Scotland's many one-season-wonder forwards, famously remarked that whenever Frank lost a scrum ball on his own put-in, he 'treated it like a family bereavement'. Heaven knows how he felt about things on the return flight to Britain.

The Australia trip was just about it for me as far as top-level union was concerned. My next important game, shortly before the 1971 Five Nations, was a Scotland trial at Murrayfield, in which I led the putative first XV against what the selectors rather dismissively branded as 'the Rest'. I went into the game feeling good about my rugby and ended it knowing that my rugby days were over. Midway through the match I saw trouble coming and shipped the ball along the line, as I tended to do when faced with the prospect of pain, but I was tackled late and disappeared beneath a heap of grunting, growling forwards. Cartilages and ligaments in both knees were well and truly mangled, with my right knee faring particularly badly. The cruciate ligament was the major problem and at that stage in the development of sports medicine, there was little or nothing to be done. The message from the specialist was clear: 'Concentrate on your career, Robertson. It's high time you made something of yourself.'

There was a playing comeback of sorts a season or two later, but it didn't add up to much. Together with my old colleague Chris Rea, who had participated in the '71 Five Nations and toured New Zealand with the Lions that summer before packing it in and heading off to make an honest working man of himself, I was invited to turn out for AS Roma in the Italian club league. It was the amateur era, but we were well looked after and as the rugby was some way short of the most challenging I'd ever experienced, I thoroughly enjoyed my six-month association with the club. The best fun was during and after a match in Sicily, against Catania. It was a relegation decider, with the loser dropping down a division, and predictably enough, the game featured a huge mass punch-up. Equally predictably, it involved 29 players rather than the full 30, yours truly being the exception. I preferred to watch as the police invaded the field and started whacking the combatants with batons. The referee restarted the game with a scrum, from which – rarity of rarities – I dropped a goal. We won 3–0. As we prepared to leave the ground, we were told: 'Careful on the way out. The Mafia are here.' So I took it upon myself to shout from the open window of the bus something along the lines of 'Bueno fortuna in secondi divisione'. Immediately, we heard three gunshots, and a bullet went through the windscreen. Later, we were told that the Mafia had not been directly involved. This made me feel a little better about life, but I was still checking for horses' heads in my bed some time later.

All this happened during my early days with the BBC, but my first job out of university had been at Fettes College – a long-established school in Edinburgh with a reputation for excellence. It was said by the celebrated thriller writer Ian Fleming, who really ought to have known, that James Bond attended Fettes after being chucked out of Eton. I could find no trace of young Master Bond in the class registers, but maybe he was there under a pseudonym. That's the thing about being undercover. One of those who definitely did attend was a certain Tony Blair and I like to claim that I taught him to read and write. This argument tends to collapse under close scrutiny, however: Master Blair was a good deal brighter than me and while I seem to remember having cause to gate him for some minor transgression or other, he generally had the last laugh by successfully avoiding games lessons – or at least, those games lessons I was charged with running. Athlete's foot, in-growing toenails . . . I vaguely recall these being the excuses for his frequent absences from rugby. I'm not sure we got on terribly well, but another senior Labour Party politician, the late and deeply missed Tessa Jowell, reported to me that Mr Blair had once described me to her as a 'wonderful teacher'. I knew Tessa well – we'd met at university in Aberdeen and been the best of friends – and I could spot one of her jokes a mile away, but she insisted this was true.

Funnily enough, I was twice booked to speak at dinners in London where Mr Blair, during his time as Prime Minister, was the star turn. As it happened, he pulled out of both events on the reasonable grounds that running the country can be rather time-consuming. On one of these occasions, he sent along his press secretary, Alastair Campbell, to fill the gaping hole on the speaking list. Having been booked to do the comedy, I made a crack about the dire fortunes of Alastair's great sporting love by suggesting that Burnley FC should be renamed Burnley Nil FC. He was not wholly amused. If only I had used the rather funnier, if slightly politically incorrect, joke told to him at the start of the Lions tour of New Zealand in 2005, for which he had been recruited as part of Clive Woodward's managerial staff. 'What's the difference between the All Blacks and Iraq?' he was asked by one of the media pack. On shaking his head a little warily, he was given the answer. 'The All Blacks *do* have weapons of mass destruction!'

The Fettes opportunity cropped up during my year at Cambridge, where I had just about sneaked my way onto a teacher training course. After playing in the 1967 Varsity match, I was contacted by the headmaster of the school, Dr Ian Macintosh, who was a highly respected figure in educational circles. I already knew him, as he'd been my own head at George Watson's. 'We're looking for an English and History teacher who could look after the sport as well,' he said after travelling down to my college to make his pitch. 'Would you be interested?' I agreed immediately. I'd already decided to go into teaching, so this was perfect: a steady job back in Edinburgh, where I'd lived all my life apart from the university years, and the chance to play an excellent standard of club rugby at weekends. The annual salary was £680 – not huge money, even in those days, but I knew I would have the benefit of lodgings in one of the four school houses where the boarders were accommodated.

I left Cambridge in June 1968 and started at Fettes in the September. I felt marginally more comfortable pontificating about English literature than I did as an alleged specialist in history, but I just about managed to stay one page ahead of the kids in all the relevant textbooks. This was no great achievement: if I'm being frank, I taught the dummies when it came to history and stuck as closely as I could to the Tudors and Stuarts, my one area of semi-expertise, doing as little in the way of wider reading as my sense of professionalism would allow.

I quickly learned how to minimise my workload in literature, too, after making the acquaintance of a colleague who was about to take up a position at Harrow School. He was renowned as an outstanding teacher – a dedicated practitioner of the classroom arts who never failed to inspire his students. Unsurprisingly, the school hierarchy thought he might inspire me as well and put us together in the same house. When he left and I moved into his rooms, which were more spacious than my own, I immediately spotted three large cupboards. I also noticed that there were no keys. The supervisors were duly summoned to break into each cupboard, the first of which was crammed from top to bottom with thousands upon thousands of handwritten pages. On closer inspection, these turned out to be virtually all the essays his pupils had ever written for him down the years . . . and they were unmarked, every last one of them. It turned out that he'd never read a single essay, telling selected initiates on the staff that 'you can guess roughly how bright a boy is by watching him in the classroom and then mark his work accordingly.' When asked by one of the keener children when an essay might be returned, he would routinely reply: 'We don't return essays, but you've been given seven out of ten for your last one. Well done.'

One last word on Fettes, which I left for the BBC a few months after suffering my knee injury. One of my pupils was Bill Gammell, whose ultimate aim as a rugby player seemed to me to outstrip his abilities by a considerable distance. At the time, the most talented youngsters ran around on a pitch known as 'Big Side', while the rest spent their time on – yes, you've surely guessed it – 'Little Side'. One day, Bill approached me and said he'd been adjudged good enough to play on Big Side by two other members of staff and was looking forward to his opportunity. 'No, Gammell,' I replied. 'You're on Big Side because all our other wings are injured.' Bill carried on regardless. 'Do you want to know my ambition?' he asked. 'I suppose it's to score a try for the First XV on Big Side,' I replied in as disdainful tone as I could muster. 'No, Sir. It's to play international rugby for Scotland.' This blindsided me just a little. 'Let me tell you this, Gammell,' I responded after due consideration. 'It is 100 per cent certain that you will never, ever, be good enough to play for Scotland.'

Four years later, after he was selected for his first cap in a Five Nations game against Ireland, he approached me at one of the pre-match press conferences. 'Sir . . .' 'Gammell, you're a grown-up now. You don't have to call me "Sir".' 'Sir, you said I would never, ever, be good enough to play international rugby.' 'Yes, Gammell. And this Saturday afternoon, you will prove me right.' Bill laughed his head off and proceeded to play bloody well. Some years later, he phoned me. 'We always had an interesting relationship,' he said. 'I'd like to offer you some sound financial advice.' As he was the son of an investment banker, had a degree in economics and accountancy and had become one of the wealthiest businessmen in the land, I was delighted to heed his words of wisdom.

The painless, virtually seamless transition from college to classroom – from the world of study to the world of work – was, looking back, just one of many examples of the good fortune with which I've been blessed. Dr Macintosh's approach came out of the blue and it put me where I wanted to be: in Edinburgh, earning myself a living and playing a sufficiently high grade of rugby with Watsonians to keep me in the minds of the national selectors. (We won the Scottish club championship in my last season there, which helped.) But if we're going to talk about luck, nothing in my life helped me more than the unusual, not to say bizarre, circumstances surrounding my arrival at Cambridge. To this day, I smile in wonder at the story. I would love to think that such a sequence of events is still possible, but I doubt it somehow.

Ken Scotland was the catalyst. The great full-back – close to 30 caps for his country in an era when caps were hard to come by; five Lions Test appearances – was an Edinburgh man and I knew him well. Indeed, I had been known to perform babysitting duties in the Scotland household. When he suggested that I might have a shot at Cambridge University and would put in a word for me, I wasn't at all sure he was making sense: it was one thing getting into Aberdeen University, but I'd never considered myself an academic genius. I politely suggested that he shouldn't waste his time on my behalf, but Ken wouldn't hear of it. He wrote to the Christ's College admissions master, an interesting character by the name of Dr Pratt, assuring him of two things: that I would win a Blue at rugby and that I'd contribute handsomely to the life of the university. Happily, he forgot to mention the astronomical odds against my winning a Nobel Prize.

I duly undertook the 15-hour coach trip from Aberdeen for my interview and arrived at Dr Pratt's door feeling more than a little nervous. On entering, a master I assumed to be Dr Pratt said: 'I'm so sorry you've had a wasted journey, Mr

Robertson. Dr Pratt has died. Just this last week. Terrible thing. Goodbye.' And out I went. I don't suppose I'd been in the room more than 40 seconds. As I re-emerged, the secretary looked at me with a peculiar expression on her face and asked me what had happened. I told her. 'Don't tell me he's played that "Dr Pratt is dead" trick,' she said. 'That *is* Dr Pratt. He hasn't used that line in 15 years. I'd go back in if I were you.' So I did.

Dr Pratt had now vanished into thin air . . . or so I thought. Suddenly, two hands appeared from behind the substantial desk, beneath which he was hiding. In his hands was a rugby ball, which he chucked at me while bellowing the single word 'Catch!' Miraculously, given my advanced state of confusion, I did as requested. Even more miraculously, I drop-kicked the ball – left-footed! – across the room and into the waste-paper basket, which was barely wide enough to accept it. The ball just sat there on top, like a boiled egg waiting to be tapped with a spoon. At which point, Dr Pratt emerged from his place of concealment, hugged me as he would a long-lost brother and said, in triumphant tones: 'You're in! Well done, my boy. Anything you need to know? Come back in an hour and I'll tell you all about the university over coffee.' On leaving his office a second time, I caught the secretary's eye once again. 'Oh dear: I suppose he's turned you down,' she said. 'No,' I replied. 'I've been given a proper grilling and I've passed.' 'But you were in there barely half a minute. How did you convince him in that space of time?' 'Without opening

my mouth. However, I'm not at liberty to divulge the details.'
And out I scurried, before anyone had a change of mind.

It may have been the shortest admission interview in the
history of Christ's College. Not bad going, seeing as it was
founded during the reign of Henry VI. There again, it may
not have been. Who can say for sure what other ruses were
used by the good Dr Pratt? What I do know is that he
believed in the university as a place for all the talents, not
simply those of the academic kind. This lesson was driven
home to me some years later when I felt it right to intervene
on behalf of one of my pupils at Fettes whom I felt had some
potential, in precisely the same way as Ken Scotland had
gone into bat for me. Dr Pratt looked kindly upon my recom-
mendation and offered the lad concerned a generous offer of
two 'Cs' and a 'D' at A-Level (Fettes following the English
method of examination grading rather than the Scottish
version). 'What about a C and two Ds?' I responded, pushing
my luck.

As it turned out, my protégé secured three majestic Ds –
and to make matters worse, Dr Pratt retired before the date
of his admission interview. I travelled down to Cambridge
to speak to his successor, the formidable literary critic Gorley
Putt, who gave me very short shrift. 'How can you show your
face here?' he barked at me, showing me the door. As I walked
across the quad, the Master of Christ's College – a Nobel
laureate in chemistry, no less – spotted me. 'Ah, Robertson.
How nice to see you again. Please join me for coffee.' After

I explained what had just happened, he said: 'I think I'll have a word with Gorley. Wait here.' In essence, he explained to Dr Pratt's successor that it was not good for the university to be entirely populated by super-intelligent types whose brains were in danger of exploding. 'It would make such a mess of the gardens,' he argued. 'You follow my meaning, Gorley? You'll see to it, I'm sure. Good man.'

Three years later, after my Fettes student had performed superbly at Christ's both in his studies and in his contribution to the wider life of the university, I received a letter from Gorley inviting me to a formal dinner to mark the end of term. 'You taught me an important lesson, Robertson, and I thank you for it,' he said. He went on to inform me that there had recently been a number of suicides among the college students, all of whom had been academically exceptional but unable to cope with the pressures they had placed upon themselves. There must be more to life than books and learning. Even at our greatest universities.

The year I spent at Christ's College was a joy, and in the early months, that joy revolved around the Varsity Match. It was the talk of the university: Dr Pratt was a genuine sports enthusiast who often invited me to dine with him at High Table, just to catch up with the latest developments. We won the 1967 game to end a brief period of Oxford superiority and if the 6–0 margin reflected the fact that it wasn't the most exhilarating of spectacles, it was typically hard-fought and there was a good deal of coverage in the national newspapers.

Rugby was high on the sports agenda that year: Keith Jarrett, the Boy Wonder from Monmouth, had made his debut for Wales against England at the scarcely believable age of 18 and, despite playing out of position at full-back, had inspired his country to victory in an outstanding encounter. Meanwhile, a more familiar Welsh maestro, the outside-half David Watkins, had caused uproar by turning professional with the Salford rugby league team. There was also the small matter of Colin Meads, the Godfather of New Zealand rugby, being sent off during a Test with Scotland at Murrayfield – only the second dismissal in the entire history of international rugby and the first since the 1920s. Yes, it was all happening.

Cambridge had a more than useful side that year. Up front there was the lock Nick Martin and the No.8 Charlie Hannaford, who would win full international honours, and the flanker Martin Green, who would coach England at the inaugural World Cup in 1987. But the real glories were to be found outside the scrum. Virtually all the backs were of a Test standard, or close to it: John Anthony, a Welshman, at full-back; Mike Smith of Scotland and John Spencer of England on the wings; Chris Saville and Peter Price at centre. Mike and John Spencer made it into their respective national teams while John Anthony had at least one trial for Wales. Chris garnered four Blues and really should have won caps as well. Between us, we produced some excellent running rugby. If we failed to showcase it on the big day at Twickenham, where Spencer scored the only try of the game, it was because of the intensity of the occasion and the sheer cussedness of what I considered to be a wholly inferior bunch of Oxford party-poopers. Dispassionately speaking, of course.

There wasn't much in the way of coaching at Cambridge during my time there. Not to put too fine a point on it, there wasn't much in the way of coaching anywhere in European rugby. England, with money and resources to burn, had waited until 1967 to appoint Don White of Northampton, an international flanker in the late 1940s and early '50s, as their first track-suited supremo. David Nash, a Lions No.8 from Ebbw Vale, had been given a similar job in Wales in the same year; Ronnie Dawson, a rather more celebrated Lion having led the tour to New Zealand in 1959, was not appointed by Ireland until 1969. Only in France, where the great Lourdes forward and Légion d'honneur recipient Jean Prat had performed the role as early as 1964, was coaching considered a necessary evil in the higher echelons of European rugby. Needless to say, the New Zealanders and the South Africans had been ahead of the game in this department, as well as all the others. Both had coaches before the dawning of the 1950s. And Scotland? We were behind the game here, as in so much else. Bill Dickinson from the Jordanhill club was the first formally appointed coach of our national team, taking over in 1971. Before him, there were only 'advisors to the captain'. Hard to believe nowadays, but true.

By this time, I was keeping myself busy running the Fettes

First XV, up there on Big Side, and I saw no particular reason why I shouldn't keep on running it for as long as the good Dr Macintosh was willing to put up with me. But it came to an end when, for the first and very nearly the last time, I made what would now be described as a 'career move'. Thanks largely to Bill McLaren, I'd been bitten by the commentary bug (aware that my playing career had come to a premature end, as well as a sticky one, he'd invited me to sit alongside him on his regular broadcasting stints for the *Rugby Special* programme) and when the chance of a full-time role with the BBC cropped up, I thought it worth a go. Bill's research notes may have been infinitely more comprehensive than my lesson preparation on the Tudors and Stuarts, but I felt there was more than one way of skinning a cat. How about a commentary style based on the gift of the gab, rather than facts and figures? To my mind, it made complete sense.

Quite rightly, the BBC put their new boy on the graveyard shift, which basically covered the whole weekend, including the Sunday overnight stint. These were hard yards as far as my social life was concerned, although breathing the same studio air as some of the great broadcasters of the age – I spent a lot of time in the inspiring presence of John Timpson and Robert Robinson, for instance – was hardly a chore. What was more, the hours gave me plenty of latitude during the week. So when a meaty Welsh prop forward and Cambridge captain by the name of Geoff Rees, one of the few front-rowers of my acquaintance ever to merit inclusion in Debrett's, asked me if I'd consider coaching the University in the run-up to the 1972 Varsity Match, there was no burning reason to turn him down. 'I'd love to do it,' I told him, 'but I could only coach the backs. I really don't understand the other creatures.' So began a long touchline relationship with the Light Blues, during which we'd establish something approaching total supremacy over Oxford, for whom I tried to feel sorry without ever quite succeeding. I'd catch the train to Cambridge after finishing work on Mondays and Thursdays – I didn't drive in those days and try not to do it much now – and after putting the best players through their paces at Grange Road, I'd head back down to London to resume my BBC duties.

It was bliss, not least because we had a heroic New Zealander running the forwards. Murray Meikle was a little older than me and was on his way to becoming an international authority on orthodontics. During his time playing rugby back home he had come up against the mighty Colin Meads, so an advanced understanding of teeth and how to put them back together probably came in handy. Most importantly from my point of view, he was a bloody good coach who, like so many New Zealanders, had a natural appreciation of the value of quick ball and how to generate it. Where were you, Murray, during the 2018 Six Nations? England could have done with you then.

I spent more than a decade on the Varsity coaching beat, which to all intents and purposes was a quick-fix process, with all the work concentrated into a period of seven or eight weeks running into the big day out at Twickenham in December. During that time, every last player with ambitions to take part in the annual showpiece drained himself for the cause and became as physically fit as he would ever be in his life. The Varsity Match may have lost much of its lustre over the course of the professional era, but nothing has changed in terms of conditioning: today's participants, without exception, are at the peak of their aerobic powers and would not lose much, if anything, to their counterparts in the full-time game. It was my job, between 1973 and 1984, to ensure that the Cambridge backs could think as quickly as they ran and play a style of rugby that would exhaust Oxford mentally as well as bodily. For the most part, thanks as much to the efforts of Murray and his successor Tony Rodgers as to my own, we fulfilled the demands of the job description. There was a six-point defeat in 1977 and another two years later. Leaving those aside, it was Light Blue heaven all the way.

And why wouldn't it have been, with the backs at my disposal? I remember Alastair Hignell materialising in front of me, mustard keen on winning his Blue as a fresher and more than capable of doing so. Yet such was our strength in depth, he posed something of a problem. 'Mr Coach,' he said with characteristic good manners after casting an eye over the first Freshers' team sheet. 'I see you have me down to play at full-back.' I hadn't actually compiled the list and told him so before asking him if he had a better idea. 'Well, I consider myself to be a scrum-half,' he replied. There was no easy way of saying it, so I plunged straight in. 'Well, Hignell. You may just have a chance of a Blue at No.15, but at No.9 we have a couple of very good players and I don't think you'll be edging past either of them.' 'Fair enough, but will I have a chance to prove you wrong?' 'Yes, of course.' And he had his chance, after which I told him: 'Right. As predicted, you won't be in the team as a scrum-half and you won't be the reserve either. Would you perhaps like to give full-back a go?' Within a few months, he was playing for England. As a full-back. Being a brilliant cricketer as well as a brilliant rugby player, he never dropped a ball for us. Being as brave as a lion, he never missed a tackle. If he was a yard short of pace, his footballing brain enabled him to make up the lost ground by reaching his destination quicker than everyone else by running only half the distance. And of course, he was, and remains, a wonderful, inspirational human being. I'm so glad I was able to set him on the right road.

Over in the pack department, things were not always so simple. The Cambridge University fixture list was extremely strong in those long-lost amateur days, but the flavour of the rugby was pleasant enough: the Light Blues were, almost by definition, younger than those playing week in, week out for Gloucester or Leicester or some horrible lot from the mining valleys of Wales, and by and large, the opposition were happy to take a gentle approach by buying into the freewheeling, adventurous spirit we liked to adopt. But every so often, our contests darkened just a little. The arrival in our midst of Eddie Butler is a prime example. Eddie was a clever sort and a very fine player who would go on to captain Wales before pursuing a successful career in both print and broadcast journalism. He was also more than a little handy when it came to looking after himself on the field – the natural consequence of playing club rugby for Pontypool, who were just about the roughest, toughest bunch of ne'er-do-wells in Britain, and perhaps beyond.

His nickname down at Pontypool Park was 'Bamber' – after Bamber Gascoigne, the question-master of the television quiz series *University Challenge*. It seemed that as far as the average Pooler forward was concerned, anyone capable of completing a form with a signature rather than a thumbprint was cut from unusually intellectual cloth. Whatever, Eddie was a vigorous No.8 when he arrived at Cambridge, and he showed plenty of that vigour during his time with us, to the extent that some of the harder teams started playing properly in response to his forthright approach. It is said that during one match, the Gloucester flanker John Watkins was about to take retribution on this uppity and annoying young pup when Eddie, pinned to the floor and in a rather vulnerable position, said: 'Before you do what you're about to do, John, could I just point out that the next time we meet, I'll be playing for Pontypool?' I'm told on good authority that John lifted him from the floor, dusted him down and continued on his way.

All that being said, the Cambridge years were 99 per cent

fun. Towards the end of my time with the team, we had some blinding back lines. In 1983, when we won 20–9, we were able to field Simon Smith, Mark Bailey, Kevin Simms and Rob Andrew, all of whom would win full England caps – dozens and dozens of them in Rob's case. A year later, when we really went to town by winning 32–6, there were repeat appearances from Rob, Kevin and Mark, together with Varsity debuts from Fran Clough in the centre and Gavin Hastings at full-back. With personnel of that calibre, I'd have had to try very hard *not* to win. As coaching jobs go, has there ever been anything better?

FINDING
MY VOICE

HE had been badly scarred in a bar fight and the lingering traces of the 60-odd stitches in his face suggested that he was not wholly committed to a life of puritanical restraint. Even without those tell-tale marks of a misspent evening, if not a misspent youth, his reputation for wild excess would have preceded him. He was a good friend of Keith Moon, the wild-eyed drummer with The Who, and was able to match 'Moon the Loon' drink for drink, late-night bar for late-night bar, lost weekend for lost weekend. He was powerfully built, blessed with enormous charisma and, having broken into the upper echelons of movie stardom with striking appearances in *Oliver!* and *Women in Love*, had become extremely wealthy. He was also very fond of rugby, to the extent that he'd recently splashed out on a set of floodlights for his local club, Rosslyn Park. And as a result of this fascination with union game, he was heading in my direction. Which made me feel just a little nervous.

'You're covering the Rosslyn Park–Coventry game this weekend, Ian, and you will have a special guest: Oliver Reed.'

So said Bob Burrows, the head of sport on BBC radio, just a few months into my career as a broadcaster. 'I don't need to tell you that he will be the main attraction. It will be about him, all of it. Not you. Him. On this occasion, we're really not interested in anything you have to say. We *are* interested in Oliver Reed. We want him on air at every available opportunity. He's the star. When he wants to talk, shut up and let him.' These were just about the clearest instructions I'd ever received in my life. Had I misunderstood them, I could justifiably have been sacked for stupidity.

I arrived at the Rosslyn Park ground in Roehampton a good three hours ahead of kick-off. This was not quite my usual practice, but I felt the occasion demanded a little extra preparation – or to put it another way, a girding of the loins. The corporation had really pushed the boat out: there was a second microphone *and* a second headset. There would also be a visual feed into the studio at White City, where footage for the following day's *Rugby Special* programme would be edited. I felt as though everyone important to my future was watching me, as well as listening to me. Even though the only person they really wanted to see and hear was Oliver Reed.

Five minutes into the game, there was no sign of the great actor. There were plenty of rugby stars on show, most of them playing for an outstanding Coventry side: David Duckham, Peter Rossborough, Peter Preece and Geoff Evans were all on the Midlanders' books at the time and they were as strong as any side in the country. What there wasn't was a star of the cinematic variety. But when I mentioned this to the sports desk, they were sticking to their guns. 'He'll be there,' they assured me. 'And when he arrives, give him the big build-up.' I was growing more uncomfortable by the second.

Another five minutes went by – and suddenly, there he was. I would almost certainly have recognised him had he been wearing normal weekend attire, for I had seen his recent box-office successes like everyone else, but as he had chosen to smother himself in the most magnificent full-length mink coat, which ran right the way down to a pair of bright yellow Wellington boots, there was no possibility of mistaken identity. He was walking, apparently none too steadily, between the crowd and the touchline, looking for a way over the barrier so he could access the commentary box. On further inspection, he was swaying and stumbling and lurching. What was more, he couldn't find his way over the advertising hoardings, despite the best efforts of some thoroughly amused spectators. Eventually, a steward opened a gate on the halfway line, thereby providing him with a route to the waiting microphone. Me? I was wondering how I could get the hell out of there, because the situation had 'danger' written all over it. Unfortunately, the great comedy show *Fawlty Towers* had yet to be written. The idea of escaping a bad situation by pretending to faint, à la Basil, did not occur to me.

The main attraction descended into the seat alongside me with an almighty thud, like a meteorite falling to Earth. This image was captured by the BBC cameras. With the words 'put him on immediately' ringing in my ears, I took the deepest of breaths and said: 'I'm happy to tell everyone that I've been joined by the film star Oliver Reed, who has done so much for this great Rosslyn Park club and helped make them one of the best equipped outfits in English rugby. Good to see you, Oliver. One of the surprises for me in these first few minutes of the match is that the Rosslyn Park pack is performing every bit as well as the vaunted Coventry eight. You would have thought, wouldn't you, that the home forwards would be completely dominated.'

The reply was as interesting, in a startling kind of way, as it was immediate. 'Would I f— ,' he replied, live on air. 'Park have a f—ing good pack.' They were the only two 'Fs' that went out: the chaps in the studio made sure there would be no more, unplugging him from the far side of London. But I'd already swallowed my mic in embarrassment. My immediate thought was that I was now unemployed – that I might as well beat the rush by leaving at half-time and going home to bed. 'What will I do for a living now?' I thought to myself. Then came some reassuring noises from the desk. 'Keep talking to him, Robbo,' came the instruction. 'No one will hear him but you, but we can't be rude.' As far as I can remember, there were no further catastrophes. I certainly can't recall the result of the game. Somehow, it didn't seem to matter.

Looking back on that extraordinary afternoon, I'd come a

long way from the classrooms and playing fields of Fettes in a very short time. The two men most responsible for this journey were Bill McLaren, of course, and Cliff Morgan. If Bill would have given anything to play rugby at Test level – he would certainly have done so, had he not contracted tuberculosis shortly after serving in the Second World War – Cliff was one of those rare rugby creatures who seemed capable of anything the moment he set foot on the inter-national field. Born in the Rhondda Valley, he helped create the myth of the No.10 factory concealed beneath a Welsh mountain, deep under the layers of coal and clay. He had all the skills in the outside-half manual and a good few more besides. He could control a match or light up a match as the situation demanded; he could bemuse and mystify the oppo-sition with his instinctive attacking improvisation; he could break their hearts with what would now be called his game management. The South Africans still refer to the classic Lions series with the Springboks in 1955 as 'the Cliff Morgan tour'. All things considered, he was impossible to ignore and a very difficult man to turn down.

Cliff had decided on a career in broadcasting after retiring from rugby in the late 1950s. He could do the lot: he could commentate, analyse, secure and conduct big-name interviews, edit current affairs programmes and produce documentaries. He also had a golden-toned voice that was naturally suited to radio – you could have been listening to Richard Burton or Dylan Thomas or some other Welsh wordsmith – and it was the cruellest irony that he spent his later years fighting cancer of the vocal cords. He went from the BBC to ITV and back again, wielding increasing influence as the years unfolded. By the time of my own enforced retirement from rugby, he was moving towards an important new role in television. With a little prompting from Bill, alongside whom I'd already done a little co-commentary work, he flew up to Edinburgh, took me out for lunch and offered me a position. 'The people at the BBC are keen on rugby and want to know if there's anyone out there who might do the job I've been doing – someone who's played a bit at a good level and might know what he's talking about,' he said. I told him I was interested, adding: 'Do you think the salary will be more than £680 a year?' Cliff smiled. 'Oh yes. It'll be three times that.'

He was the most wonderful company: even if he hadn't looked after me during my early years in radio and become a really good friend, I'd have been heavily influenced by him just by being a part of his professional circle. He was very bright, extremely witty and had a command of language that was the envy of everyone who knew him. He could be as ribald as anyone, but only in the appropriate surroundings; he could also let rip if things went wrong in the studio. But generally speaking, he was a charming man – and that charm was of the greatest value to the BBC when it came to contractual negotiations. Cliff cared about rugby (to my knowledge, he had no other serious sporting interests) and he made it his business to maintain, if not increase, the game's profile on the airwaves. Every so often he would travel to Twickenham to talk to Bob Weighill, the long-serving secretary of the Rugby Football Union. 'Now, Bob. Let's talk about the next three years. Could we do the same again, at the same price?' Bob would shake his head, sorrowfully. 'Can't do the same again, Cliff, nice as you are. We have to put it up a bit.' 'Okay, how about a one per cent increase for inflation?' 'Are you able to go to three per cent?' 'Don't think we can, Bob. Which is a shame, because we so love covering it.' 'One per cent it is, then.' As they say, if you can fake sincerity you've got it made.

While Cliff hadn't been on the BBC staff in any formal way – he was a freelance contract man at that time, an arrangement that gave him the scope and freedom to do the things that really excited him – my employment terms were more basic. As a five-day-a-week staff sports broadcaster, I was expected to do anything and everything, at all hours of the day and night. After arriving at the corporation in March 1972, towards the end of the rugby season, I found myself reading out the racing results. I was comfortable in the role, partly because I had an interest in the horses anyway and partly because it was far from an insignificant job. Hundreds of thousands of people up and down the country enjoyed a flutter on the gee-gees, just as they do now, but back then, there were very few ways of staying in touch with events. Unless you were at the course or happened to be within walking distance of one of the larger bookmaking concerns, results were hard to come by. Who wanted to wait for the following morning's newspapers to discover the fate of a £5 yankee?

By far the most important programme of the week in our corner of the BBC operation was the Saturday afternoon live production. My first Head of Sport – emphasis on the capitals, because the position was considered to be very grand indeed – was Angus Mackay, who, with a name like that, should definitely have been on my side. It quickly turned out that Angus wasn't on anyone's side. The only thing he cared about, quite possibly over and above everything else in his life, was the show, which culminated with *Sports Report*, an hour-long bulletin originally broadcast on the BBC Light Programme before moving to the Third Programme, Radio 2 (where it was situated in my early days) and, finally, to its present home on Radio 5 Live. Angus edited that hour himself and seemed to regard it as his personal property, which was probably fair enough, given that he had been responsible for the launch way back in 1947.

When I encountered him he was on the brink of retirement, but he lived up to his reputation as a 'stern, methodical Scot', as one account describes him. He also had a temper. I was in the office one Saturday morning, still trying to find my feet, when he appeared before us in a fearful mood. 'Bloody hell – bloody Bill Bothwell's left us right in the lurch,' he seethed. This was surprising news. Bill Bothwell was a highly respected football commentator based on Merseyside and as far as I was aware, he had no track record of irresponsibility. Angus then enlightened us. 'The bugger's had a heart attack and he's in hospital. On a Saturday! What a time to choose. Who's going to cover the big game now? He's completely f—ed up my programme. And he's always been so reliable. Can't understand it.' I still laugh whenever I think of the incident, but in a way the story is profoundly sad as well as funny. There is, after all, such a thing as life outside of work.

There again, working at the BBC in the early 1970s sometimes seemed like the elixir of life. It was a golden age of sports commentary and I'll always be grateful for the experience, even though my own contribution was low-carat in the extreme. The cricket commentators were rightly celebrated as the grandees: John Arlott, Brian Johnston, Don Mosey, Alan Gibson, Rex Alston, a young Henry Blofeld, an even younger Christopher Martin-Jenkins. *Test Match Special* had been going in ball-by-ball form since 1957 and had developed a flavour all of its own, with John Arlott quickly achieving legendary status through the warmth of his Hampshire burr, the vivid imagery he summoned seemingly at will and the occasional surge of righteous anger, generally in response to some act of perceived committee-room vandalism on the part of the MCC establishment, of whom he was generally more than a little suspicious. My first London home was a flat in Highgate and I quickly discovered that John lived only half a mile away. We would bump into each other on occasion and he would congratulate me on a piece of commentary before explaining, with great subtlety, how I might have done it better.

Brian Johnston was easier to get to know – a less serious man than Arlott, I felt – and was rarely anything other than exceptionally funny. He enjoyed watching rugby and once told me he had been an enthusiastic wing at school, if only for the brief spell between taking the field for his first game and being tackled for the first time. When he was in his 70s, he was asked how he would respond if told that he could no longer watch cricket at Lord's. He said he would buy a rope at the local hardware shop and shin up the side of the ground, daring the stewards to interrupt his progress. 'They couldn't stop me,' he said. 'It's my life.' How lovely is that?

Alan Gibson scared me a little. He was a formidably learned figure who had graduated from Oxford University with a First – having not attended a single lecture, it was said – and been elected President of the Union. It struck me that there must have been a good deal more behind his Oxbridge admission than the ability to drop-kick a rugby ball into a wastepaper basket. He reported on rugby as well as cricket, as did Don Mosey, another senior figure in the BBC sports department. Indeed, Don was my first rugby producer, a role in which he could be very intimidating indeed. On one of my first trips north, to cover the touring All Blacks, he made his position abundantly clear. 'Okay then. Obviously, you'll do the first 20 minutes of each half, because you're on my patch. I repeat: *my* patch. And you're the junior.' Very good broadcaster. Quite belligerent. That sums it up.

Two men with expertise in both rugby and cricket were unfailingly supportive of me: Peter West and Rex Alston. Peter was frightfully well spoken and attended the Royal Military Academy at Sandhurst before moving into broadcasting. He had an enormous range: there were spells as Dan Maskell's support act at Wimbledon; he knew his way around the Olympics; he was perfectly at ease hosting the original *Come Dancing* series. He could write as well. 'Spot on, Robertson,' he would say after one of my fledgling commentaries. 'Well done. Keep it up.'

As for Rex, who was in his 70s by the time I materialised at the BBC, there was never a moment when I didn't feel he wanted me to succeed. It's a slightly macabre story, but whenever Rex is mentioned now the death notice tale crops up. He famously phoned *The Times* to complain about an obituary he had read that morning, demanding to be put straight through to the department responsible. When the switchboard operator told him all such issues were dealt with by the information office, he refused to be fobbed off and insisted he speak to the appropriate editor. 'Our obituaries are generally submitted from outside the office, but our contributors are trusted by *The Times* and we're sure all the facts are right,' insisted the telephonist. 'I'm fairly sure your correspondent has one fact completely wrong,' said Rex. 'It's an obituary of Rex Alston . . . and I'm Rex Alston, very much alive.' End of argument.

The BBC being the broadest of broad churches, there was more to my education than a regular rubbing of shoulders with the rugby-cricket fraternity, whose sporting passions were often interchangeable. I found the football men – and they were all men back then – to be equally generous with their backing. Bryon Butler was the correspondent when I joined and he gave me two precious pieces of advice. The first concerned the Saturday programme's outstanding presenter, Desmond Lynam, who was as accomplished a broadcaster as I ever worked alongside. I learned so many tricks of the trade, just by watching and listening to Des as he brought the show together, but it was through Bryon that I discovered what it was that made him tick.

'What's he doing?' I asked on entering the office one quiet Monday morning and spotting Des crouched over his desk, headset on, listening to something or other with the utmost concentration. 'He's listening to himself,' Bryon replied, 'and if you want to be a top broadcaster, you'll follow his example. Des always listens back to the previous Saturday show, all five hours of it. There is no fast-forwarding. He goes over the whole thing – every question, every link, the lot. And he makes notes. He wants to know how he could have done things better, because there's always an improvement to be made somewhere. It has to be done, old boy, so you'd better make a habit of it. You've been here two years now. Can you honestly stand there and tell me that you haven't said something you subsequently regretted – that you haven't once forgotten to remind people of the score at the start of the second half, or that you haven't occasionally left the listeners with three or four seconds of dead airtime, which feels like a week when you're sitting in your car, wondering what the hell is happening? You have to be your own reviewer and be hard on yourself. It's the only way.' And I did as I was told. I'm not sure I was ever quite as devoted to my self-assessment duties as Des was to his, but down the years I've spent many hours with the tell-tale tapes. Fluency is everything in radio commentary – every 'um' is an embarrassment, every 'er' a humiliation. If you don't review your work with complete honesty and acknowledge your sins, you put yourself at risk of repeating them.

Bryon's second flash of enlightenment, given almost 40 years ago, was on the subject of technology – something I have made it my business to avoid at all costs. Which was his point. 'There is a lot of machinery in our world now,' he said to me. 'Lots of things to plug in, lots of buttons to press, lots of connections to be made. It will only increase. If you're wise, you'll play dumb. Even if you understand how to work this stuff – which I do, as a matter of fact – don't let on to the BBC. Don't let them know you know. If you claim to be technologically ignorant, they'll send someone with you. Someone who will do all the plugging and pressing and connecting and leave you to do something more interesting. It's far easier that way, believe me.' And I did believe, each and every word of it. As many a long-suffering colleague will confirm, I treated Bryon's instruction as my own Eleventh Commandment.

Without trying to be in the least sacrilegious, the other Ten Commandments were handed down to me by Bill McLaren – the master, as far as I'm concerned. He was the nicest, most caring friend and colleague; the most dedicated, professional and inspirational of commentators. It is difficult to imagine a happier combination: a marvellous broadcaster who also happened to be a marvellous human being. People forget now that he was a natural educator. Like a vicar performing services in different churches around his parish, Bill was a peripatetic teacher. I think he was a regular at four schools in his beloved Border country and was still running physical education classes in far-flung corners of Scotland well into his 60s, decades after he had become the most familiar voice in rugby broadcasting. He was also a quality coach: some of the very best players from his native Hawick – Jim Renwick, Colin Deans, Tony Stanger – came under his wing as they made their long journey towards the full Scotland team. All this speaks to his innate generosity of spirit.

And when his day's work was done, he would turn to his preparation for the commentary match ahead of him. Somewhere around 18 hours of prep per game, on average. Out would come the charts, on which he would compile thousands of facts, and the coloured counters he used as memory tools. A white counter bearing the number two might, down the years, have referred to John Pullin of Bristol or Peter Wheeler of Leicester or Brian Moore of Harlequins – England hookers all. A green counter marked with the figure seven would stand for one of the many and varied Ireland breakaway forwards who played championship rugby down the decades: Fergus Slattery or John O'Driscoll, Nigel Carr or Philip Matthews. The counters, dozens of them, would disappear into a bag and be shuffled around. Then he would draw one out and recite everything worth knowing about the relevant player – height, weight, inside leg measurement, place of birth, school, injury record, number of caps, number of points, number of times he blinked during his waking hours. His famous charts, works of art for those of us who shared his profession, were therefore a back-up – a safety net. If he could broadcast the information without taking his eyes off the action, he felt he was doing a proper job.

Bill had taken an interest in me while I was playing the game and had been exceedingly kind about my style of rugby, highlighting the attacking flourishes while drawing a discreet veil over the defensive frailties. If I made a half-break that petered out, he would not criticise me for disappearing up a cul-de-sac. Instead, he would talk about a 'wonderful break that would surely have led to a try had the support been there'. When I was handed the Scotland vice-captaincy and was obliged to attend press conferences, he would lob me an easy long hop of a question and smile gently as I smacked it to the boundary. After the knee injury that ended my international career, we kept in close touch: he was supportive of my decision to go into teaching because he was a teacher himself and considered it a wholly honourable profession. And when he invited me to join him in the commentary box – almost always in Scotland, for he rarely set foot in England on club rugby duty – he spent hours talking me through the 'dos' and 'don'ts' and explaining my role in detail. 'Never repeat what the commentator has said,' he told me. 'You're job is to add to it.'

Slowly but surely, we developed our broadcasting relationship. A typical exchange: 'The ball has gone into touch eight yards' – not seven or nine – 'from the Hawick line. That was a fine kick.' 'Yes, and it was the right thing to do because there was no overlap, and while Langholm have the throw they have to propel it over the head of Willie Hunter, who's 6ft plenty.' 'Aye, he's like a lighthouse in the desert, Willie Hunter. He won't have a clue what to do with the ball when he's won it, but win it he will.' After which he would present me with a Hawick Ball – one of the boiled sweets he always carried with him, with the same solemnity as he carried his charts. We clicked, purely and simply, and I couldn't have wished for a better education. If a commentary went well, he'd give me a smile and a 'you're on fire, son'. If I made a cheeky remark about his obsessive preparation – if I suggested that as one team were playing in green and the other in red, there was nothing else we needed to know – he'd roll his eyes and call me a 'right tease'.

So many things about Bill amazed me, not least the tiny hint of vulnerability beneath those comforting layers of hard-earned expertise. It seems extraordinary to say it, but he was never entirely convinced that his BBC position was safe and occasionally gave voice to his suspicions that some commentator somewhere was after his job. Some time after I had flown the nest and spent years travelling the length and breadth of Britain watching the best club rugby around and had a few Five Nations and foreign tours under my belt – sometime in the late 1980s, it must have been – I told him that I, for one, would never replace him, even if the corporation offered me a king's ransom. 'Why?' he asked. 'It's the best job in the world.' 'It's really not,' I said. 'You cover Hawick versus Jedforest four times a season. You go to Gala versus Melrose and – oh, the *big* one – Watsonians against Glasgow High. This is you, 40 weeks a year. Soul-destroying.' 'That's not fair, son. All the top Scottish players are here. I love it.' 'But look at me: I do all the Five Nations games, all the autumn internationals, a tour every year. Every corner of the world. When you go away, it's to Kelso or Langholm – and even then you can't wait to get back to Hawick. You should remember that while it's heaven on earth to you, there are other people who see a day out of Hawick as a day well spent.' 'You may have a point there, son, but I still think you're after my job.' 'Bill, I would rather die.' 'I believe you, son, but allow me a quick look in your bag, just in case there's a knife in there.' Then he grinned at me. He knew he could trust me.

Quite why a commentator as skilled and revered as Bill suffered from a lack of self-belief, I've never been able to fathom. I know this much for certain, however: there were no knives concealed amongst the charts and Hawick Balls in the McLaren brief case. I can't think of a player who didn't like him and that fact alone speaks volumes, especially in an age of deep suspicion between the practitioners of rugby and the chroniclers of it. How did he achieve the seemingly unachievable by spending 50 years in sports journalism without making a single enemy? His most heartfelt advice to me provides the explanation. 'Remember, son,' he said. 'When you're commentating, you're not a tabloid newspaper in human form. You're not seeking blood. If a full-back drops a high one, you don't destroy his life – you don't say things that will hurt his mother or his granny or his wee bairn. He isn't a war criminal or a homicidal maniac – not as far as you know, anyway: all he's done is drop a rugby ball, which we can't be completely sure didn't drift on the breeze or spin an inch off-line just as it reached him. Instead of vilifying people you should make a point of mentioning all the good things they do, and if there's something wrong you simply point it out rather than make a West End production of it. "The worst pass I've ever seen", "the most pathetic tackle in the history of the game" – it's not nice and it's not necessary, all that nonsense. Be kind. You gain nothing from being an assassin.'

I've tried to follow that advice, almost to the letter. If I've never completely drawn a veil over a significant error, I can't remember ever really going after someone on air. How could I, having been taught by Bill? For years, he would listen to my commentaries and give me his thoughts. 'I heard you on Saturday, son,' he would say on the phone. 'Very good. Very good. Just one thing, if you don't mind my mentioning it . . .'

Steadily, with the priceless support of Cliff and Bill, I increased my footprint on the BBC's rugby coverage. Rex Alston had finished, as had Alan Gibson, and Peter West was heading towards retirement. That left more work for the rest of us and I was happy to go wherever the corporation felt like sending me. That first taste of tour broadcasting, when I joined Cliff and the party-loving, highly gifted Welsh commentator Alun Williams for the last two Tests of the '74 Lions tour in South Africa, left me wanting more: my job there was to conduct interviews, not describe the action or pass judgement on it, but those mighty games in Bloemfontein and Johannesburg and the events surrounding them produced enough memories to last a lifetime.

On my return, I quickly found myself contributing to the Five Nations coverage. This was the big time and I was loving it. I did not, however, head out with the 1977 Lions party, who, led by the great Welsh outside-half Phil Bennett, travelled to New Zealand for a 21-match tour that was probably the wettest ever. Day after day it poured with rain, leaving the British and Irish players homesick at best and clinically depressed at worst. For my part, I enjoyed the English summer to the full by joining Peter Bromley, as great a commentator as Bennett was a rugby player, on the horseracing beat. Not everyone got on with Peter like a house on fire – he could be very sharp-tongued, especially to those poor producers of the live Saturday programme who had the effrontery to resist his trademark 'come to me now' command for more than a split-second – but I felt there was a warmth between us. He really was something else when it came to horse identification. I recall being with him at a running of the Steward's Cup at Goodwood: 40 horses sprinting six furlongs from a hidden start down in the dip, not so much a challenge to a commentator as his worst nightmare. Peter called it like a dream, without a word – still less a horse's name – out of place. It was close to genius, and it left me dumbstruck.

Yet even when a career is gathering pace, as mine was with the increasingly high-profile radio commentaries and the regular television spot on *Rugby Special* (initially produced on something less than a shoestring and broadcast from a locker room with adjoining toilet until a belated move to proper studio accommodation at the BBC's White City headquarters), there is always the chance that someone unexpected will come up with a tempting job offer. It happened to me in 1980, when the *Sunday Times* decided I might be the man to fill their vacant Rugby Union Correspondent position. Why did I accept, when I was making solid progress in broadcasting? Money had something to do with it. I was living in London, with a young family, at a time when the capital was growing more expensive. When a substantial hike in salary was put on the table, I couldn't think of many good reasons to turn it down. A match report and a feature each week, plus guaranteed attendance at all the games that really mattered, wherever they might be in the world? It was a fantastic offer, especially as the BBC were happy for me to continue broadcasting as a freelance, both on the radio and on *Rugby Special*.

It did not take me terribly long to work out that print journalism was a very different beast to broadcasting, but I felt reasonably at home with my match-reporting duties, despite the unsympathetic deadlines. Those were the days before mobile phones and the internet, of course, so it was vital to source the means of communication before arriving at the ground for a big Saturday match. Happily, one of my predecessors on the paper had been Vivian Jenkins, who had played international rugby for both Wales and the Lions as well as first-class cricket for Glamorgan. It was to him I went in search of guidance.

'Here, Ian, is my old contacts book,' he said, handing me a small volume thumbed to within an inch of its life. 'You'll find it comes in useful. Now, where's your first game?' 'It's at Moseley this weekend.' 'Moseley? Moseley? How wonderful.' And he cried tears of laughter. 'Go to this address, just by the ground at The Reddings,' he continued. 'There you will find a very helpful couple who will give you sandwiches for lunch – proper sandwiches with the crusts removed – and allow you to use their phone to file your dispatch after the final whistle.'

I took him at his word, arriving at The Reddings on a beautifully hot autumn day for my debut as a Sunday journalist. I knocked. There was no answer. I knocked again. No answer. I was panicking now. Where would I find another phone at this late juncture? More than that, I was peckish. To my great relief, a shadow finally appeared through the frosted glass in the door . . . and there stood a striking young lady with barely a stitch of clothing upon her frame. 'Sorry,' she said. 'We've been sunbathing.' At which point she was joined by her identical twin sister, identically underdressed. 'What can we do for you?' said the first. 'I think you've done quite enough already, but my name is Robertson and I hope you're expecting me.' The penny dropped and in I went for my sandwiches, prepared in advance as always by their mother. And when I'd finished my lunch, I sank to my knees in prayer and said a heartfelt thank you to Mr Vivian Jenkins. The following week, my sports editor, John Lovesey, asked me where I was planning to go next. 'Wherever you like, John,' I said. 'London Scottish? Perfect. And I notice that the following week, Moseley are playing at home. . . '

I was reasonably comfortable with the live reporting side of the job: it was rather like dictating radio analysis down the phone to a copy taker, none of whom ever subjected me to the treatment meted out to the late Chris Lander of the

Daily Mirror, who was famously asked by a weary typist halfway through his match piece: 'Is there much more of this shite?' However, the feature work was more testing. 'Correspondents usually come into the office on a Friday to write their main piece,' John Lovesey told me, gently, 'but perhaps you should come in on a Thursday.' I would sit in a corner of the sports department, struggling to get my paragraphs in something vaguely approaching the right order and failing miserably. If there had been a dunce's cap handy, I'd have been wearing it.

Then came the day when the sports hierarchy suggested a feature interview with the finest of all Welsh full-backs, JPR Williams. He was a busy sort, being a surgeon at a hospital somewhere down Gwent way, but he agreed to meet me for two hours after completing his morning caseload. I made the trip down from London and waited, notebook in hand, for the great man to appear. 'Sorry,' said JPR, looming into view. 'I have to attend a very important meeting, so the interview's off.' I tried to dig in my heels. 'Well, I have to write 2,000 words about you for Sunday's paper and it will be a lot easier if I can ask you a few quick questions. It will certainly look a lot better with some Williams quotes. Twenty minutes should do it.' He wasn't having it and I left with a blank sheet of paper. On returning to the office, I knocked out a rather tough piece. Early on the Sunday morning, with the paper on the streets, I received a phone call. 'I've just read your demolition of JPR Williams,' said the voice, 'and it's absolutely brilliant.' 'Who's that?' I asked, a little nervously. 'It's me, Chris, his brother. You coached me at Cambridge.' It was a funny moment, but I've since had my regrets over that article. When my dear friend and colleague Alastair Hignell was diagnosed with multiple sclerosis, JPR made contact immediately. 'Are you doing something for Higgy?' he asked. 'We're putting on a dinner.' 'I'd love to come along and I'll bring one of my Lions Test jerseys to auction.' I don't mind admitting that I shed a tear.

My spell on the *Sunday Times* was far from an unmitigated disaster: apart from anything else, I had two colleagues – Michael Green, the very funny author of the bestselling *Art of Coarse Rugby*, and Norman Harris, a New Zealander who did much to popularise mass running in this country before the dawning of the city marathon era – who put a smile on the face of the working week. But I didn't feel as settled in newspapers as I had in the broadcasting world, so when Peter Lorenzo, then a familiar football voice at the BBC, made contact and suggested I might like to retrace my steps, I was more than ready to discuss the fine detail. The 1983 Lions tour of New Zealand was on the immediate horizon and he told me I'd be going on it if we reached agreement. 'Will I have a title?' I asked. 'I didn't have a title last time.' 'We'll be calling you "Rugby Correspondent",' Peter replied. 'I think that'll do just fine,' I said. 'When do I start?'

A THINKING
MAN'S GAME

IT can be cold and wet in the South Island of New Zealand in the months of June and July. Make that *very* cold and *extremely* wet. It can also be highly instructive. Midway through the British and Irish Lions trek through All Black country in 1993 – from memory we were in Dunedin, where the tourists had just been soundly beaten by a typically vigorous and energetic Otago side – I was enjoying a contemplative coffee with Ian McGeechan, the head coach of the party, when we spotted a woman of advanced years searching for a seat in the bar. Being the gentleman he is, Ian shifted to one side and invited the lady to take the weight off her ageing feet. She had barely finished thanking him when she said: 'Hang on a minute – aren't you Ian McGeechan? Want to know where you're going wrong?'

Ian was well acquainted with this kind of thing. He had spent enough time in New Zealand to know that when it comes to rugby, everyone has an opinion – that you can't buy a packet of chewing gum at the corner shop without the owner saying: 'That'll be 20 cents – and by the way, your flankers are rubbish.' But he was also a careful listener, as all great coaches are, and he paid full attention to this latest free-of-charge tutorial. 'I've watched the last three matches,' the lady informed him, 'and your kicking game is completely muddle-headed. It's plenty long enough, but you're booting the ball into open field and giving us too much time and space to run it back. Why would you want to do *that*? If you give us both sides of the field to attack you, you're bound to lose. What you should be doing is going to the lines. It's elementary.' It was the most brilliantly detailed analysis, to the extent that Geech had no argument to put against it. 'Yes, yes . . . you're quite right,' he said when the class ended. And after bidding his instructor farewell in characteristically polite fashion, he took the lesson on board. For the rest of the tour, the Lions kicked more intelligently and to far greater purpose. Partly as a result, they almost won the series.

As the BBC's rugby correspondent, I had a range of roles: it was not simply a matter of delivering an accurate, entertaining commentary on match day. There was an analytical side to the job, and as there can be no analysis worthy of the name without understanding, it was essential to build relationships with key figures in all the major teams – people who knew exactly what was going on, because they were the ones in charge. Captains and senior players were in that group, as were those administrators and rugby politicians who had access to the inner sanctum. But the principal insiders were the coaches and it was my good fortune over the course of almost five decades to meet and work with some of the greatest and most successful practitioners of the art, from Carwyn James in Wales in the 1970s to Clive Woodward of England in the late 1990s and early 2000s; from Ronnie Dawson and Syd Millar in Ireland during the early days of top-level coaching, to the likes of Graham Henry, Steve Hansen, Vern Cotter, Joe Schmidt and Eddie Jones – significant rugby thinkers who launched their careers in New Zealand and Australia but understood the importance of experiencing different rugby cultures and made it their business to take on prominent roles a very long way from home. These people are living proof that in the union game, as in so many other walks of life, travel broadens the mind.

In my list of coaching greats, Ian McGeechan occupies the very top position. I must have played against him at some point towards the end of my own career, for there was only a short period of time between my final appearance for Scotland in the 1970 Test against Australia and Geech's international debut against the All Blacks in 1972. He was primarily a centre, but he had the all-round game to stand his ground as a high-class No.10 and he was picked in that position by the Scottish selectors on more than one occasion. Indeed, he played an entire Five Nations tournament at outside-half in 1975, forming a useful combination with the redoubtable Dougie Morgan.

But my first really clear memory of him is in South Africa with the Lions in 1974, where he was an extremely important, if rather under-celebrated, member of Willie John McBride's 'Invincibles'. Some players in that extraordinary party returned home as unquestioned 'greats' of the sport, from JPR Williams and Phil Bennett and Gareth Edwards up there in the fresh air outside the scrum to Ian McLauchlan, Fran Cotton and Mervyn Davies down there at the coal face. Come to think of it, Willie John also made quite a name for himself by putting the Springboks to the sword in that famous series, as did Andy Irvine and JJ Williams and Gordon Brown and Fergus Slattery and God knows how many others. It is fair to say that by comparison, Geech and his midfield partner, the Irish centre Dick Milliken, received less in the way of public acclaim, despite the crucial nature of their contribution. But it was obvious to me as I witnessed the second half of the Test series at first hand that Geech, a long way short of a physical powerhouse, was a tactical giant in the making, and in retrospect, it was possible to glimpse the future coach concealed inside that red No.12 shirt.

Why did I rate him so highly as a player? Two reasons. Firstly, he was blessed with almost all the technical gifts – if I wanted to save time and energy, I'd list the things he couldn't do rather than those he could – and what was more, he seldom made a mistake. It was a surprise when he so much as hinted at an error, even when his relatively slight frame was tested in defence. He certainly put in more tackles than I had managed during my international career – frankly, it could hardly have been otherwise – and if he didn't smash opponents backwards in the modern fashion, he always brought them to ground one way or another. During that '74 Lions trip, he proved as resilient as anyone. Lest we forget, those tourists undertook a 22-match itinerary that included fixtures against the most intimidating and downright brutal provincial opponents as well as the Springboks themselves, yet in the Test series there were only two changes to the starting team, with Andy Irvine replacing his countryman Billy Steele on the wing for the third match in the rubber and Chris Ralston of England coming into the second row for another Scot, the magnificent Gordon Brown, who had suffered a serious injury when a South African forward head-butted him so hard on the fist that his fingers were damaged and his wrist broken. At least, that was how Gordon told it. The Springboks had a different version.

Secondly, and perhaps more importantly in terms of the coaching career ahead of him, Geech was a brilliant reader of situations. If many of the best players and the vast majority of the most successful coaches are committed students of the game with an inexhaustible thirst for knowledge, Geech was as studious as any rugby man of the modern era. During his time on the field with Scotland and the Lions, he was remarkably alert to the dynamics of a contest and even more attuned to the broader tactical and strategic ideas that might give his teams a narrow but decisive advantage. He was never loud or domineering with regards to his teammates: the notion of shouting the odds, of taking the 'my way or the highway'

My idea of heaven: running free with the ball
… and no tackler in sight

Bill McLaren: the master commentator and
my mentor

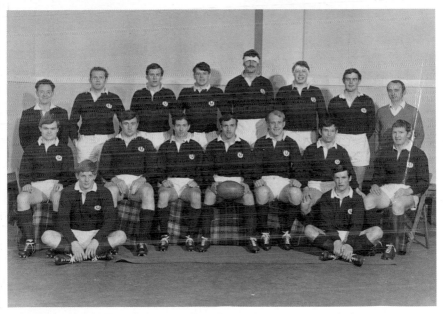

A fine body of men: the 1970 Calcutta Cup-winning Scotland team, with skipper
Frank Laidlaw holding the ball and me sitting to his right

A quartet of rugby geniuses: clockwise from top left – Carwyn James, Cliff Morgan, Barry John and Ian McGeechan

The greatest player of them all? Gareth Edwards scores yet another try – yes, against Scotland

Broadcasters United; preparing for a big Test commentary with Alastair Hignell, front, and producer Ed Marriage

The victory of a lifetime: Colin Meads, the fearsome All Black lock, congratulates the Lions on their 1971 triumph

A team for all the ages: the 1974 Lions during their unbeaten tour of South Africa

Rugby royalty from north of the border: John Rutherford, above, was the prince of Scottish outside-halves; Jim Telfer, below, was the warrior king of the forwards

Rob Andrew in his pomp. I taught him all he knew during his university days!

The most iconic of sporting moments: Francois Pienaar receives the Rugby World Cup from President Nelson Mandela

Pure box-office: the All Black powerhouse Jonah Lomu (above) and the Wallaby wizard
David Campese were the greatest wings in the game

Elizabeth Taylor had stardust in her veins. In case you're wondering, that's me in the picture – not Richard Burton

Mad, bad and dangerous to know? Oliver Reed was a one-off – especially as a co-commentator

Australia is over there somewhere! A paparazzi moment with the star of stars, Dame Edna Everage

approach, was entirely foreign to him. Yet he persuaded people to listen. Whenever Geech suggested this or that, those around him knew he was making a serious argument for the right reasons and were happy to give it a go.

When he set his coaching career in motion, he quickly proved himself a clever motivator. Almost irrespective of the character of the player he was addressing, he knew how to push the right buttons: he disseminated advice in such a way that the player left the conversation not only more confident than ever in his own ability, but also fully equipped to capitalise on the weaknesses of his direct opponent. Geech was also the smartest of selectors. On Lions tours, he repeatedly sprung surprises in piecing together his Test teams: if any pundits can say, hands on hearts, that they always expected the Scottish loose-head prop Tom Smith and the Irish tight forwards Paul Wallace and Jeremy Davidson to force their way into the elite side in 1997 at the expense of an English trio as good as Graham Rowntree, Jason Leonard and Simon Shaw, they should have quit journalism for a new life in the money markets and made themselves a packet.

Furthermore, Geech was an outstanding nurturer of raw talent. To take my own position of outside half as an example, players as outstanding as John Rutherford and Gregor Townsend benefited from being around him. If he was still an active coach of Scotland today, the thrillingly talented Finn Russell would reap similar rewards. Finn has a streak of maverick unpredictability about him, just as Gregor did.

If I had to back one coach to make a success of turning Finn into a complete No.10 rather than an exciting but unreliable trickster, it would be Geech.

Yet for all his softness and subtlety as a guide and mentor, he was no one's idea of a pushover. On his first tour as Lions coach, to Australia in 1989, he was very clear that if a heavy defeat in the opening Test was to be avenged, his players would have to take a no-nonsense approach – an approach that ultimately paid handsome dividends, even if the rugby was a little on the tasty side for a while. Geech has never hidden from his role in events. In his own published account, he emphasised the importance of getting under the skin of the outstanding Wallaby scrum-half Nick Farr-Jones, writing: 'I was quite ruthless. I just said to the players: "We have got to play him out of the game. You've got to hit him late, hit him early, but hit him! Just whatever it is, take him out."' I don't think anyone could accuse the coach of sending out mixed messages in the course of that little address!

He could also fume with the best of them when he felt his team had been badly treated by the referee, although he preferred to do his seething in private. There were a couple of occasions on Lions tours when I witnessed his fury, most famously after the first Test against the All Blacks in Christchurch in 1993, when his opinion of the Australian official Brian Kinsey was not so much low as subterranean. Kinsey had awarded an early try of profound dodginess to the New Zealand centre Frank Bunce and then virtually condemned the Lions to defeat by blowing for an extremely late penalty against Dean Richards and handing the unerringly accurate Grant Fox a shot to snatch the spoils.

Kinsey was in no mood to offer explanations to the media in the immediate aftermath. Along with a bunch of newspaper journalists, I sought him out and asked the pertinent question, along the lines of: 'What the hell was *that* about?' He gave us short shrift. 'Are you going to question me about every decision I made out there?' Kinsey responded. 'Who do you think I am? The memory man of the world?' I drew a deep breath and pressed on. 'Well, you must know what the final decision was for.' No luck. 'I told you, mate: there's 80 minutes of decisions out there.' In other words: 'Time gentlemen please, that's all for tonight. Get yourselves home.' By all accounts, he was equally unforthcoming when the Lions management posed a query or two of their own, which explains why Geech was so livid. He would have needed the patience and tolerance of a saint to stay completely calm in the face of such rank injustice.

Calmness was his factory setting, however: he saw no value in allowing emotion, positive or negative, to cloud his judgement. And anyway, if Geech needed someone to send a charge of electricity through one of his squads – someone who could make himself very plain in telling it how it was – he could always turn to Jim Telfer. To my way of thinking, the softly-spoken tactical mastermind from the Scottish midfield and the stentorian disciplinarian from the back row of the scrum made the perfect pairing, and if anyone is seriously willing to argue the point, they are welcome to look at their record as a coaching partnership. Together, they delivered that greatest of rugby rarities, a Scottish Grand Slam, in the 1990 Five Nations. Together, they guided the Lions to a series victory over the Springboks in 1997 – an outcome that seemed more than a little far-fetched at the outset of the tour, given that the South Africans were reigning world champions. They were massively productive when working in harness and if Ian was largely responsible for the strategic framework of a particular project, Jim was equally influential when it came to the delivery side of things. Especially the delivery of quick ball from set-piece and breakdown. If Ian's ideas were to come to fruition, he needed the raw materials. Without Jim, those materials may not have been available to him.

Jim was a ruck man as a player and a ruck man as a coach, and he drilled his forward packs accordingly, because the way he saw it, Scotland were far better equipped to play a fast game with the ball on the ground than they were to match a meaty bunch like England or France or South Africa in the mauling department. Some of his instructions were blood-curdling, especially to poor little shrinking-violet paci- fists like me. 'You get there first, you get there in numbers and you smash 'em,' he would say during my time in the Scotland side. 'The referee will award penalties against them, even while their blood trickles down into the mud. And when it comes to tackling, we won't just tackle them to the ground, will we Robbo? We'll knock 'em back, won't we? Throw 'em back. All of 'em. Twenty-stone locks, the lot. Isn't that right, Robbo?' And I'd be nodding and muttering 'Yes, Jim; of course, Jim; three bags full, Jim,' while trying to work out ways of getting the hell out of the way without anyone noticing.

You had to be fit to play Jim's style of rugby and no one knew that better than Jim himself, because he'd been as fit as anyone during his days as a rampaging back-rower. When, in the years before the appointment of full-time coaches, he led preparations as captain, he'd have us running from touch-line to touchline at pace, grant us a nice long break of 10 seconds maximum, and then have us going from side to side again. If he'd possessed real pace – that extra yard or so of express straight-line speed – he'd have been one of the greats of the world game. A Kieran Read of the 1960s, perhaps, with added aggression. All the Scottish players of the time knew of his physical capabilities and those of us who had the misfortune to be associated with teams other than Melrose, where Jim played all of his club rugby, could hazard a guess at what might be coming our way on a Saturday afternoon.

I don't actually remember facing Melrose during my spell with Watsonians: what I *do* remember is pulling out of a game against them, which may tell a tale. You have to look at it from my point of view. As I've already mentioned, Jim wasn't entirely convinced by my defensive game. If he was convinced of anything, it was that I didn't *have* a defensive game. Had he found himself in a position to test my fortitude at first hand under match conditions, he'd have done it with the greatest relish. I wasn't especially keen to give him the opportunity. I know my limitations.

There was method to the Telfer madness, undeniably. Back in the amateur era, when rucking was considered not only legitimate but absolutely central to the development of a fast, free-flowing brand of rugby, the Scots were second only to the All Blacks in freeing up ball on the floor while staying on their feet and moving quickly to the next point of contact. Much of this was down to Jim and his conviction that the rucking style was the natural one for Scotland to adopt. He knew that to be successful, we had to play to the strengths of our mobile forwards. Other packs in the northern hemisphere game were bigger, stronger and heavier than anything we could put on the field. What they weren't was faster. As a general rule England were markedly slower as a forward group and while the French had some phenomenal back-rowers – a Walter Spanghero and a Benoît Dauga here, a Jean-Pierre Rives and a Jean-Claude Skrela there – the ruck was not in their playbook, perhaps because they had more than enough on their plate in domestic rugby without the additional problem of boots on bodies. Jim recognised this early and when his partnership with Geech began in the late 1980s, they found themselves to be of the same mind.

Between the two of them, they left an enormous mark on the game north of the border and breathed new life into a

Lions concept that, in the eyes of some, did not fit easily with the realities of a newly professionalised sport. Both had an innate authority about them and if Geech's version was quieter and more contemplative than Jim's harder-edged brand, there was something about the dovetailing of the two that gave added value to both. Together, they generated tremendous respect. What was more, they came up with a distinctive style of rugby that was recognisably Scottish and, given the limitations of our game in terms of playing numbers and resources, highly successful. If anything else could be asked of a coaching partnership, I'm really not sure what it might be.

Scotland have not been blessed with a coach of Geech's quality in recent years, but then, it is not easy to find an all-rounder who is as productive in the long-haul national environment, where players of differing standards are thrown together and moulded into a side over a period of seasons, as he is on a Lions tour, where the very best talent in the British Isles congregate for a two-month race against the clock. For some years, the search seemed futile. When Geech finished his second spell in charge, back in 2003, the union turned to Matt Williams, an Australian, in the hope that he would bring something fresh to the mix. He lasted two years, winning only three of his 17 Tests. Next up was a home-grown option in the shape of Frank Hadden, a man of Dundee who, by pure coincidence, had played club rugby with Geech at Headingley and, being an outside-half, had understudied him during the great man's absences on international duty. Frank's record was fairly good, given the struggles of the time, but he parted company with the national team in 2009 and was replaced by Andy Robinson, the former Bath and England flanker who had been a major cog in Clive Woodward's coaching wheel at the triumphant 2003 World Cup but had found the top job just a little harder to handle. Once again, Andy made progress of sorts, and very nearly reached the break-even stage in terms of results. But when Scotland failed to find a way out of their World Cup pool in New Zealand in 2011 – the first time this had happened to them in the history of the tournament – and then contrived to lose a home match with Tonga the following autumn, there was nowhere for him to turn.

Enter another Australian, the flamboyantly informal Scott Johnson, who had not been particularly prominent either as a player or a coach in his homeland, but suddenly surfaced as a skills specialist with Wales after an invitation from a certain Graham Henry, who was then honing his own methods in the principality before returning to his native New Zealand and performing no end of wondrous deeds. My dealings with Scott were not 100 per cent harmonious: he liked to put on a performance in front of the media and my instinctive response was to take him on at his own game. 'That's a very funny reply, Scott,' I once said to him, 'but the question I asked was actually a serious one. We're very lucky here in Scotland: if we want humour, we have Billy Connolly.' Exit Johnson stage left. End of press conference.

I thought our rugby fortunes took a significant upturn when Scott's period as interim coach ended in 2014 – he disappeared upstairs with the title 'Director of Rugby' on his headed notepaper – and Vern Cotter, a hard-eyed New Zealander, took over the running of the national team. There was no joke-cracking with Vern, no funky language or super-trendy business-speak, no vaudeville act. Here was a man who understood the fundamentals of the game and considered it his job to put them in place. Everything about him spoke to his image as a Kiwi countryman with a tough, ultra-realistic, deeply unromantic view of the game and an equally ingrained reluctance to waste words. He seemed to be made of granite, or some equally hard material. If the New Zealanders ever decided to create their own Mount Rushmore as a way of celebrating their finest rugby coaches, they wouldn't need a sculpture of Vern. A simple line drawing would have the same impact.

Wherever he had worked, he had won things. He made a success of his first coaching job, with Bay of Plenty in the North Island of New Zealand, and won two Super Rugby titles during a three-year spell as forwards specialist with the Christchurch-based Crusaders. (In the 'fallow' year, he had to settle for the runners-up spot.) On moving to Clermont Auvergne in France, where he formed an extraordinarily fruitful partnership with his compatriot Joe Schmidt, there was a first Top 14 title for the team to go with a European Challenge Cup victory. Clermont also reached a Heineken

Cup final and three further domestic deciders under his guidance. To my mind, it was no surprise that in Scotland he wasted little time in setting us on the right road. Between 2014 and 2017 he recorded a 53 per cent win rate – the first time any coach had finished on the right side of the ledger since Geech's brilliant initial spell in the late 1980s and early 1990s. What was more, he was within one bad refereeing decision of taking Scotland to a World Cup semi-final for the first time since 1991. I liked the way he coached and I loved the way he presented himself and his team in public. Suddenly, we were a serious rugby nation once again.

If I'm being honest, I'd have preferred Vern to stay on past 2016. Two of my great friends in New Zealand, the long-retired All Black centres Bruce Robertson and Bill Osborne, assured me right at the start that Cotter was highly regarded in his homeland, and if you're highly regarded there it's pretty certain that you'll pass muster everywhere else. Had I been situated somewhere near the top of the Scottish Rugby Union, my plan would have been to draft Gregor Townsend in from Glasgow as attack coach under Vern with a view to him taking on the top job after the 2019 World Cup in Japan. In fact, I mentioned this to one or two long-standing acquaintances who wield some power and influence at Murrayfield. But with Glasgow performing so well in both domestic and European competition, Gregor was a much sought-after figure, particularly by big-spending clubs in France. 'This is our chance to keep him here in Scotland,' said my SRU contacts. 'We have to nail it now.' So it was that Vern went back to the club rugby scene across the water with Montpellier and Gregor took over as the main man. I'm sure he'll be fine. He's an unusually gifted individual – some of his ideas on the game are truly original – and a thoroughly nice man into the bargain. He's already taken Scotland to an all-time high ranking of fifth in the world and if, under his leadership, we've let slip a couple of games against beatable opposition in Fiji and the United States, we've also obliterated the Wallabies, run the All Blacks extremely close and sent the English homewards from Murrayfield to lick their wounds. Not bad for starters.

It has been the nature of my job with the BBC to spend more time south of the border than in northerly lands, so my relationships with England coaches have been at the heart of things. Some of the early Red Rose bosses are all but forgotten now – John Elders, John Burgess, Peter Colston – and no one delivered on the results front until Mike Davis, who won a bunch of caps as a lock in the 1960s despite playing relatively low-key club rugby in Devon, took hold of Bill Beaumont's team midway through 1979 and put together a run of results that rewarded the Twickenham faithful for their endless patience. His first game in charge was a single-point home defeat by the All Blacks. It was a poor spectacle, but as the New Zealanders fielded players as good as the scrum-half Dave Loveridge, the lock Andy Haden, the No.8 Murray Mexted and the great captain Graham Mourie, it was hardly a source of shame. From there, England won a first Grand Slam in almost two decades, and some of the rugby played by Bill and his colleagues in a formidably experienced pack – Fran Cotton, Peter Wheeler, Phil Blakeway and Maurice Colclough; Roger Uttley, Tony Neary and John Scott – was outstanding. And England being England, they chose Calcutta Cup day at Murrayfield to make a statement. Five tries, three of them from the Orrell wing John Carleton, underlined their superiority.

They would not taste such success again until Geoff Cooke, that down-to-earth son of Yorkshire's broad acres, was appointed to the top job following the failed World Cup campaign of 1987, when England flopped out at the quarter-final stage. I got on well with Geoff and certainly felt he deserved the plaudits that came his way. He was a very fine selector – his appointment of Will Carling as captain, despite the fact that the Harlequins midfielder had only seven caps to his name, was as close to a master-stroke decision as any to come out of Twickenham in living memory – and he moved heaven and earth to re-establish England as one of the game's major forces. There was a consistency of approach that had been almost foreign to the Red Rose operation for longer than anyone cared to remember and the rewards were great. A Grand Slam and a World Cup final in 1991; a magnificent follow-up Slam in 1992; a convincing victory over the touring Springboks, back in the international fold after years of apartheid-driven isolation. These were heady days for English rugby and it was a pleasure to witness, and commentate on, the major occasions as they rolled in one after another.

Yet it was not until Jack Rowell replaced Cooke at the end of the 1994 domestic season that we in the media found ourselves in the world of the personality cult. I wouldn't argue for a second that Jack was the type of human being to seek out publicity: he did not go out of his way to put himself in the spotlight. But he was as big a character as he was a physical specimen – very few players, leaving aside the odd second-row giant, could look him squarely in the eye without the use of a trampoline – and with his commanding air and waspish approach to conversation, he could not avoid being the centre of attention. Under his meticulous and frequently inspirational style of management, Bath had become the most successful side in Britain, by a country mile. They were awash with magnificent players, largely because virtually every A-list player in the land wanted to be a part of things down there at the Recreation Ground, and they had some of the brightest, toughest-minded, insanely competitive individuals to be found anywhere in European rugby. Jeremy Guscott, Richard Hill, Gareth Chilcott, Graham Dawe, John Hall, Andy Robinson and, most prominently, Stuart Barnes . . . these people took an awful lot of beating, and they were not beaten very often. It is said that Stuart lost 10 serious games of rugby in as many years. I suppose it depends on your definition of the word 'serious', but if that figure is even remotely accurate, it is an astonishing record. It is little wonder that, during a club training session on a Monday or Wednesday night, Jack felt able to cut a fully-fledged international down to size by saying: 'That may be good enough for England, young man, but it isn't good enough for Bath.'

His way of doing things on the banks of the River Avon could not be translated easily to the Twickenham environment, where players from Wasps and Quins and Leicester were either unwilling or unable to respond quite so readily to the brutal 'shame culture' that had taken root in the Bath dressing room, and there were times when Jack felt a little uneasy under interrogation from the press. But I was lucky in my dealings with him. 'Ian!!! Ian Robertson!!! Are you ready?' he would bark, by way of demanding my presence for a private interview. When some newspaperman or other made the point that all one-on-one discussions had been declared off-limits, Jack would wave a hand dismissively and say: 'He's special.' I would then mention quietly to him that such a response was not entirely helpful in terms of my popularity amongst fellow journalists, but he never cared a jot. There was a mischievous streak a mile wide in Jack's character and he took the greatest pleasure in playing the media contingent off against each other. He was also adept at wrong-footing his interlocutors, at making them think twice about the reports or broadcasts they were putting together. On the frequent occasions that he made a remark I suspected was a wind-up, I'd say: 'Really?' And he'd reply: 'Maybe.' And he'd smile, a little wolfishly, before turning on his heel and walking off, leaving me wondering exactly what I would be telling the BBC audience in a few minutes' time.

Yet Jack was perfectly approachable if you did it in the right way and had earned his trust. Like most coaches, Jack placed a very high premium on trust. I could phone him at his home and ask him specific questions about specific issues and he would answer them freely, on the understanding that I wouldn't go blasting the details all over the airwaves. It was one thing to use the information anonymously to give weight to my reporting; it was quite another to quote him directly in a headline news item. The understanding of this difference was absolutely key in building the relationships I needed if I was to do my job effectively. If I betrayed a confidence, there would be no more illuminating chats. I knew that. There was no earthly point in saying to Jack, or any other coach, 'I swear I didn't give that information to any other member of the press pack', if I'd just broadcast it to millions of people tuning into a radio bulletin. Some people think that a journalist's job is to tell everything he knows to everyone who might be reading or listening or watching at any given moment. That's fine in theory. In reality, it's a little more complicated.

Jack enjoyed some mighty moments during his Twickenham tenure: the comprehensive 32–15 victory over the Springboks in Pretoria in June 1994 was a stunning beginning; the Grand Slam campaign in the late winter and early spring of 1995 was very convincing indeed and set things up perfectly for a meaningful challenge at the forthcoming World Cup back in South Africa. There followed some equally mighty moments that he enjoyed rather less, including Jonah Lomu's extraordinary demolition of England on semi-final day in Cape Town and the peculiarly inept home defeat by France in the 1997 Six Nations, when a 20–6 lead deep in the second half somehow went missing. A lurking microphone picked up Jack's thoughts as things went pear-shaped. 'I don't believe what I'm watching,' he said, to no one in particular. Neither did anyone else, least of all yours truly as I looked down from my radio commentary position in the clouds on the weirdness and bone-headedness unfolding at pitch level.

It was the last we saw of Jack on home soil. His subsequent games at the head of the England operation were in Cardiff, Buenos Aires and Sydney, and at the conclusion of that little jaunt to faraway lands – as most English sporting folk will confirm, the Welsh capital seems more foreign than almost anywhere on the planet when it comes international rugby – his day was done. Rumours were circulating that key elements on the governing body wanted to bring in Graham Henry from New Zealand as Twickenham's new overlord; other reports suggested that Jack, a successful businessman in his other life, was reluctant to commit himself to the England role on a full-time basis, despite the union game's sudden abandonment of the amateur ethic and its embrace of professionalism. It was a confusing time for those journalists charged with covering the fortunes of the national team and it seemed to me that something entirely unexpected was about to happen. Enter Clive Woodward as Jack's successor. 'Well, you can't get anything more unexpected than this,' I remember thinking on the day of the announcement.

Of all the England coaches I've encountered during my broadcasting career – and barring the old Northampton flanker Don White, who was appointed while I was still playing for Scotland and packed it in during my spell of teaching at Fettes in Edinburgh, I've had dealings with everyone who has held the position – Clive was undoubtedly the most fascinating, the most compelling, the most quixotic and the least predictable. He was also the most successful, thanks to his remarkable achievements in that year of years, 2003. Which was why I found it hard to criticise him two years later, when he led the British and Irish Lions to New Zealand. In '03, England had secured the most exceptional of Grand Slams – their clinching victory over a pumped-up Ireland side in Dublin was a masterclass in all sorts of ways – and gone on to beat both the All Blacks and the Wallabies down there in the Antipodes. This was unprecedented. Oh yes, almost forgot. They also won the World Cup.

As is often the case when a team dominates at international level to this degree, some historical revisionism takes place, generally aimed at taking some of the credit away from the man in charge and placing it somewhere else. But I have never been tempted to take anything away from Clive and his central role in England's conquest of the rugby world. He had the intelligence, and indeed the humility, to change his plans when it became evident they were not working; he introduced players into his starting line-up at critical moments and reaped the benefits; he modernised the way things were done at the top end of the sport in his country; he sent surges of energy and ambition and optimism through the committee rooms and private bars of Twickenham, where those qualities had not always been particularly noticeable. It was possible to disagree with Clive about certain aspects of his manage-ment of the side and it was certainly possible to be bemused by him. But I found it impossible to dislike him. He was extraordinarily enthusiastic and upbeat and was always the best company. If we see his like again in Twickenham high office, I'll be pleasantly surprised.

So yes, the criticisms I felt obliged to make in 2005 stuck in my throat. But criticise I did. It seemed to me that Clive's selection skills, quite outstanding for so much of his career, had suffered a drop-off since his acrimonious departure from the England job a little under a year previously and I also felt that his planning for the Lions tour, with its separation of the coaching teams for weekend and midweek teams and its 44-strong playing party (not including replacements), was flawed. I was hardly alone in reaching this sorry conclusion. In the official history of the Lions – yes, the *official* history – I read the following: 'It must be recorded that the New Zealand team was a class apart from the Lions who, for whatever reasons, failed to perform to their ability on the field. Their courage under the intense pressure exerted was never in doubt, but what was apparent is that they were badly let down by a coaching staff that devised an outmoded and doomed tour strategy.' The piece goes on to argue that Clive was 'caught in a timewarp' – a direct reference to his selection for the first Test in Christchurch, where almost half the team consisted of England players who had started the World Cup final in 2003. By the time they faced the All Blacks, some of those players had clearly lost their edge, either temporarily or, in one or two cases, permanently.

If I didn't judge them quite that harshly, it was because the Lions were playing some unusually strong opposition. But I *was* critical on air. When I bumped into Clive's wife Jayne at the team hotel, she mentioned this criticism, adding: 'I thought we were all friends.' She was smiling, but she was also making a point. 'Jayne, I'd like to believe we are friends,' I replied, 'but I have to report what I see and say what I think. Clive has been outstandingly good for years, but it's not working out right now. I'm being mildly critical of his current approach, not trying to destroy his reputation. And by the way, have you listened to the whole of my last report? For the first half of it, I'm reminding everyone how imaginative and resourceful he was in piecing together that World Cup-winning side and delivering on the big occasion. Only in the second half do I question his work here. Nothing would give me greater pleasure than to say he's at his absolute best on this tour, but he's not.' To their great credit, both Clive and Jayne accepted that I was commenting in good faith. We remain excellent friends to this day, to the extent that Clive continues to be an indefatigable supporter of my charity work. He's an extraordinarily generous man when it comes to backing a good cause.

The record books tell us that the Lions lost that Test series 3–0, and it is clear to me that if the itinerary had included a fourth international, as in the pre-professional era, the outcome would have been 4–0. In the face of that, it is some-times forgotten that Ian McGeechan was also working on the tour, heading up the secondary coaching team charged with preparing for the midweek matches. Geech had such a rich history with the Lions, such a profound understanding of the unique dynamics involved, that I failed to see how the 'dirt-trackers' would lose any of their five games, even though sides as strong as Wellington and Auckland were on their to-do list. Keen to put my money where my thinking was with a small investment at the nearest bookmaking outlet, I headed off in search of some reasonable odds the moment I arrived in the North Island.

'I'd like to back the Lions to win all of their midweek games, starting with Taranaki next Tuesday night,' I said to the first bookie I could find. 'We don't offer prices on that kind of thing,' he replied. I was taken aback. 'You must do,' I argued. 'You're a bookmaker.' 'Nobody ever asks, apart from you, and I don't go to the trouble of fixing odds for one Scot all on his own. You're the only bloke in the country looking to place a bet.' After another few minutes of back and forth, he relented. 'I'll offer you 5–1 on the clean sweep,' he said. Being just a little deflated by this Scrooge-like behaviour, I decided to push my luck. 'I think 5–1 is a touch on the tight side. The Lions will be saving all their best players for the Tests, so Wellington and Auckland, two of your very strongest teams, will be taking on the second-raters. It should be 25–1.' And I walked out. A couple of days later, I walked back in again. 'How much are you looking to bet?' the bookie asked, wearily. 'Fifty dollars tops.' 'I'm not going as far as 25–1, but 20–1 is just about possible.' 'Done.' My money was on the counter in a fraction of a second. Of course, Geech ensured that it wasn't wasted. It was not the biggest windfall of my gambling career, but I still felt the warm glow of triumph when I collected my winnings en route to the airport for the flight home.

Clive has not coached since – not at any visible level, at least – and there is always a temptation to look back on a rugby man's final piece of work as the defining act of his career. That would be completely unfair in this case. Clive presided over the most spellbinding period in English rugby history, a seven-season ride so gripping that the union game frequently fought football to a standstill in the scrap for space on the back pages of the national newspapers. Every now and again, rugby even forced its way onto the front pages too. It takes a charismatic coach, as well as a successful one, to drive that kind of coverage, and Clive was indisputably a box-office figure. He had a connection with the rugby public, he was willing to take on the establishment when he felt the battle was worth having and he gave the Twickenham crowd a sense of belief. In short, he had style.

As with Geech, it was possible, with hindsight, to detect the essence of the future coach in the player. Clive liked to do things differently on the field and could not countenance the prospect of following all of the rules all of the time. He prized his individuality and frequently bamboozled opponents with the originality of his running lines in midfield and his highly developed sense of timing. When he was brought into Bill Beaumont's side during the 1980 Five Nations as a direct result of the broken leg suffered by the Sale centre Tony Bond during the opening match against Ireland – that fixture at Twickenham marked his international debut – he quickly made his mark as a distinctive figure. The hallmarks of that formidable side were experience, organisation and discipline (leaving aside, perhaps, the bad-tempered, mean-minded punch-up with Wales in the third match of the tournament): back-line players like Dusty Hare, Mike Slemen and Paul Dodge were models of strength and security under pressure. Clive was happy to move away from the playbook. In that sense, he was an old-fashioned free spirit of the kind I had often encountered during my own playing days.

Yet as his coaching career developed, Clive showed himself to be a multi-faceted sort: there was a cold, calculating side to him that few had spotted during his early days in the England job. He was quite ruthless in fast-tracking Jason Robinson into his international starting line-up, even though there was still so much rugby league to be found in the wing's sporting DNA. He was hard on the likes of Graham Rowntree and Simon Shaw, two high-performing tight forwards who would have walked blindfold into most, if not all, of the rival teams at the 2003 World Cup, but could not find a place in England's squad. He was pretty brutal in doing away with the likes of Richard Cockerill, the bullet-headed Leicester hooker, when he felt they had served their purpose. And he was also sufficiently detached from his own emotional side to name an experimental side for a World Cup warm-up game with France in Marseilles, even though victory there would have kept England on course for the longest winning streak in rugby history. Clive picked only three first-choice players – Josh Lewsey, Ben Cohen and Mike Tindall – for that game, while the French went in fully loaded with the likes of Christophe Dominici, Yannick Jauzion, Frédéric Michalak, Fabien Galthié, Fabien Pelous, Serge Betsen and Imanol Harinordoquy.

I could tell, the moment the teams were confirmed, that England's run of 14 straight wins was likely to end on the shores of the Mediterranean. 'Clive, this is so sad,' I said. 'There's a record on the near horizon and you're giving it up. You can't win with this side.' 'I have to see these other players perform,' he explained. 'A record would be nice, but a world title would be better. To win one of those, I must get my squad right. If we're going to get what we want, this has to be done.' England lost by a point. Had they won that night and gone on to record the same results at the World Cup and the following Six Nations, their run of success would have stretched to 25 matches – and that would have taken some catching.

So yes, there was a cool, analytical, single-minded side to Clive's make-up. There were, of course, other sides, and some of the stories told to me by his players were, and remain, very funny indeed. Matt Dawson, an outstanding international scrum-half during English rugby's most memorable years and a very valued friend and BBC colleague in more recent times, was once phoned at five in the morning by the head coach, who had an important message to deliver. 'Matt, I'm really sorry,' Clive said to his bleary No.9 at the start of Test week, 'but I'm not putting you in the team for Saturday. The reason being that in the last game, things went really well for us, especially at scrum-half, and that line-up needs another chance to play together. Don't worry, though: you'll get another opportunity. Do you see where I'm coming from?' 'Not really,' said Matt, gathering his wits as best he could at that ungodly time of day. 'The scrum-half in the last match was me.' 'No it wasn't . . . oh, wait a minute . . . oh Christ . . . yes, you're right. In that case, you're back in the team. As you were.'

And then there were the flip charts. Clive liked a flip chart when it came to presenting tactics and strategy to the team and one day at the England base, he was taking his side through the ways and means of beating the All Blacks at Twickenham a few days hence. Written on this particular chart were the two line-ups, side by side, from full-back to No.8. 'I've gone through it over and over again and I'm telling you now: I would not swap a single one of my players for one of theirs.' There was a theatrical pause, eventually broken by Jason Leonard, speaking in his Barking best. 'I'd have that Jonah Lomu just ahead of Austin Healey, that's for sure.' There was instant support from Jason's fellow Londoner and sporting soulmate, Lawrence Dallaglio. 'Hear hear,' shouted Lawrence.' 'Right, that ends the meeting,' said Clive, struggling to re-establish his authority in the face of hysterical laughter.

As it turned out, the New Zealanders did not trouble England during the 2003 global campaign, for the very good reason that they were never drawn against them. Instead, Clive had to find his way past South Africa (who were weak by Springbok standards); Wales (who were not expected to ask serious questions of their great enemy, having lost 13 of the previous 15 matches against them, but staged something of an uprising on quarter final night before being kicked to defeat by Jonny Wilkinson); France (who were short of confidence, especially when the Sydney weather turned wet ahead of the semi-final), and Australia, who were inexperienced in certain areas but had players as threatening as Lote Tuqiri, Stirling Mortlock, Stephen Larkham, George Gregan,

Phil Waugh and George Smith in their corner, together with home advantage. Again, it was Wilkinson who made the crucial contribution with the boot, but England's sole try – only their second during the knock-out stage – came from Jason Robinson. As the Yorkshireman had also created Will Greenwood's crucial score against the Welsh with a long and bamboozling run from his own half, it was fair to say he justified his double-quick promotion into the elite combination.

There would be subsequent attempts to bring the best of rugby league down south and turn them into the best of rugby union, but the success rate was some way short of sensational. Clive had already capped Henry Paul, the New Zealander, off the bench in 2002, but when Andy Robinson took over the England role two years later and tried to make Paul a more central figure, things went very wrong extremely quickly. Andy's successor was another Bath coach, Brian Ashton, and as a 13-a-side aficionado of long standing – he was born in Leigh, after all – he was perfectly prepared to give the league contingent a chance if he felt they justified it. Hence his experiments with Lesley Vainikolo, a Tongan-born New Zealander built by the same construction firm responsible for the mighty Lomu, and Andy Farrell. Neither were unqualified triumphs. When Martin Johnson was appointed in place of Brian, we saw Shontayne Hape and Chris Ashton join the ranks of the international cross-coders. Of the two, Ashton made all of us sit up and take notice – but then, he was a wing, like Robinson, and wings find the transition far easier than those performing other roles.

And so we come to Stuart Lancaster and his own dabblings with the rugby league community. Under his stewardship of the England team, three midfielders – Kyle Eastmond, Joel Tompkins and Sam Burgess – were handed the white shirt. Of these, the last was far and away the most controversial. It was such an extraordinary move to select a non-union player in a World Cup squad at such an early stage of transition, as Stuart did in 2015, that I still wake up wondering if it really happened. If Clive was bold with Robinson, Stuart was bold with Burgess. The difference? Only one of those players understood enough about what he was meant to be doing to make sense of the coach's decision. To my eye, Sam Burgess might have been a good blind-side flanker at the 2019 World Cup. What he was not, patently, was a good midfielder at the 2015 tournament. He simply hadn't played enough rugby union to merit a place, and anyway, he was picked out of position.

I cannot remember a more catastrophic selection call in the whole of my time in the game, either as a player or as a correspondent, and to this day, I struggle to work out what the hell went on and why. Whether or not his selection was down to Stuart alone, or whether the head coach was railroaded into it by other members of the coaching team, has never been fully ascertained. All I know is this: when I asked Sonny Bill Williams, the All Black cross-coder, how long it had taken him to feel properly equipped as a union player, he said '24 months'. When Sam Burgess, hired at great expense as 'England's Sonny Bill', was picked in the World Cup party, he had barely played 24 matches.

For all that, Stuart deserves a good deal of credit for his efforts in the top job. He inherited a mess in the Red Rose sense – the England team was in meltdown after the 2011 World Cup, where their performance off the field was significantly worse than their showing on it, which was saying something – and as the Rugby Football Union was in extreme turmoil at a political level, the phrase 'poisoned chalice' sprang to mind when he took on the role, initially on an interim basis. He may not have been a Brian Ashton, who was blessed with a rugby imagination rich enough to concoct whole new ways of attacking with ball in hand, but at the same time, he was not a Martin Johnson either. When Martin was appointed, I was near the front of the queue for an interview. My long-suffering and wonderfully supportive producer, Ed Marriage, was the man holding the microphone, for the very good reason that I could not reach much higher than the new boss's chest, even with my arm fully extended. Ed was keen that I should ask a couple of straight questions, rather than throw in some clever curveballs, but I decided to go my own way. 'Don't worry, Ed: he can't thump an old man in spectacles,' I said, reassuringly. When it was my turn to play interrogator, I ventured forth with confidence. 'On the credit side, Martin, you're one of England's greatest ever players and possibly their greatest captain. On the *debit* side, you've never coached anyone, anywhere. Do you have a blueprint?' Ed cringed, his face losing colour, while I received the Johnno stare. Somehow, we got through it. And while I could not, with my hand on the Gospel, claim that I had a warm relationship with Martin during his three years in charge, he was never less than courteous and, like Clive, was more than happy to give up his time for charity.

My relations with Stuart, on the other hand, were entirely positive: partly because he was an established coach armed with an excellent, if not terribly high-profile, set of credentials who went out of his way to explain what he was trying to achieve; and partly because he was such a thoroughly open, honest and approachable human being. I think we trusted each other: certainly, he was perfectly happy to chat at length about selection, tactical minutiae and other team matters, to the extent that when we approached some slightly sensitive territory, it was often me rather than him who would sound the alarm. 'I really don't think you'll be wanting my opinion this week,' I once told him during the build-up to a Calcutta Cup match. 'If you listen to me, you'll find yourself picking the worst England team in history.'

Too many people have done too much forgetting as a result of the World Cup failure in 2015. When Stuart was summoned from the depths of the RFU organisation and brought out into the light, I didn't have an opinion one way or the other as to whether he was the right man for the task. But very quickly, he won me over, together with countless thousands of supporters, through his complete commitment to the restoration of England's reputation as a Test team. There was a salvage operation to be done, and difficult though it was, he did it. If his departure from Twickenham was a painful moment for everyone who witnessed it, his recent resurgence across the Irish Sea in Dublin has been a delight. Leinster have been setting the pace in European club rugby once again and Stuart must be placed very high on the list of those who have taken them back to the summit. He has a lot more to give and I look forward to seeing how his career unfolds.

I dare say there are those in Ireland who would like to see him succeed Joe Schmidt as head coach of the national team – a move that, for different reasons, would be almost as testing as the England role. It won't be easy for anyone to follow Joe if and when he returns to his native New Zealand: I put Joe, so quiet and understated yet so razor sharp in the rugby intellect department, very close to the top of the heap among modern-day strategists; indeed, to my mind, he is the finest coach of the Ireland side since Ronnie Dawson and Syd Millar were in the thick of it back in the 1970s.

Comparisons across the ages are frequently said to be point-less and it is true that when Ronnie, a hooker from Dublin who captained the Lions in New Zealand in 1959, became the first national coach, rugby union was far from the all-encompassing business we see now. Yet he was at the heart of coaching development in that country, an Irish Geech before the real Geech emerged in Scotland, and there were some superb wearers of the green shirt – the wing Tom Grace, the prop Sean Lynch, the piratical flanker Fergus Slattery – who launched formidable international careers under his guidance. And Syd? A prop from Ballymena who played nine Lions Tests across three tours and then coached the greatest touring side of them all in 1974, he drove Ireland up the mountainside to a very high altitude during his time in charge. They were a seriously good side in those years and when they outscored England by five tries to one at Twickenham during the '74 edition of the Five Nations, having drawn with the All Blacks earlier in the season, it was possible to think that Mike Gibson, Ray McLoughlin and Willie John McBride might go on to beat everyone. If those were the early days of coaching in the northern hemisphere, Syd was a long way ahead of the game.

But if I have to place one coach alongside Ian McGeechan and Clive Woodward, it must be a man who famously – indeed, notoriously – was not granted the opportunity to work with his national side. Why did Carwyn James never coach Wales? He was too opinionated, too modern-minded and far too challenging for the rugby establishment west of the River Severn: I imagine his conversations with them to have been similar in spirit, if not in tone, to those Brian Clough must have had with the Football Association. So he was left to work his magic with Llanelli at club level, with the Barbarians at one-off level and, most wondrously, with the great 1971 Lions at full international level. And magic it was. A fervent Welsh nationalist, there is a photograph of him taken at an Eisteddfod in Haverfordwest in 1972. He is wearing ceremonial clothing that to my eye gives him the look of a wizard. Could anything have been more appropriate, given what he had just achieved with the Lions?

When I joined the BBC that same year, largely at the behest of Cliff Morgan, it was common knowledge that Cliff and Carwyn were great friends. In one sense, they had been adversaries: Carwyn would surely have won more than two caps for Wales had Cliff not made the fabled No.10 shirt his personal property with the quality of his performances. Yet their camaraderie far outweighed their rivalry and the two men were as thick as thieves. Both were masters of the spoken word whose language had the force of poetry; both could be almost musical when they talked of rugby and its glories. I met Carwyn through Cliff and it was immediately clear to me that he was an intellectual with the rare ability to communicate his ideas on the union game to all those prepared to listen. He had such a soft, gentle voice, but concealed beneath it was an iron will. 'No,' he would say. 'That is *not* what we should be doing if we're serious about winning this game.' It might have been barely audible, but nothing could have carried greater weight.

If I'd met Carwyn a year or so earlier, I would have listened to the prediction of my countryman Doug Smith, manager to his coach on the Lions trip to New Zealand, when he predicted, not once but several times and with what turned out to be uncanny accuracy, that the All Blacks would be beaten by two Tests to one, with the remaining match drawn. And once I'd listened, I would have made my way to the nearest bookmaking concern, safe in the knowledge that with Carwyn in charge, assumptions about New Zealand superiority would be proved wrong. The Wales team of the 1970s made a decent fist of things without him by winning the Five Nations title far more often than not. How good would they have been *with* him? There you have the romance of sport in a nutshell, for we'll never know.

If Carwyn Jones was a prototype of what we now call the 'supercoach', Eddie Jones is a living example of this rarest rugby species. He took an underpowered Wallaby side to the World Cup final in 2003, was a crucial member of the Springboks' staff when they won the global title four years later, and worked a major miracle in guiding Japan to the brink of a knock-out place in the 2015 tournament. It would be remiss of me not to include him among the mighty names discussed in this chapter, not least because he reeled off 17 consecutive victories after succeeding Stuart Lancaster as England's head cook and bottle-washer. If we include the 'dead match' win over Uruguay in 2015 – Stuart's last game in charge – it amounted to a record run of success for England and equalled the achievement of the All Blacks under Steve Hansen.

Looking back on his career which is still unfolding, Eddie has enjoyed more than is fair share of triumph. Looking ahead, who knows what the future holds.

THE STATE OF
THE NATIONS

THERE are many mansions in the house of the BBC and the extension work shows no sign of ending, thanks to the internet and its limitless capacity. By the time I arrived at the corporation, the enduringly popular *Sports Report* feature had already moved home twice, having been broadcast both on the BBC Light Programme and the BBC Third Programme. Now, it was a fixture on Radio 2, and would stay there until the creation of Radio 5 and, thereafter, Radio 5 Live. Yet this is not the half of it. When it comes to the big rugby events – Lions tours, World Cups, one-off meetings with the great teams of the southern hemisphere and, as February dawns each year, the Six Nations – the entire network is interested, from super-trendy Radio 1 to the global World Service operation. Yes, even Radio 4 demands a piece of the action. Which is where things get a trifle serious.

The *Today* programme is the channel's flagship news offering, capturing the attention of all movers and shakers from the Prime Minister down, and over the course of my broadcasting career, I have found myself in public conversation with some of the very biggest names in radio journalism: John Timpson and Robert Robinson, Brian Redhead and Peter Hobday and James Naughtie. I cannot claim to have faced the relentless brand of questioning inflicted on Home Secretaries or Chancellors of the Exchequer or the chief executives of multi-national corporations, but just occasionally I have found myself squirming in my chair. I still break out in a cold sweat when I recall one discussion with the formidable John Humphrys, who, being Welsh, tends to talk rugby in a very particular way.

I had been previewing the start of the 2000 Six Nations – the first such event, thanks to Italy's admission to the championship – when John lobbed an inquisitorial hand grenade in my direction. 'Just before you go, Ian,' he said, 'tell me this: what are Italy doing in the tournament?' I could have argued that as the Azzurri had beaten Ireland, Scotland and France in the previous few years, they deserved their promotion. I could have said that the old Five Nations was in need of some freshening up and that global expansion had to be the name of the game if rugby union was to make progress as a world sport. But I played the cultural card instead. 'You're assuming, John, that this is all about the 80 minutes on the field,' I remarked. 'It's about far more than that. These championship weekends are pilgrimages. Who would turn down a trip to a wonderful city like Rome, with the Vatican and the Colosseum? Who wouldn't want to go to Paris for three nights with the Louvre and Montmartre and the Eiffel Tower on your doorstep? Or Edinburgh, steeped in history all the way from the castle down to Holyrood? Or Dublin, the most convivial city in the world? Or London, with the West End, the Houses of Parliament and Buckingham Palace? Every one of them a precious jewel.' I could hear the silence. 'And?' John finally said, after what seemed like hours. 'And,' I replied, with great hesitation, 'I suppose, in a sort of a way, a weekend in Cardiff . . .' 'What do you mean by "you suppose"?' roared the great man of . . . yes . . . Cardiff. 'You suppose? In a sort of a way? *In a sort of way? What's wrong with Cardiff? Explain yourself.*' The volume was rising by the syllable. I couldn't have been more on the back foot had I been wearing the No.10 shirt of Scotland and found myself on the painful end of a Colin Meads tackle. 'The point is,' I replied, desperately searching for an escape route, 'I played only one international in Cardiff, during the course of which I created a brilliant try – for Wales,' I said, praying that a little self-deprecating humour might calm the waters. 'Barry John charged down one of my clearance kicks. People said it was the closest I'd ever been to an opponent.' It was the best I could do, having failed to include Cardiff among the great must-visit locations on the planet. John calmed down, but only slightly. 'You've wriggled out of it,' he said. 'Just.'

That same weekend, the Italians marked their entry into the top tier of European rugby by beating Scotland at the marvellously evocative little Stadio Flaminio, no more than a mile or so beyond the Piazza del Popolo, which, appropriately enough, had once been used as a prime site for public executions. The final score was 34–20 to the home side and while the Scots outdid their hosts in the try count, 29 points from the boot of Diego Dominguez was too much in the way of resistance. Dominguez was no Barry John as an attacking outside-half. (No one could ever quite identify what it was that made Barry such a titan of a No.10. How did he glide like that? Where did he learn that sidestep, if not from God himself? Who bestowed upon him an instinct so highly developed that it allowed him to stay a dozen steps ahead of his opponents rather than a mere one or two?) Dominguez had few, if any, of those gifts, but he was a heck of a kicker and his game management skills were not to be underestimated. As Scotland discovered to their acute discomfort that day in the Eternal City, there is no end to the mysteries of rugby at international level.

Nowhere in the whole of rugby are those mysteries more unfathomable than in the Six Nations, the best annual tournament in the union game by a very great distance. During his long tenure as the chief executive of the Rugby Football Union, a spell that was never less than interesting and occasionally proved cataclysmic, Francis Baron ventured to suggest that the final game of the tournament should always be between England and France – the implication being that they were naturally the strongest sides in the competition and that as their rugby economies would ensure they would grow stronger still at the expense of everyone else, the public deserved a climax worthy of the name rather than a damp squib. Since when, both Ireland and Wales have won more Grand Slams than either of their two supposed betters. Which is another way of saying that things rarely go wholly to plan.

The French, in particular, have had their rough spells and are no strangers to finishing below the fold in the final table, yet while the worst performing of the old Five Nations contestants have, far more often than not, had their Wooden Spoon blushes saved by the Italians, the Azzurri newcomers have still found ways to record tournament victories over all opponents except England (whom they should have beaten on more than one occasion but never quite found the composure). Who could have predicted England's long-awaited clean sweep in 2016, just a few weeks into Eddie Jones' stewardship of a team still stained by their failure to find a way into the knock-out stage of their own World Cup? By the same yardstick, there were not too many people prepared to bet that Jones and his men would be beaten three times in the 2018 edition of the competition. The moment we say we know for sure how the grand rugby weekends of February and March will pan out, the Six Nations makes us look stupid.

I would like to think – and it would certainly be good for the growth of the game around the world – that the southern hemisphere's take on our tournament, the Rugby

Championship, was offering something similar: not just in terms of competitive unpredictability, but also in the wider sense of cultural experience. Sadly, it isn't – and I don't think it can hope to do so. Between Argentina's inclusion in 2012 and the end of the 2017 competition, the All Blacks lost only two of their 33 games and had a positive points difference of almost 600. Over the same period, the Wallabies, second in the performance table, lost 15 matches with a negative points difference of nearly 100. Whatever that is, it is not the definition of competitive. As for the broader issue, the distances between Auckland and Johannesburg, Sydney and Cape Town, Buenos Aires and everywhere, are simply too great. You can't fly from Dunedin to Mendoza for a rugger weekend and be back at work on Monday morning unless you're Buzz Aldrin. The commercial jet engine is a wonderful thing, but it's not *that* wonderful. When all is said and done, we are lucky up here in Western Europe. We are in the right part of the world, with the right geography, the right number of strong teams and the right kinds of contrasting but closely linked rugby traditions. As long as we look after what we have, we'll be able to indulge our appetites for many decades to come.

We are beginning to hear voices in support of a Six Nations expansion policy to include one, perhaps two, of the Eastern European teams, the obvious contenders being Georgia and Romania (who were on the brink of making the leap to Five Nations status before the dismantling of the Berlin Wall, the drawing back of the Iron Curtain and the upheavals in the Eastern Bloc in the late 1980s). Even the Russians have their ambitions in this direction. But if you accept my argument that this is a rugby-plus tournament – that the games themselves are a part of the experience but not the whole of it – you must also accept that a weekend in Tbilisi will entice fewer supporters than a weekend in Rome, even if high tea with the Pope is not on the general itinerary. Georgia are currently the strongest of the second-tier nations, but what can they offer? There is nothing in their record of on-field achievement to suggest that a Seven Nations would be in their interest, let alone anyone else's. They have beaten the Scottish and Italian second-string sides, but that leaves them some way short of Italy's body of work ahead of their own inclusion almost two decades ago. As things stand, six is the right number.

My own little sojourn in the land of the Caesars, back in the early 1970s, left me well disposed to Italian rugby, Mafia gunshots or no Mafia gunshots, and that historic victory over Scotland in 2000 was an important statement, even though it came across as just a little rude from the point of view of rugby folk in my native land. If I'm honest, I'm not sure that result took me entirely by surprise, for there was rather more to the Azzurri side of the time than Signor Dominguez and his golden boot. Alessandro Troncon was the best scrum-half ever to pull on a blue shirt and their pack was very powerful, even by their own impressive standards: Massimo Cuttitta,

Alessandro Moscardi and Carlo Checchinato were tight forwards who could hold their own against all-comers; the flankers Massimo Giovanelli and Mauro Bergamasco were among the most passionate, fire-and-fury street fighters in the international game. What *did* surprise me were the events at Murrayfield seven years later.

I was in Dublin for the Ireland–England game – the first such fixture to be held at Croke Park, that grand cathedral of Gaelic sport and, as a consequence of a particularly problematic slice of Anglo-Irish history, an occasion with a fair bit of emotion and nervous energy around it. I decided to go to the ground early, enjoy a bite of lunch and watch the game from Edinburgh, which was kicking off some two and a half hours earlier. Annoyingly, the big screen in the media room went blank just as Scotland took the field. Someone replaced the plug after six and a half minutes and when the picture reappeared, it was perfect. What wasn't perfect, obviously, was the scoreline in the top corner. It read Scotland 0 Italy 21. This was clearly an impossibility. 'They've messed that up,' I said to whoever was within earshot. 'Someone should sort out the graphics.' And then it dawned on me that the Italians were indeed leading by what amounted to a match-winning score, having accumulated three converted tries in the time it had taken the electricians to replace a dead fuse. It then emerged that the Scots had pretty much scored those tries against themselves. 'Own tries', effectively. Bergamasco had taken advantage of a chargedown after 19 seconds; Andrea

Scanavacca intercepted a loose pass to double the tally three minutes later; and Kaine Robertson did something very similar almost immediately. The plucky Scots managed a response of sorts, but it was nowhere near enough to spare the national blushes. When Troncon rubbed it in with a fourth Italian try at the back end of the game, there was nothing left for me to do but turn what was left of my befuddled mind to commentary of the match at hand. As it turned out, England were beaten far more heavily than Scotland had been – the difference being that Ireland scored the vast majority of their 43 points through their own efforts.

Just occasionally, England found themselves in a difficult contest off the field as well as on it. Amid the political fall-out of the sudden shift to professionalism after the 1995 World Cup in South Africa, the search for television money and the life it breathed into the sport grew ever more frantic. The great and the good at Twickenham fell out comprehensively with their Celtic neighbours within a year of the 'open game' declaration when they claimed a larger share of the Five Nations proceeds on the grounds of size. They found a supporter in the shape of Rupert Murdoch, who had moved his BSkyB television company into the rugby mainstream, but very little backing in Cardiff, Dublin and Edinburgh. There was an unholy row, every word of which I had to follow and report, and things calmed down only when a compromise deal was agreed, allowing the Rugby Football Union to take the satellite route while everyone else stayed grounded with terrestrial broadcasting. The agreement was designed to last 10 years. Instead, it lasted three.

In 1999, less than a month before the start of what would be the final Five Nations before expansion, England were expelled from the competition after pushing once again for a more substantial piece of the financial cake. Barely a day later, they were readmitted. I had an inside track on this for I was on good terms both with Allan Hosie, a former international referee and fellow Scot who was chairman of the tournament committee, and with Bill Beaumont, with whom I went back a very long way, having followed his outstanding career as an England lock and captain with microphone in hand, written about his exploits at great length in the *Sunday Times* and participated with him in the authorship of more than one book on the game. When the two men popped into the Drum and Monkey pub in Glasgow for some beer-fuelled diplomacy, I knew precisely what was afoot before the first pint was pulled. When peace in our time was agreed, I was able to give BBC listeners the news in what would now be called 'real time'. England were back in, the big-money sponsors were happy and all was right with the world, for the time being at least.

What then occurred on the field, as opposed to off it, beggared belief. England were good value for their victories over Ireland in Dublin and France at Twickenham, and with a tight win over the Scots already in the bag, they travelled to Wembley for an 'away' finale against the Welsh, who had relocated while construction work was completed on the new Millennium Stadium in Cardiff. On the last weekend, Jim Telfer marked his abdication as head coach by pushing Scotland to a magnificent five-try victory in Paris, with virtually all the havoc wreaked before the interval. It left the Auld Enemy in need of victory if they were to clinch the title.

One writer described Wembley as 'a Welsh suburb' as Clive Woodward's men took the field, with my friend Lawrence Dallaglio performing the captaincy duties. They were in control as the clock ticked down, but not so completely in command that Lawrence was justified in rejecting two simple penalty shots in search of further tries. All England needed was a three-pointer to make sure of the championship, but opportunities were spurned in favour of close-range line-outs. I thought to myself more than once during the last quarter: 'Lawrence, you may live to regret this.' And sure enough, Wales made their way down field, won a line-out of their own and ran Scott Gibbs, their bull of a centre, on the perfect angle as his fellow Lion, the No.8 Scott Quinnell, delivered a flat pass. As I remember it, my commentary went along the lines of: 'Gibbs beats the first man . . . beats the second . . . he goes for the line . . . he's over the line . . . he scores the try that, with the conversion, means Scotland are the Five Nations champions, now and for ever more.' I really couldn't help myself, even though the Scots weren't actually playing in the game I was covering. And if I remind Lawrence of those events when we're together at rugby functions, as I sometimes feel driven to do, a familiar look of pain spreads across those chiselled features of his. 'Enough, enough,' he shouts, every time. 'Can't we just leave it?' One day, Lawrence. One day.

MADIBA AND
THE WORLD

THE career-defining acts of our greatest rugby players are those performed on the grandest stages, and these days, one stage is infinitely grander than all the others put together, with the single exception of a Lions Test series: the World Cup. It's a sign of the times. Think of Rob Andrew and you think of Cape Town in 1995 – a dramatic and decisive late drop goal in a World Cup quarter-final against the Wallabies. Think of Jonah Lomu and you think of the four tries he put past England in the same city, one week later. Think of Daniel Carter and it's the 2015 World Cup knock-out stages that spring to mind. Think of Jonny Wilkinson . . . well, you know where I'm going with that one. In my own small way, I know the feeling. Of my thousands of commentaries and the zillions of breathless sentences I've broadcast over the airwaves, it is a single passage of 51 words, lasting no more than 23 seconds, that sums up my career. 'Thirty-five seconds to go . . . This is the one . . . It's coming back for Jonny Wilkinson . . . He drops for World Cup glory . . . It's up . . . It's over . . . He's done it . . . Jonny Wilkinson is England's hero yet again and there's no time for Australia to come back . . . England have just won the World Cup.'

Let's put that to one side for a moment. Yes, I'm proud of it as a piece of commentary, but there is more to life – and far bigger things *in* life – than a game of rugby union, irrespective of its scale. An example: if you had the good fortune, as I did on more than one occasion, to meet Mr Nelson Rolihlahla Mandela, the entire world of sport is placed in its proper perspective. Of all those who encountered him, even for the briefest of moments, I imagine only a tiny minority would not remember it with great fondness. We talk too freely these days of the 'extraordinary', the 'incredible', the 'amazing'. We are too quick to throw around words like 'charisma' and 'aura' and 'unique'. When you find yourself in the company of an individual as transfixing as the late president of South Africa, you are reminded that language can too easily be cheapened and stripped of its meaning.

It would be profoundly wrong to suggest even for a second that in the case of Madiba, the President's clan name that was used across the globe as a mark of affection and respect, a walk-on role at a World Cup final encapsulated everything he achieved over the course of a tumultuous lifetime. But the photographs of him that day in Johannesburg in June 1995 – clad in a Springbok cap and shirt, shaking hands with the home captain François Pienaar before kick-off, handing an exhausted François the trophy at the end of a shudderingly physical final in which the intensity was maintained all the way through the 80 minutes and into extra time – are among the most captivating and life-enhancing, and indeed the most significant, ever taken at a sports event. The word 'iconic' is another victim of our frivolous approach to language. If you want the true definition, cast your eye once more over those pictures from Ellis Park.

My first meeting with Nelson Mandela was not at the World Cup, but in Johannesburg some three years earlier. The Springboks had just emerged from sporting isolation; Mandela had just emerged from 27 years of imprisonment, 18 of them spent in a tiny concrete cell on Robben Island, situated in Table Bay off the Cape Town coast. He was by now the president of the African National Congress, but it would be another couple of years before he assumed the presidency of his country. The Boks, in many eyes the unflinching representatives of the 'white man's game', were due to play readmission Tests against New Zealand and Australia and, as this was one of the major sports stories of the moment, the BBC decided I should cover both games. The match with the All Blacks would be played in Johannesburg and the tension was almost oppressive. How would the Afrikaners of the highveld respond? The ANC, an increasingly powerful political force in the land, had sanctioned the fixture on the understanding that it would not be used to 'promote apartheid symbols' – in other words, that there would be no waving of the official South African flag or singing of the national anthem 'Die Stem', both of which the party considered provocative. I had to be alive to the wider implications of the event, so when I discovered that Madiba would be attending a reception with F.W. de Klerk, then in his third year as State President, I thought it would be a good idea to hover nearby in the hope that an exclusive interview with perhaps the world's most famous man might somehow fall into my lap.

Off I went, tape recorder hidden in my pocket. I did not have a clear idea of how I might find a way into the function, but I had the germ of a notion at the back of my mind. If I told the security people, of whom there would be plenty, that I was there to see someone as important as F. W. de Klerk on official BBC business, I might have an outside chance. Immediately, I was stopped by a doorman who managed to look both extremely official and distinctly unaccommodating. Time to try it on. 'F. W. de Klerk himself has demanded that I attend,' I said, a trifle pompously. It didn't get me very far. 'You're not allowed in here,' I was told, firmly. 'You have no identification, you have no accreditation, you have no invitation.' All to play for, then. 'It's no problem for me,' I responded, moving swiftly into 'do you really think I care?' mode. 'But I should tell you that Mr De Klerk was quite adamant. It's he who wants me in there. In fact, his people said that if he doesn't get his own interview on the BBC World Service with its 300 million listeners, someone will hang.' At which point, I walked away – very slowly. Then came the shout from the doorman. 'Come back! You can go in, but don't tell anyone who let you in.'We shook hands and over the threshold I ventured.

As I crossed the room, Nelson Mandela was in a corner surrounded by half a dozen bodyguards. I approached, just a little meekly, and waited until he'd finished speaking. 'I'm representing the BBC World Service,' I said, still with no particular hope of success, 'and I'd love to have a quick word. Nothing about the game, nothing about rugby, purely about the occasion and what it means to the country.' He looked away. 'Oh well, it was worth a try,' I thought. Then he looked back, just as I was being manhandled in a gentle but fairly decisive manner by his attendants. One last chance. 'Mr Mandela, the BBC have told me that if I don't get this interview, there'll be a fate worse than death awaiting me when I get home.' Suddenly, he had a quizzical expression on his face and a question in his mind that needed asking. 'What is this fate worse than death, my friend?' I had to think quite quickly, which is sometimes beneficial – and sometimes the opposite. 'I've been told that without an interview, they'll send me to Robben Island for 27 years,' I told him, grimacing inwardly with every word. As the bodyguards responded to this bare-faced cheek by lifting me clean off the floor, the miracle happened. Madiba smiled, laid his hands on my shoulders and pushed softly in a way that returned me to the ground.

He led me to a corner of the room, where there was a tiny little door opening into a tiny little room with two chairs and a table. I'm short, but even I had to duck to get inside. It was empty. We sat down, I asked five or six questions and bagged myself a 20-minute interview about sport being a healer, about the whole country coming together, about the importance of unity and sport's role as a catalyst. He was so gentle, so friendly, so attentive. Everything was said and done with full eye-to-eye contact. I couldn't believe it. I was speaking in private with a man whose invisible presence over almost three decades had won him support and loyalty in every corner of the earth, and who was now a free man at the very heart of South Africa's fragile and perilous move towards democracy. He was full of talk about the new world, about transition. He spoke about his great love of football – in this respect, he was no different to the overwhelming majority of his people – but he recognised that rugby union was the game of the existing establishment, the game in the headlines, and was therefore of considerable importance. He also talked of his love of the BBC as a positive force. I don't think I was overawed at any point: I'd conducted more than my fair share of big-name interviews and was confident that I wouldn't dry up or make a fool of myself. But I was completely won over by his personality. I will never forget those few minutes in that room, not much bigger than a prison cell.

As it turned out, the match at Ellis Park did not quite go to plan. The national flags were waved and the national anthem was sung with considerable gusto by an overwhelmingly white audience. Unsurprisingly, there was one hell of a row. Yet in the aftermath of that setback, Mandela remained committed to the idea that rugby could, and should, be used as a unifying force. Against stiff initial opposition from within the ANC, he won the argument. The extent of that victory would become clear for all to see at the World Cup final three years later.

My second meeting with him was 12 months before the great tournament. I was in Cape Town, following England's eight-match tour of South Africa under the leadership of Jack Rowell. Before the second and final Test, I was staying at the lovely Vineyard Hotel, handily situated for the Newlands stadium where the match would be played. Mandela was also there for some kind of lunchtime gathering. He was now the leader of his nation, not just of his party, and the bodyguard count was even higher than it had been that day in Johannesburg. As I emerged from a revolving door near the function room, our eyes met. We stared at each other for 30 seconds or more. 'This is ridiculous,' I thought. 'He won't remember me. He can't *possibly* remember me.' I moved away, towards the hotel restaurant. Then came the familiar voice, booming out across the room. 'Hey!! My friend from Robben Island. Now you ignore me!' I was flabbergasted. He must have done several million interviews in the intervening time, yet for some unfathomable reason he recalled talking to a little Scottish clown who had crawled into his cupboard with a microphone two years previously. This time, I couldn't think quickly: it was one of the few occasions in my life when I found myself stuck for words. I kept walking towards the restaurant to give myself time to think. Then I turned. Everyone was staring at me, their glasses of wine half way to their mouths. There was complete silence. 'I'm so embarrassed,' I said. 'When I walked in and our eyes met, I recognised you immediately.' Theatrical pause. 'I just couldn't remember your name.' Madiba's tummy, which was now quite substantial, wobbled in and out with laughter. 'My friend,' he said, putting his arm around me. 'We'll have lunch together to celebrate our reunion.' I'd like to say I sat next to him and had a passionate discussion about the great political issues of the day, but in fact, the conversation was far more general and involved several other people. I didn't have my tape recorder on me anyway.

We must now spool forward to the World Cup itself. It was my good fortune to spend the tournament, and its aftermath, on the best of terms with two of the key figures in the Springbok squad: François Pienaar, the captain, and Kitch Christie, the coach. François had played against England the previous year, leading the Boks to a squared series: indeed, he never played for his country without being skipper. Kitch, who had coached François with considerable success at Transvaal, was completely convinced of the flanker's motivational skills and, on succeeding Ian McIntosh at the head of the national team, immediately decided that as far as the World Cup captaincy was concerned, there was no issue to discuss. I knew something of Kitch's background: that he had Scottish family links and had been educated in Edinburgh, at the Leith Academy – a little less expensive than the schools with which I had been associated as pupil and teacher, for the very good reason that it charged no fees at all. But as we'd never actually met, I couldn't claim to know Kitch personally. Imagine my surprise when, as I checked into the Sandton Sun hotel on my arrival in South Africa, there was a message for me behind reception. It was from Kitch, informing me that I'd be having dinner at his house that evening and that he'd pick me up. I'm not sure to this day who or what lay behind this unanticipated approach, although Kitch did mention his love of the World Service, to which he listened avidly. Did François put in a word for me? It's possible. One of these days, I'll make a point of asking him.

Throughout the competition, both men were generous with their time. It put me in a good place journalistically because as the games unfolded, it became clear that the Springboks were genuine contenders for the title. Privileged access to them was worth its weight in gold. At one of their early training sessions, the President was watching and we had a chat over coffee. Thanks to Kitch, I had two further meetings with him during the build-ups to the semi-final and final. Madiba recognised that the World Cup was about the team – that the Boks were front and centre of proceedings. His job, he felt, was to do everything in his power to unite the country behind them. No one who was present in South

Africa during those wonderful weeks was left in any doubt as to the success of the mission.

The most memorable of the training runs was on the eve of the final. Kitch had promised me an interview – the only one-on-one interview he was willing to give that day – and as dear Bill McLaren, my honoured mentor, was standing next to me as I conducted it, I felt doubly blessed. 'Not bad, son,' said Bill, with whom I would share commentary duties on the big day. High praise indeed! Kitch also allowed me to lurk around the edges of the session and get a feel of the mood in the Springbok camp. It was spine-tingling. They knew they were up against it, for their opponents, the All Blacks, were hot favourites. That New Zealand team had illuminated the tournament with the fizzing ambition of their rugby, which allowed attacking players as exciting as Glen Osborne, Jeff Wilson, Walter Little, Andrew Mehrtens, Josh Kronfeld and Zinzan Brooke to show the best of themselves. They also had Lomu, who, in the course of one sensational display in the semi-final against England, had propelled the entire sport into the stratosphere. Influential people who had never considered themselves to be rugby followers – politicians, business leaders, broadcasting giants – were suddenly taking an interest. Jonah was the biggest name in town, as well as the biggest wing in history. Yet with Kitch and François stoking the fires, the Boks felt there was a way to win and that they were capable of turning that sense of possibility into reality. I remember Kitch saying to the group as the training session ended: 'Go to your rooms and be at peace with yourselves. You're playing for your family, your loved ones; you're playing for 40 million South Africans, black and white. Above all, you're playing for Madiba.' And how they played. The gang-tackling of Lomu, the ferocity of François and his fellow forwards around the breakdown, the energy and bravery of Joost van der Westhuizen and James Small and the other relatively small men in the back division, the chilling drop-goal efficiency of Joel Stransky when the moment to strike finally arrived, the joyous response of the crowd . . . it was unforgettable.

I should mention one other thing at this point: through all of this – the tactical and strategic planning, the coaching, the selecting, the nervousness and inner turmoil – Kitch was suffering from leukaemia. He'd been fighting the disease since the late 1970s and it had worked its evil, yet his levels of energy and commitment were extraordinary. He rarely, if ever, referred to his condition during our discussions and he did everything he could to stop it interfering with his work on the training field. If he was weak in body, he was unusually strong in mind. It is said that on one occasion, he joined a Springbok 'huddle' after training and was squeezed so hard by the players either side of him that he was left nursing two fractured ribs. The story goes that Kitch said nothing. He didn't even flinch. Remarkable.

As if there wasn't enough happening on the field at the '95 tournament, rumours of off-field discussions about an

Australian-led professional breakaway along the lines of the Kerry Packer-driven upheaval in cricket during the late 1970s were reaching the ears of everyone who went within a mile of the Springbok, All Black, Wallaby, English and French teams. In the event, these moves towards meltdown persuaded the rugby establishment to strike a deal with one of the most influential Australians of them all, Rupert Murdoch, allowing him to secure the rights to a reshaped rugby offering in the southern hemisphere – a decision that led directly to a formal declaration of the end of amateurism just a few weeks after the conclusion of the tournament. They were confusing days of conspiratorial whispers and counter-whispers and while it wasn't easy, I kept on top of developments as best I could. It was all about money, of course, as these sea-changes in sport always seem to be. As coincidence would have it, I had a little financial business of my own to conduct. It would not change the course of rugby union, but it certainly had a positive effect on my wallet.

I was in Durban, preparing for the last of England's pool matches against Western Samoa. The All Blacks, who I considered to be the most likely champions, were playing Japan on the same day. I was waiting by the hotel lift when a Welshman emerged. 'Okay, BBC rugby man: you like a bet, don't you?' I could not deny it. 'Well, do you have a spread betting account?' 'No, but I know someone who does.' 'What do you think the spread is on the New Zealand–Japan game?' I thought for a second. It would clearly be a massacre, so I went big. 'If I had to guess, I'd say 97–100 points.' 'Wrong. It's 42–45, and furthermore . . . ' I didn't wait to hear about the 'furthermore'. I pressed the lift button, whizzed up to my hotel room and phoned my spread-betting pal to make sure that the information was true. On his confirmation, I phoned the bookmaker concerned and gambled £50 a point – way more than I'd ever risked in previous investments.

The bookie knew me well enough and offered some advice. 'You should know that the All Blacks have picked just about their weakest 15 for this match,' he said. 'That's why they'll win by dozens,' I replied. 'They know they're in the quarter-finals. They also know that if they put out the best side, none of them will be full-on. Why would they risk getting injured by going down on the ball or tackling someone? They'll all play like pacifists. These second-string guys know it's their last match of the trip, so they'll be "full steam ahead".' 'Oh Christ,' said the bookie as he contemplated the error of his ways. 'I didn't think of that.' The final score was 145–17 and it wasn't in favour of the Japanese. Marc Ellis scored six tries all by himself; Eric Rush and Jeff Wilson each contributed a hat-trick; there were nine further tries by various wearers of the silver fern. As for the second-string fly-half Simon Culhane, he landed 20 conversions. Yes, 20. When I phoned for my winnings, the bookie asked, through gritted teeth, whether I was ecstatic, or merely delighted. I said I was bitterly disappointed. 'Eh? Do you think New Zealand should have scored even more?' 'Not at all,' I replied. 'It's just that I didn't expect them to concede two tries and 17 points to the bloody Japanese. That flanker chap of theirs [I was referring to Hiroyuki Kajihara, who twice managed to find his way across the New Zealand line in acts of mind-boggling defiance] has cost me the best part of a grand!' Try as I might, I couldn't feign frustration for long. After all, I'd pulled in thousands.

Having covered every World Cup to date, bookended by the All Blacks' one-sided romp in 1987 and their compelling triumph over more testing opposition in 2015, I am in no doubt that the 1995 tournament was the greatest of the lot, for a wide variety of reasons. But I have another favourite and there are no prizes for guessing which one. I had spent long enough in close proximity to the England team, and formed enough lasting friendships among its senior figures, to pray for their success in 2003. Yes, there are times when a rugby man with a beating Scottish heart must extend his hands and best wishes across the border. I felt that as the sport's best teams gathered in Australia, there were reasons to believe that Clive Woodward and his unusually battle-hardened and experienced side would go very close to breaking the southern hemisphere's monopoly on global superiority. It would not be easy, especially in a corner of the union landscape where England's win-rate had been a long way short of impressive, and on balance, I thought the All Blacks under John Mitchell, until recently a frank and forthright member of the Red Rose coaching staff, held a slight advantage. But there was a very strong chance that England would not face the New Zealanders until the final, and in a one-off contest under the greatest imaginable pressure, anything could happen. Besides, England had just beaten New Zealand in New Zealand despite losing two forwards to the sin bin and being forced to stare down the home side with a six-man pack. The white-shirted fortitude that night in Wellington said a lot about the character of Clive's team.

Such was my confidence, I engaged in another round of odds-hunting and risked £100 of my monthly salary on an English triumph. 'Just hang on a moment,' said my regular bookie, suitably alarmed at the size of my stake. 'We've been putting up with you for more than 20 years now and as far as I can remember, your biggest bet with us was a few quid each way on a 4–1 favourite. Now you want to stake £100 on England? In Australia?' I had my explanation off pat. 'Are you suggesting that I don't have nine friends who all want to stick a tenner on England as well?' It turned out for the best, of course. I could have bought a house in Glasgow with the winnings.

As I've indicated, some of the most important driving forces behind England's victory were, and remain, good pals: Lawrence Dallaglio, Jason Leonard and Matt Dawson in particular. We've chatted and laughed and enjoyed a glass or three of wine in so many bars in so many parts of the world, I have no hesitation in counting them amongst my friends. My connections with players since 2003 have not been as

close. Is it simply a generational thing, the inevitable consequence of a man old enough to carry a bus pass covering the
activities of people young enough to be his grandchildren?
I'm not so sure. Lawrence and Jason – and, indeed, Clive
Woodward – knew what it was to enjoy their rugby in the
amateur era, when relationships between players and the
media were wholly informal, free of the barricades erected by
agents, public relations specialists, marketing executives and
all the other human paraphernalia who somehow connect
themselves to major sporting concerns in the professional
age. Which is not to say that I don't get on extremely well
with some of the players in or around the current England
squad: Ben Youngs, the Leicester scrum-half, has always been
a thoroughly approachable sort with his own views on the
game and the strength of character to express them; James
Haskell, the much-travelled flanker, comes across as half-
bonkers, but I've had my fair share of fun with him over the
years and will no doubt continue to do so, even if he's
becoming just a bit of a threat on the after-dinner circuit.
But all things considered, friendships across the player-media
divide were far easier to form and develop back in the day.
Which is a shame.

Given the respect I had for Lawrence, Jason, Matt and
several others in the 2003 squad, there was no question of
divided loyalties. None of the Celtic teams were in much of
a position to challenge for the big prize, although Wales gave
England all the trouble they could handle during a tense

quarter-final in Brisbane. But for Will Greenwood's try just after the interval – a score created by Jason Robinson, who in a rare outbreak of multi-tasking split the opposition defence with a trademark run from deep *and* passed the ball at the optimum moment – they might not have made it through, although I suspect Jonny Wilkinson, albeit some way short of his best in that contest, would have found a way to win it off the kicking tee however many indignities the Welsh attackers inflicted on the English defence. Jonny had his issues during the tournament, without a shadow of a doubt. He contributed four-fifths of England's points in the crunch pool meeting with the Springboks in Perth (not that the Boks were in much of a condition to crunch anyone at that low point in their recent history) and after that match, there were few reasons to think that he would not build on a productive start and hit top form when it mattered. Then came Samoa . . . and peril. While Jonny was suffering one of his extremely rare off nights in an England shirt, the islanders hit the favourites with what the French would have called a 'try from the end of the earth' and generally made a hard-hitting nuisance of themselves. To make matters worse, England broke the most fundamental of rugby's laws by playing with 16 men during a chaotic spell in the second half. Had the tournament administrators really gone after them, England's title ambitions would have been seriously under-mined. In the event, they escaped with a slap on the wrist.

It was by no means a done deal that England would beat

France in the semi-final in Sydney – they simply weren't playing well enough. But the weather turned grim, the French seemed to convince themselves that they could not hope to win a wet-weather game in the face of their opponents' organisation up front and game management skills in the decision-making positions outside the pack, and as the contest progressed, Jonny was increasingly in his element. Suddenly, there were flashes of vintage Wilkinson, as opposed to the tentative Wilkinson we had seen against the Samoans and the Welsh. When England secured their place in the show-piece, every bit as comfortably as the 24–7 scoreline suggested, they knew their main source of points was back on song. Jonny had been responsible for all the points: five penalties, three drop goals. He had been on the field in Paris when Jannie de Beer, the Springbok No.10, dropped no fewer than five goals to end England's interest in the 1999 World Cup at the quarter-final stage. This was a sweeter feeling, by far.

As the BBC's rugby correspondent, it was down to me to make a connection with Jonny. He was, after all, the star attraction of the team – the top-of-the-bill act. There were some genuinely outstanding players in that England side, from Jason Robinson, Will Greenwood and Matt Dawson to Phil Vickery, Martin Johnson, Richard Hill, the insanely competitive Neil Back and the Leonard-Dallaglio metropolitan axis. But none of those, with the possible exception of Lawrence, transcended the sport in the way the quiet, painfully shy man in the No.10 shirt managed to do. I would describe my own relationship with Jonny as neutral, as 'vanilla'. He was always polite, always made an effort in an interview, was always where he said he'd be when he said he'd be there. But he was by no means at ease in the media environment. Jonny was already famous by the time we reached semi-final night and there was no getting away from it: in the months and years after the World Cup victory, when he repeatedly looked career-threatening injury problems in the eye and overcame them through what appeared to be a process of mind over matter, he grew more famous still. Yet if that fame – or at least, the handling of fame – did not come naturally to him, he always did right by those who worshipped the ground on which he walked. Time and again, I saw him spend an hour or more signing autographs. He was always there, pen in hand, for as long as it took.

On one occasion, before his late-career move to Toulon from Newcastle (to whom he had shown great loyalty when other talented players headed out of Kingston Park in search of club rugby's glittering prizes), I received a request from one of my favourite charities. The Make-A-Wish Foundation works on behalf of children and young people afflicted by potentially terminal medical conditions and does everything in its power to lighten their load, if only for a day, by giving them a special experience. It just so happened that Jonny was the number one hero of a boy who had been given just eight weeks to live. The foundation phoned me, and I phoned Jonny. 'All he wants is to have his picture taken with you and kick a few rugby balls back and forth.' The request was heard and granted. Jonny met the lad and his family at Newcastle airport, checked them into their hotel, took them to that day's training session, passed on some insider's knowledge on how to kick World Cup-winning goals in front of a global audience, and spent some quality time improving his starstruck student's technique. He then took the family to his house, where there was a pool, and asked the lad if he'd like to swim. As Jonny took off his towel at the poolside, the boy said: 'Scars? You call those *scars*?' And as he removed his own towel, the effects of a lifetime of surgery were there for all to see. Jonny knew what it was to undergo an operation, but the tell tale marks on his troublesome shoulder did not amount to much by comparison. He was deeply moved. And virtually every day for the rest of his life, which tragically ended all too quickly, the lad wore a rugby shirt signed, needless to say, by the great man himself.

Jonny's attention to detail, his unflinching commitment to covering all the bases in pursuit of perfection, would have been the stuff of legend had it not been completely factual. Everyone, from coaches and players to journalists and supporters, knew one thing about him: that he pushed dedication beyond the limits usually associated with the union game. In the world of sports broadcasting, some of the biggest names put in a similar amount of preparatory work, Bill McLaren among them. I've never pretended to go anywhere near as far as Bill did in putting together the facts and figures relating to a game, although major international matches demand many a long hour of study. To me, broadcasting is the last of the great ad-lib shows – and by definition, ad-libbing is hard to plan. I believe the best commentaries are delivered in the moment, based not on what a broadcaster assumes will happen but on real events unfolding in real time. I've always recognised the importance of homework in advance of a match and I make sure I have the fine detail and the relevant history at my fingertips. But exhaustive preparation does not mean you don't have to be on your toes. Many commentators down the years have arrived in the broadcasting box fully equipped with statistics, only to find themselves stuck for words in the face of the unexpected. Bill McLaren was the perfect commentator: he did *all* the spadework and was *never* dumbstruck. Me? I could never claim to match my mentor in the first of those disciplines, but I was similarly blessed with the gift of the gab. I'm glad it was that way round. There have been occasions – not many, but enough – when I've attended a club rugby game expecting to provide regular score updates, only to find myself filling in with full commentary for 10 or 15 minutes because a football match has been abandoned or some other unforeseen complication has thrown the radio schedules out of synch. When you hear the presenter say 'We'll stay with the rugby because there's an exciting finish in prospect and the big horse race is still half an hour away', you're hardly in a position to say 'Will we *@?!'. Oliver Reed might have tried something along those lines, but it's not much of an option for us mere mortals.

Ahead of the final in 2003, there was bound to be extra preparation and additional research. Why? Because the interest generated by England's advance was off the scale – way beyond anything I'd ever experienced in all my time at the BBC and in Fleet Street. Even if I'd locked myself in my Sydney hotel room and drawn the curtains, the magnitude of the event would have dawned on me soon enough. For one thing, the Australian press was full of rugby union – a rare event, given that their airtime and column inches are invariably dominated by rugby league, Aussie Rules and cricket. For another, Radio 5 Live's head of sport and the overall station controller were in town. Yes, something big was definitely happening.

There was a whole week available to cover the necessary ground: unlike the football World Cup, where people can play three times in six or seven days, the physical fall-out of rugby at the top level dictates that the knock-out stages have to be run from weekend to weekend. Still, the pressure was on – and not just because I had the top brass of the BBC in my rear view mirror. Clive Woodward gave me an early indication of his thinking in terms of selection, which helped. So too did the arrival of my occasional expert analyst, Rob Andrew, who was always a terrific reader of the game and could bring the right kind of perspective to bear, having played at three World Cups and featured in some of the most dramatic matches in recent rugby history. But I was the one in the hot seat because it was down to me to hold the thing together. Radio commentary is a very different beast to the television version: you have to keep talking irrespective of what may or may not be happening on the field, because there is no alternative. Would I capture the mood correctly? Would my judgement be sound enough to spot the way the contest was going? Would I strike the right balance between objectivity and excitement? In short, would I rise to the occasion?

When the crux moment came, in the last minute of the final period of extra time, it was not without its sense of trauma. England's decisive move was clean-cut and largely trouble free from the broadcasting point of view: the hooker Steve Thompson's throw to the tail of the line-out; the substitute flanker Lewis Moody's catch and delivery; Mike Catt's full-pelt carry into the guts of the Wallaby defence; Matt Dawson's 'dummy trigger' snipe (which took me a little by surprise); Martin Johnson's extra drive, which forced one or two would-be Australian charge-down men back onto their heels; Dawson's crucial pass to Jonny. As Matt would put it later: 'I suppose ideally, Jonny would have liked it on his left foot. But I thought 'he's missed three off his left already, so try one off your right.' I guess I made him look even better than he was.' My problem was that amid the frenzy and exhilaration of one of the most famous three-pointers in history, I didn't quite believe my own eyes. I thought it was

Jonny's drop goal. I was utterly convinced it was Jonny's drop goal. And then, with the ball still in the air and everything happening at once, I heard that little nagging voice in the back of my mind: 'That was a right-footed drop, and Jonny is left-footed.' For one grisly, gruesome moment, I was saying to myself: 'Christ!!! It wasn't Jonny at all. It was bloody Mike Catt!!!' I nearly gave it the full Anglo-Saxon treatment out loud, straight into the microphone. Early retirement beckoned. But then, with Rob screaming like a banshee, I rescanned the field with my binoculars and realised it had been Jonny all along. Instead of punching myself in the face, I punched the air. Metaphorically speaking, that is. And within a few seconds, the restart had been safely gathered and that same Mike Catt had hoofed the ball all the way into Queensland to end the game. John Inverdale, one of the finest sports presenters on the airwaves, walked straight up to me from six seats away and said: 'That was definitely *not* the worst commentary you've ever delivered.' I knew then that it was alright. Jonny wasn't the only one who had passed the test.

All that was left for me to do that night was . . . an ocean of work. First, I had the pleasure of describing the trophy presentation – a ceremony transformed into something out of the ordinary by the Australian Prime Minister John Howard, who seemed less interested in congratulating the visitors in the traditional fashion than in practising his passing game by propelling the winners' medals at the England players with all the velocity he could muster. From there, it was off into the bowels of the stadium to file pieces of varying lengths to every BBC radio outlet under the sun. When we were finally done, the entire team, led by our ever-amenable and magnificently organised producer Ed Marriage, headed back into Sydney – a fair lick from the out-of-town Olympic Stadium complex in Homebush – for a ceremonial dumping of the gear at the hotel. Only then could we think in terms of alcohol and a proper celebration. We did not spare the horses. There was no reason to think that England would not challenge for the big prize at subsequent World Cups, but there could be only one first and we'd been the ones blessed with the opportunity to witness it, describe it and revel in it.

It seems strange to us now, but the idea of a World Cup was not universally welcomed when, in the mid-1980s, both the Australian and New Zealand unions threw their weight behind the launching of a global competition. Such ideas had been percolating through the thick layers of rugby adminis-tration for years, but had failed to take hold where it mattered, with the sport's most senior governing bodies. Even when the Antipodeans, rather less traditionally minded than their counterparts in most parts of the British Isles, finally won the argument, it was not by much: there were only eight nations with decision-making powers and it was by no means sure that the northern hemisphere countries would support the proposal. As it turned out, both Ireland and Scotland withheld their backing while England and Wales, after much agonising, signalled a reluctant willingness to give it a go. Things could so easily have turned out differently, and if they had, we might never have had those images of Lomu and Wilkinson and Carter imprinted on our minds.

Right from the start, I could see the potential in a World Cup-type competition. I also thought it was inevitable, although I could not say how or when it would find its way off the drawing board. But even now, I understand some of the reservations put forward by the Scots and the Irish at the time. Apart from anything else, the organisation and delivery of such an event within the confines of the old amateur structure was fraught with difficulty. Could it be guaranteed that all the best players from all the top countries would be able to participate? These people had to work for a living and there was only so much absenteeism the average employer could be expected to tolerate. Rugby was full of examples of players who simply could not find the time or money to join Lions tours to New Zealand or South Africa, which took place once every four years. If the international calendar was to accommodate a new tournament that would take more than a month to complete, loss of earnings would be an issue.

But once it was there, with a starting date of 22 May 1987 – New Zealand versus Italy in Auckland – the World Cup developed its own momentum and justified its existence, even though the All Blacks were so far ahead of the competition at that point. I think it is true to say that no team has ever won the title more easily than those New Zealanders won the first one. They were such a vibrant, adaptable side, full of moving parts that seemed to move far faster and more smoothly than anything we had previously seen, and they had game-breaking talents across the field: John Gallagher at full-back, John Kirwan on the wing, the master strategist and goal-kicker Grant Fox at No.10, new-age front-rowers in Steve McDowell and Sean Fitzpatrick, a space-age lock in Gary Whetton and one of the finest back-row trios ever to band together in common pursuit of the loose ball. We could call them The Good, The Bad and The Unbelievable. Alan Whetton, the blind-side flanker, would have been a superstar had his partners not been such larger-than-life individuals: he was tough, resilient, highly skilled, utterly dependable – a go-to man when the contest was at its hottest. Wayne Shelford, or 'Buck' as he was known by the legions who idolised him, had the self-same qualities, with added extras. There was a dark yet blazing ferocity about him, an air of menace. You just knew that anyone getting on the wrong side of him, as the Wales lock Huw Richards did during a semi-final slaughter at the Ballymore stadium in Brisbane, would finish a distant second. When the unfortunate Richards recovered from a Joe Frazier-like punch on the jaw delivered by his rival, it was he, not Shelford, who was sent off. And then, just to top it off, we had Michael Jones in the No.7 shirt. God, what a genius. Faster, stronger, more ruthless in the tackle, more creative with ball in hand, more predatory – here was a breakaway forward who played not just in different parts of the field to his opposite numbers, but in different halves of the field. But for crippling injuries and a powerful sense of religious devotion that prevented him playing rugby on the Sabbath, there would be no doubting the identity of the greatest open-side flanker ever to grace a rugby field.

I was in Brisbane for that New Zealand–Wales semi-final, just as I had been in Sydney the previous day for the Australia–France tie – one of the stand-out games of the entire World Cup era. Here was a contest that did not follow the script, as tends to happen when the French are on one of their missions. It is not always possible to tell when Les Bleus will turn it on, for the very good reason that they are as confusing to themselves as they are to the rest of us. But that day at the Concord Oval, just as they did a dozen years later at Twickenham and eight years after that in Cardiff, they pulled a rabbit from the hat, that wondrous full-back Serge Blanco claiming a late try in the corner to leave Wallaby assumptions of a place in the final broken and scattered in the dust of New South Wales.

If the trophy decider was something less than a cliffhanger – as so often happens, the French had played their final one round early – I returned from the adventure convinced that the World Cup, still fighting for its place in rugby's landscape, was here to stay. It had been a relatively modest beginning, played by people who, as the revered Wales wing and Lions manager Gerald Davies points out in his history of the tournament, would stay modest for some time to come. Gerald turns to Fitzpatrick, that All Black hooker for all the ages, for a sobering account of the victory celebrations. 'We had won, but it was not a big night,' he quotes him as saying. 'We went to the pub and had a few beers and Craig Green (who played on the wing in the final) turned to me and said: "We've just won the World Cup, but on Monday at 5.45am I'll be standing on the corner of my street with my lunch box, waiting to be picked up to go roofing. It will be a normal day." It was bizarre.'

It was not until the 1991 tournament, presented in Britain and Ireland on a bigger canvas to bigger audiences with greatly enhanced television and radio coverage, that the World Cup started to make good on the claims the early enthusiasts had made on its behalf. This was no doubt helped by the fact that England, the principal hosts, went so close to winning the trophy, and would surely have done so had they not attempted to play a gifted but deeply inexperienced Wallaby side at their own game instead of sticking to what they knew best: scrums, line-outs, mauls, territory, pressure. There again, they might not have made the final at all had my pal Gavin Hastings kicked a penalty from in front of the sticks at the tipping point of a tight semi-final in Edinburgh. It was later revealed that Gavin was concussed and did not have any clear idea of what he was doing or why. I was so shocked when he missed, I could easily have slipped off my broadcasting chair, smacked my head on the floor of the commentary box and joined him in La-La Land. However, I've long since forgiven him.

Perhaps the greatest glory of covering eight World Cups over three decades has been to see the finest practitioners of the sport sweep the doubters aside by producing their best rugby when it mattered most. We saw it from two stellar Wallabies, the centre Tim Horan and the lock John Eales, in 1999 (if ever a player merited the nickname 'Nobody', as in 'Nobody's Perfect', it was the staggeringly gifted Eales). We saw it in 2007 from some ultra-competitive Springboks: the wing Bryan Habana, the scrum-half Fourie du Preez, the hooker John Smit, the flanker Juan Smith and the completely dominant engine-room partners Bakkies Botha and Victor Matfield. And if I'm not sure we were treated to such riches of individual performance when the competition returned to New Zealand in 2011, where standards on the field were almost as grim as the behaviour of an out-of-control England party off it, normal service was resumed in 2015 when Daniel Carter seized the day.

As the tournament approached, I found myself wanting all four home nations to meet expectations, and for at least one to exceed them. I'm not completely partisan, but it is hard not to fear for the future of the sport if the big three southern hemisphere countries win all of the top prizes all of the time. My prayers were not answered. England had a dreadful time of it, Ireland under-performed, Wales could have beaten the Springboks on quarter-final day but didn't, Scotland were messed up by the referee. From my point of view as a broadcaster, we needed a focal point for the last two weeks of the event. Step forward Carter, the saviour of 2015.

Throughout that fortnight, the New Zealand outside-half from a tiny South Island country town – no larger than a village in our terminology – was the emotional centrepiece. He had blinded us with his brilliance against the Lions in 2005, yet six years later, the World Cup he had been expected to dominate unfolded without him. The injury demons that dragged him down to his lowest point in 2011 seemed to be affecting him still as the 2015 tournament loomed into view. When England travelled to New Zealand for a three-Test series some 15 months before the big event, he was struggling for fitness once again and off the selectors' radar. Yet All Black followers the length and breadth of the country were hoping against hope that he would be back on his feet soon enough and put himself in a position to claim his rightful reward.

On that trip in 2014, my old friend Bill Beaumont, travelling as chairman of the Rugby Football Union, mentioned that the patriarch of the Carter clan, Neville, was throwing open the doors of the family home and wondered if I'd like to join him. I jumped at the chance, obviously, and we set off together. There was what amounted to a rugby museum in the house – memorabilia signed by Jonah Lomu and Richie

McCaw and heaven knows who else – while in the Carters' garden, there stood a set of rugby posts. Here was the site of the infant Daniel's first kicking sessions. I asked Neville if he had a ball handy. 'Yeah, I'll get one from the museum,' he said, without hesitation. 'No, no – not one of those valuable ones. If you'd ever seen me kick, you'd know I can find the nearest stream with my eyes shut. Just a normal, bog-standard ball will do fine.' Suitably equipped, I promptly sent a drop kick sailing between the sticks. 'Wayhaay, three points,' I said, assuming Neville would be impressed. His response? 'Now try it with your left foot.' That set me thinking. 'What would Dan's strike-rate have been during his formative years?' I wondered. 'That would be 93 per cent, dropping goals from right back there on the road as well as up close.' 'Well, I'm stopping now with a record of 100 per cent. And you can tell him that.'

A year or so after his majestic performances in the knock-out stage of the World Cup, culminating in two match-winning kicks from desperately difficult positions in the final against the Wallabies, I travelled to Leicester for their European Champions Cup match with the Parisian side Racing 92, where Daniel had just materialised as an overseas capture. Unsurprisingly, the BBC rather fancied the idea of a Carter interview. 'I have a chance,' I told the people back at central control, 'but I happen to know that he's been bought up by television and they won't be happy if he starts speaking to someone else.' A few minutes later, Dan emerged from the

Racing 92 dressing room. 'I have just two questions,' I said. 'Sorry, can't do it.' 'And also . . . I have a statement to make.' He looked at me quizzically. 'When I was in your back garden . . .' Realisation dawned immediately. 'Ah right. My dad told me about your drop kick.' I went in for the kill. 'Yes, and Neville also said that you would always give me an interview if I really needed one. I hope you'll stick to your father's word.' Dan laughed, nodded his head towards the open door and said: 'Quick. Come into the dressing room.' As I remember it, he said more to me than he had to the television people. What a star.

ONCE IN A
RED MOON

AT some point during the closing months of 1970, while teaching at Fettes in Edinburgh, I received a letter from the British Lions – the British and Irish Lions, as they are now more popularly known. It was a polite inquiry about my potential availability for the following year's 24-match tour of New Zealand, which, with a couple of warm-up games in Australia added to the itinerary, would begin in early May and end in late August. This was almost as long as one of my after-dinner speeches and very definitely more exciting. It was also a high point of my rugby career. Just to be considered as a vaguely conceivable candidate for one of the outside-half berths was akin to striking oil, or gold, or some other rare commodity behind the clubhouse at Watsonians. The Lions? Really? Now we're talking.

Almost before the ink had dried on the notepaper, I informed John Lawrence, the team's liaison officer, that I would definitely be in a position to make the trip if selected. Not that I expected to be selected, even with that precious missive in my possession. I certainly wasn't counting any chickens. I knew that the Lions officials, the most prominent of whom were my countryman Doug Smith as manager and Carwyn James as coach, would be chucking around plenty of these letters. It wasn't like throwing confetti, exactly, but there would be 60 or more players on the long list. Anyone in the starting line-up of any of the home nations was almost certainly on the correspondence roster and, at that point, I was Scotland's first pick in the No.10 position and had played all four matches in that year's Five Nations. I remember thinking to myself, once I'd calmed down: 'If you *hadn't* received a letter, Robertson, what then? You'd be worse than rubbish.'

I also knew that a certain Barry John was playing rather well for Wales and as he already had experience of Test rugby with the Lions, having toured South Africa with them in 1968, the place in the Saturday side was most unlikely to be up for grabs. Yet there was still an outside chance of an outside-half place. Barry's young understudy, a genius of almost equal stature by the name of Phil Bennett, had not yet staked a full claim to Lions ascendancy, while in Ireland, the hugely influential Mike Gibson, who had travelled as a No.10 in 1968, was now spending the vast majority of his time at inside centre. His successor in the green shirt was Barry McGann of Cork Constitution, who, despite being blessed with a cultured passing game and a kick like a mule, was not the most fleet-footed No.10 in history. Tony O'Reilly, that touring superstar of the 1950s who was an even greater wit than he was a Lions wing, once said that if you ran twice around Barry, you qualified as a bona fide traveller. As for the England candidates, neither John Finlan of Moseley nor Roger Shackleton of Harrogate was likely to be mistaken for Barry John, even on the darkest of nights.

So there were moments of anticipation and excitement when I received that letter, even though I knew, deep down in my heart of hearts, that I'd fall short. Back then, a Lions tour place was the ultimate for any rugby player raised in these islands – and that was before the victories over the All Blacks and the Springboks in the 1970s, events that raised the profile of our game and changed it forever. Ahead of the '71 trip, the Lions had not returned home triumphant since before the Second World War. There had been a squared series with the Springboks in 1955, largely because my friend and inspiration Cliff Morgan had shown the best of himself as a playmaker of the highest calibre, but apart from that, there had been nothing but defeat. 1950, 1959, 1962, 1966, 1968 . . . those five tours, three to New Zealand and two to South Africa, had yielded three draws and one win in 20 Tests. But for the Lions' regular successes in Australia, where the meetings with the Wallabies were considered secondary to the main events, there would have been almost no reasons to be cheerful. Yet there was still a kind of magic that attached itself to the name. To be a *Lion*? That was the dream, for all of us.

As it turned out, my knee went 'pop' – and my career went

'pop' with it – some months before the '71 squad was chosen. As for McGann and Shackleton and Finlan, there was no tour for them either. Carwyn placed all his faith in Barry John, who, alarmingly enough, had shown a degree of reluctance about committing himself to such a long stint in All Black country. Once the coach had sweet-talked Barry into making the trip, partly by assuring him that he would be spared the worst excesses of the physical jerks programme in training, it was possible to make do and mend in the No.10 position depending on the circumstances. My fellow Scot, occasional guardian angel and great friend Chris Rea, very much a centre by instinct and upbringing, played outside-half twice on the tour, against a combined South and Mid-Canterbury/North Otago side in Timaru and a Poverty Bay/East Coast collective in Gisborne. Even Arthur Lewis, that forthright centre from Ebbw Vale, was press-ganged into duty in the pivot position, and by all accounts he was suitably bemused. 'I don't kick off my left foot, I don't kick off my right foot . . . I don't bloody kick at all,' he was heard to say. Somehow, he found a way through. On the other occasions when Barry needed a rest or, in the case of the mega-violent meeting with Canterbury in Christchurch a week shy of the first Test, simply had to be protected, the positionally flexible Mike Gibson filled in. But even with alternatives at his fingertips, Carwyn still asked an almighty amount of Barry. The 'king' played no fewer than 17 of those 26 matches. On two occasions he played three times in eight days. On one occasion, he played four times in 12. Can you imagine that happening in this day and age? Me neither. I think the true miracle of Barry in 1971 was not that he scored 180-odd points and inspired the Lions to a first ever series win in New Zealand, but that he made it home in one piece.

Players made remarkable sacrifices to be a part of a trip that redefined what it meant to be a Lion: my Scotland teammate Ian McLauchlan was told by his employers at Glasgow council that he couldn't possibly take more time off work to play rugby, so he packed in his job, sold the family car and came to some arrangement with the bank over the mortgage. By way of adding fuel to the fire of a three-month separation from normal life with his loved ones, his son was a week old when he left. I would, without thinking twice, have made sacrifices of my own had a place been offered and I'd been in a physical condition to accept it, but I had to acknowledge that my chance, slim as it may have been, had gone.

It was therefore a moment of genuine excitement when the BBC sent me to South Africa for the final two Tests of the Lions' next trip in 1974. I was very much the underling, as Cliff Morgan was still master of all he surveyed when it came to the broadcasting of rugby on the radio and Alun Williams was his co-commentator. But just to be there, hoovering up interviews with various Lions and attending some fairly sour-faced Springbok press conferences (losing the first two Tests and every provincial game to date had come as something of a shock to them), was an experience and a half. There were people on that tour I'd played with and against on the international stage: the 'Mighty Mouse' McLauchlan, Sandy Carmichael, Gordon Brown and Billy Steele amongst the Scottish contingent; JPR Williams, Phil Bennett, Gareth Edwards and Mervyn Davies amongst the Welsh; Mike Gibson, Ken Kennedy and Fergus Slattery from Ireland.

Talking of Irishmen, I had also come up against Willie John McBride, the captain of that party. And what a captain he turned out to be. Whenever that formidable Ulsterman and the rest of the razzle-dazzlers from the Test team were not playing, they made it their business to support the midweek 'dirt-trackers' every step of the way – not just by watching those games from the stand, but by shouting and hollering and punching the air in support. As they expected no less from their colleagues when it came to the big Saturday games, they considered it their duty to return the favour. Partly as a consequence, there was never the slightest hint of a split in the party: the kind of split that badly undermined several subsequent tours – 1993, 2001 and 2005 especially. Willie John stood by his men through thick and thin. After an uproarious evening in the team hotel, during which it was proven beyond doubt that a chandelier looks much better hanging from a ceiling than it does laying on a floor in bits, he was approached by an extremely irate manager. 'Your players are out of control and I can take no more,' said the host. 'I'm calling the police.' Puffing away on his pipe, Willie John pondered awhile before putting the matter to rest in seven brilliantly chosen words. 'Tell me: how many will there be?' he asked. 'Good reply,' said the manager, diplomatically. 'Would you help me sort out the damage?'

As a further illustration of Willie John's success in bringing people together and holding them together, this is a classic. I had not been long in South Africa and was attending a drinks party after a midweek game. 'What time will we be leaving?' I asked some of the press boys on the trip. 'When Willie John says we're leaving,' came the reply. 'Just watch him. You'll know when it's time.' Sure enough, there came a point in the evening, with plenty of food and drink still available for consumption, when Willie John walked towards the door. He didn't say a word. He just walked. And all 29 of his fellow players, together with the management, bade their farewells to the hosts and followed him out. As did the men from the media. It was deeply impressive. He was a rough, tough kind of a sod, Willie John – people say he was the first player to return the compliment after being punched by Colin Meads, the fearsome 'Godfather' of All Black rugby. Yet he never raised his voice. He understood the importance of the collective, and the collective recognised and respected that understanding. Which was why they did as they were told, without fail.

Contrast this with Graham Henry's approach to team togetherness when the Lions toured Australia a little over a quarter of a century later. Many good judges felt the New Zealander, the first overseas head coach in Lions history, had a very strong bunch of players at his disposal – perhaps the strongest since the 1974 group, which I still consider to be the greatest team of my rugby lifetime, along with the World Cup-winning All Black sides of 1987 and 2015. Amongst Henry's 35-strong party were some really significant talents, from a young Brian O'Driscoll in the centre, Jonny Wilkinson and Rob Howley at half-back, and some of the most formidable forwards of the age: Keith Wood and Phil Vickery, Martin Johnson and Danny Grewcock, Richard Hill and Lawrence Dallaglio and Scott Quinnell. The Wallabies, by contrast, were hanging on to the best of themselves for dear life, but two years after their deeply impressive World Cup title campaign, they were beginning to creak.

From the outside, everything suggested that the Lions might achieve that rarest of feats by winning a second consecutive series. From the inside, sadly, things looked very different. Quite quickly, I picked up mutterings from players about rifts in the camp driven from the top. This was the consequence of blundering insensitivity rather than the application of a fully thought-out policy, but there is no escaping the fact that in a particularly frosty press conference after a defeat by Australia A in Gosford that was rather heavier than the 28–25 margin suggested, Graham made it abundantly clear that any continuing interest he might have in the affairs of the midweek team would be strictly limited. The main concern, apart from a rash of injuries, was the perception that the Test team had been decided well in advance of the first meeting with the Wallabies in Brisbane. This perception was hard to shift, especially as some players had, before the very first tour game in Perth, noticed a team list mistakenly left on a table that looked uncannily like a first-choice side. Either that or the coaches had decided that Wilkinson, Johnson and a variety of other titans were wildly overrated and would spend their trip down among the 'stiffs'.

It seemed to me that Graham didn't quite grasp the Lions concept, which has always been based around the building of an elite team in real time, based on form in the matches leading into a Test series. You have to keep people engaged, because the moment they become disengaged – the moment they feel they are out of the running for a Test place no matter how well they play – the problems kick in. If the senior side is nailed down before a single match has been played, the head coach might as well reveal his hand in the Heathrow departure lounge by saying: 'Right, you lot will be flying with me on this gleaming new supersonic jet over here; the rest of you can tag along behind in that rickety old single-propeller job over there, because if you crash, it's not going to matter a damn.'

In 1974, there was not even a suspicion of internal upheaval. 'There was never any griping about selection from me or any of the other guys who missed out on the Test team,' said dear old Sandy Carmichael many years after the event. 'That must have been the strongest Lions squad that ever toured and just to be a part of it was astronomical.' Those words hit the nail on the head. Without a buy-in from everyone on the trip, it's terribly hard to get a return. During my short but magical month with Willie John's men, I came to understand that. I also experienced for the first time the power of the electrical charge that runs through a Lions Test match.

On 13 July, the atmosphere at the Boet Erasmus Stadium in Port Elizabeth was more spine-tingling than anything I had previously encountered, even as a player. The Springboks were 2–0 down in the four-Test series and would have nowhere to turn if they lost: as a consequence, they had picked some of their more renowned hard cases in an effort to beef up their pack and had trained behind closed doors to minimise distractions and maximise the intensity of their preparations. They had come to fight – the speed at which they flew out of the tunnel told me that much – and if the Lions were to clinch the spoils, they would have to match them in the physical stuff. This they did, and more. The fabled '99' calls – the Lions' version of the NATO principle that an attack on one was an attack on all – came thick and fast and after each mass dust-up, the ones left standing were the tourists. As Clem Thomas, a Lion himself in the same country almost two decades previously, subsequently wrote: 'Some of the big Springbok forwards actually ran away from the battle,' adding that at the after-match banquet in the Ostrich Hall, the most influential figure in the whole of South African rugby, Dr

Danie Craven, declared that he was ashamed of his countrymen. It was almost as if he considered the 26–9, three-tries-to-none defeat to be not just the low point of Springbok rugby, but the nadir of South African manhood.

The series safely under lock and key, it was my great pleasure to wallow in comprehensive victories over Border in East London, Natal in Durban and Eastern Transvaal in Springs before heading to the Afrikaner citadel of Ellis Park in Johannesburg for the final Test, where victory would give the Lions an unimprovable record of 'played 22, won 22'. There were more than 80,000 spectators in the ground for this 'dead' game and if someone forced me to count the times I have heard Fergus Slattery insist that he grounded the ball for a winning try late in the contest, I'd end up having an uncomfortably close relationship with my pocket calculator. The fact remains that the South African referee Max Baise – no neutral officials in those days – disallowed the score and the game ended in a 13–13 draw. The rugged Welsh hooker Bobby Windsor has been heard to claim that when the official was quizzed about the decision, he replied: 'Look boys, I have to live here.' I can't confirm that one way or the other, which is probably for the best.

I would not refresh my first-hand acquaintance with the Lions for almost a decade. The BBC felt they were better served by my enthusiasm for the horse racing scene in 1977, so I was not on the plane with Phil Bennett's happy band of warriors, who quickly became unhappy as the winter weather in New Zealand did its worst and extreme training demands drove what was left of their spirits deep into the mud. It was a good tour to miss, I think. I would certainly have appreciated the opportunity to travel to South Africa for the 1980 tour under Bill Beaumont's avuncular leadership, but I had just moved from the BBC to the *Sunday Times* and there was enough industrial unrest around the national newspaper scene to keep me off the travel list.

I believe now that my absences had led me to make some false assumptions about the Lions when, now back at the BBC, I headed to the land of the All Blacks, my first visit to the country, in 1983. I thought it would be 1974 revisited – that there would be a Gareth Edwards figure, a JPR Williams figure, a 'Broon frae Troon', a 'Mighty Mouse' and a 'Merv the Swerve'. But these were no more than hopes and fancies. The most pertinent of the relevant facts was that the Lions had lost their last two series, and that the sense of superiority had evaporated. Which is not to suggest for a moment that the party was bereft of talent. Willie John himself was there, albeit in a managerial suit and tie rather than a trademark headband, and with Jim Telfer enlisted as coach, there would be plenty of motivation and a high level of conditioning. But the tour was short by the standards of the time, there was less opportunity for meaningful team-building and some of the front-line players – in particular the Cardiff scrum-half Terry Holmes, the Pontypool flanker Jeff Squire and the Bridgend prop Ian Stephens – were hit by injury and failed to play a Test between them after the first, highly competitive match of the rubber in Christchurch. The simple, sad truth of the matter was that thereafter, the Lions could not play rugby quite well enough to subdue a New Zealand team who were that little bit better in too many areas.

One of those areas was the line-out, where Ciaran Fitzgerald's repeated failures to hit such potent ball-winners as Bob Norster and Maurice Colclough ensured that the Irish hooker would attract all the criticism he could handle, and then some. Much of this stick stemmed from the fact that precious few people outside the selection panel felt Fitzgerald was the best hooker in the British Isles – or even the second best, come to that. For him to be picked ahead of a double Lion and all-round class act like Peter Wheeler of England, and then to be handed the captaincy, thereby ensuring that a No.2 as accomplished as Colin Deans of Scotland would be condemned to a supporting role, was controversial indeed. Time and again, particularly during the second Test in Wellington, the Lions wrapped up their precious first-phase ball in tissue paper, placed it in a presentation box with a nice pink bow on top and handed it to the New Zealanders. Even Francis Palmade, the highly experienced referee from the far south of France, felt sorry for them. He was nearing the end of a Test career stretching back to 1973 and to judge by his reaction, he had seen nothing to resemble this flagrant surrender of priceless possession in all his born days. His favourite word, it seemed to me when discussing these events, was 'mal co-ordonné'. You did not have to be Marcel Proust to know what he meant, or to whom he was referring.

In the end, the Lions were whitewashed, or Blackwashed, and the last of the four beatings they took from their hosts was truly horrible: a 38–6 hammering in Auckland, the headline feature of which was a hat-trick of tries from the wing Stu Wilson. Only two players, the All Black centre Frank Mitchinson and the Springbok wing Tom van Vollenhoven, had previously achieved the feat. They did it in 1908 and 1955 respectively. Yet until the final match, I never felt the Lions were entirely outgunned. And anyway, I was having the time of my life, enjoying everything the country had to offer. Most gratifyingly, I had struck up a friendship with three of the New Zealand backline of the 1970s, the wing Bryan Williams and the centres Bill Osborne and Bruce Robertson, all of whom had been wined and dined at my old house in Highgate, no more than a street away from where I live now, and it was delightful to spend time with them in far-flung corners of their homeland.

I was also pushing myself professionally far harder than at any point in my career to that point. I was not needed for television work as Nigel Starmer-Smith, who had played scrum-half for England when I enjoyed my one and only Calcutta Cup victory in 1970, was the man on screen duty. But I did full radio commentary on every tour game, with no second voice to help me out. There was also the question of getting my words of wisdom on air back home in Britain, where it mattered. I am not a master of technology, as my broadcasting colleagues and support staff will readily agree: in the same way that I couldn't knock back steaming great forwards in a way that might have made Jim Telfer wonder whether I had a defensive game worthy of his respect, I don't think I could have left Bill Gates or Steve Jobs for dead in the field of gadgetry. All I knew was that by some strange process involving pipes under the ocean, my dead-of-night descriptions of the Lions' endeavours on the field and my reports of events in camp could be received loud and clear at home – always assuming, of course, that I made the right arrangements. This involved booking phone lines long enough in advance – 12 hours or more was the general rule of thumb – and then pressing the correct buttons in the correct order. I spent longer in the post office than I did in the bar. The things I've sacrificed for my art!

With the Springboks off-limits because of the South African government's continuing internal adherence to the racial policies that had caused so much protest and upheaval across the world, there was a six-year gap before the Lions packed their bags once again. The destination this time was Australia . . . and nowhere else. Not since 1899 had the Lions (who weren't even called 'Lions' then) devoted themselves lock, stock and barrel to the land of the green and gold. Back then, eight of the 21 games were staged in Sydney, another four elsewhere in New South Wales, eight in Queensland

and one in Melbourne. It said something about the spread of rugby union interest in Australia. Something similar was being said 90 years later. New South Wales and Queensland still dominated the geography of the game in Wallaby country and as the whole caboodle was over and done with in the space of a month and a half and no more than a dozen games (one of them against a joint Aussie-Kiwi confection, who took the field calling themselves the 'Anzac XV'), it was possible to see the direction of travel for these tours. No more four-Test series, no more long adventures. It should also have been possible to see some other pointers to the future, if only the eyes of the travelling media had been properly peeled.

In the early game against Australia B in Melbourne, the No.10 role was performed by a very young man – the rugby equivalent of a spotty kid – by the name of Tim Horan. The tight-head prop was equally youthful, at least by front-row standards: Ewen McKenzie. A week later, in the game with Queensland B up in Cairns, young Master Horan appeared in the centre alongside another fourth-former, Jason Little. Three days after that, at the beautiful North Sydney Oval, the New South Wales team featured Marty Roebuck at full-back and Phil Kearns at hooker – two more infants. All these players would, two years later, be in Wallaby shirts on World Cup final day at Twickenham, and all of them would play a significant role in beating England to the trophy. For the real Mystic Megs amongst us, Andrew Blades and David Wilson also showed up in provincial games on that tour – forwards who would help the Aussies secure another world title in 1999. And then there was the fiery little hooker who turned out for New South Wales B in Dubbo just before the first Test. Eddie Jones was his name. I wonder what happened to him?

One person we all knew about was David Campese. It was impossible to be remotely interested in rugby and not know of him. He was the most thrilling of attacking players, blessed with quick feet, super-fast instincts and a tongue so rapid that it left those other virtues for dead. Because Australia was short of all sorts of numbers when it came to rugby union – short of money, of teams, of playing resources – the great man of Queanbeyan, a smallish place situated in the Southern Tablelands area of New South Wales, was as difficult to shake off on that tour as he was to stop. He played in almost half the fixtures, so there was no getting away from him. By the end of the trip, he had doubled down on his reputation as one of rugby's most compelling figures and a credit to his home town, which can also claim a world squash champion in Heather McKay and a Formula One driver in Mark Webber among its sporting products. Yet by hook or by crook, the Lions prevented Campo scoring. Not a single point was registered against them by the most brilliant running wing we had seen in decades.

I've spent a good deal of time with him since that series: he has always made himself available when I've asked him for an interview (a blessing for any broadcaster, given his inability to get through a single sentence without saying something interesting) and we've socialised on many occasions. He is the best of company and I treasure my friendship with him. When I remind him of his crucial contribution to the Lions' victory in that series – the famous botch-up behind the Wallaby goal-line when Campo, deciding to spice things up with a long-range attack, attempted to find his full-back Greg Martin with a switch pass and presented the ever-alert Welsh wing Ieuan Evans with a match-turning try for free – he takes it in good heart. 'Who was it at fault?' he often asks. 'Me, or the 14 other people in Wallaby shirts who didn't get close enough to take my pass?' I like to stick up for him if I can and have done so on Australian television stations. 'If he'd been French and thrown a pass like that on his own line, his fellow backs would have second-guessed him, gone the length, won the game and ensured him a state funeral and burial in the Pantheon,' I once argued. 'They'd even have waited until he had died. You Aussies were quite happy to bury him alive for the crime of ambition.'

One last story about '89. We were in Canberra for a game against Australian Capital Territory, a midweek game separating the first and second Tests. The Lions were in a betwixt and between kind of place: they had been badly beaten by the Wallabies in Sydney the previous weekend, but the key players were beginning to pump themselves for a real tilt at the opposition in Brisbane a few days hence. And there they were in Canberra, which I wasn't alone in viewing as a strange kind of place with its coldly formal administrative air. If you can imagine a civil service department expanded into something on the scale of a new town like Welwyn Garden City, you're somewhere in the ballpark. 'Where's the best place to eat around here?' I remember asking a local. 'Doyles on The Rocks.' 'But that's in Sydney.' 'Yep.' I was writing a book on the tour and was a little behind with the word-count, so I told the press pack I'd be avoiding them for a night. 'I'll grab something on my own because I have work to do,' I said, heading to the hotel restaurant for a quick bite.

It was rather a large restaurant, with several tables pushed together in the middle to create a single canteen-like arrangement for 30-odd people. Those people turned out to be the Lions, who were busily feeding their faces at the trough ahead of the following day's training session. I found myself a small table for one and opened the menu, just as the door swung open, followed by a single word in a broad Northern Irish accent. 'Robbo!!!!' In came George Best. Yes, *the* George Best. The football genius, the front-page glamour kid, the trend-setting symbol of an entire generation, the man who had been labelled 'the fifth Beatle'. *That* George Best. I'd known him for a while, having shared several long evenings on the after-dinner circuit, and here he was in Canberra, of all places on God's earth. He was doing some soccer coaching, it turned out. 'Drinks, Robbo,' he shouted. 'What'll you be having? Red or white?' I plumped for a glass of red. 'Waiter!!! A bottle of white and a bottle of red for your man here.' So much for the glass idea. As we chatted away, up came Gavin Hastings, my fellow Scot and the Lions' Test full-back – the same Gavin I'd coached at Cambridge University. 'The boys are all saying the same thing,' he told me. 'They're saying "Christ, Robbo knows George Best". Do you think you could get him to pop over and say hello to us?' George being George, he fronted up. For some strange reason, the Lions treated me with increased respect from there on in.

Of course, everyone thought they knew George – and that includes the 99.99 per cent of the human race who never met him or saw him play football on anything other than a television screen. Some idolised him, others were not so impressed. When you reach his level of fame, opinions are two a penny. In my dealings with him, he was the warmest of men who, for all his well-documented problems, was a natural storyteller and comic wordsmith as well as one of the most brilliant sportsmen of the century. One of my favourite stories concerns his late-night tryst with a very successful beauty queen at an expensive hotel in London. He had just been to a casino and won himself a mint, to the extent that when a waiter entered the room with the bottle of 'Shampoo' George had just ordered, there were thousands upon thousands of pounds thrown carelessly on the bed. 'Shall I open the champagne?' he asked George and his young lady. 'Or will you do it yourself?' 'You open it,' said George, 'and here's a tip for your trouble.' The waiter looked at the bunch of bank notes he had been handed and blinked in disbelief. 'This is my annual salary,' he said. 'Just one of these notes will be plenty.' 'Get on and take it, please,' came the reply. 'And by the way, we'll be wanting another bottle of Shampoo in half an hour.' As the waiter reached the door, he turned. 'Can I ask you a question?' 'One question? Go ahead.' 'Tell me, George: where did it all go wrong for you?'

The Lions needed that series victory in Australia: a fourth consecutive defeat in the southern hemisphere would have significantly weakened them reputationally and may even have set in train a series of events that would have threatened their very existence. It was also vital that the tour was a happy one. From everything I'd read and heard about the 1977 and 1980 trips, enjoyment seemed to be at a premium, and while I'd revelled in my 1983 adventure, it was no use pretending everyone on that visit had felt the same way. When I look back now, the really joyful Lions tours in my experience were 1989, 1997, 2009 and 2013. Not all of them were victorious – the Lions lost, desperately narrowly, in South Africa in '09 – and they were far from plain sailing on the news side of things. Each and every one of them had spikes of controversy: most of them on the field of play, one or two of them in the area of team management and selection. But despite the upheavals, they were the greatest fun. I'm sorry to say that in 1993, 2001 and 2005, the opposite was true.

That 1993 challenge in New Zealand was a tough one, with a brutal itinerary: North Harbour, a very good side at the time, in midweek; Canterbury, never less than a serious proposition even if they weren't trying to beat you up, in midweek; Waikato, then the reigning domestic champions, in midweek. By the end of the tour, some of the 'dirt-trackers' had raised the white flag. Will Carling, who, contrary to most expectations including his own, found himself out of the Test side after the opening match of the series in Christchurch, has said some very strong things about the deterioration of the second-string side, up to and including the suggestion that certain people stopped competing. I have to admit that from where the media were sitting, that's how it appeared.

That being said, I thought Ian McGeechan, back on board for a second consecutive tour of duty as coach, did a top job with the senior XV. He made bold selection decisions – dropping a figure as prominent as Carling was no soft option – and was courageous enough to back a green-about-the-gills lock from Leicester by the name of Martin Johnson, who had not been included in the original party and would have remained surplus to requirements had Wade Dooley, a prominent Test Lion in 1989, not suffered a sudden and deeply upsetting family bereavement and returned home. There followed one of the more insensitive episodes in Lions history. Geech and the squad wanted Wade to return after the funeral; after careful thought, Wade decided he was up to the task, and the secretary of the Four Home Unions, Bob Weighill, set about putting things in motion. Bob had no option but to run this by a variety of administrative bodies, of which rugby union has always had more than its fair share, and those bodies agreed that while Wade was welcome to return to the country, he would not be allowed to actually play. It was not one of our lords' and masters' finer moments.

I contrast this with the events of 1997 in South Africa, where Geech, in charge once again with Jim Telfer at his side and the invaluable Fran Cotton on managerial duty, showed the kind of flexibility necessary to keep virtually everyone happy, virtually all of the time. Along with 1974, which was such a fresh and invigorating experience for me, the '97 Lions trip was the best of those I covered as a broadcaster. It was the first of the professional tours and the last of the amateur tours at one and the same time. In terms of the nuts and bolts, the hard reality, these Lions were being well paid to do a proper job of work. In terms of the spirit of the thing, it was just like the old days. Of the original 35-strong group of players, the overwhelming majority had played international rugby pre-1995 and the declaration of the 'open' era. Even the exceptions – the England backs Tim Stimpson, Nick Beal and Will Greenwood, and their grunt-and-groan countrymen of the forward persuasion, Mark Regan and Simon Shaw; the Irish forwards Jeremy Davidson and Eric Miller, the inexperienced Welsh hooker Barrie Williams – had played at the highest club level under the amateur code. As ever in a tour party, some individuals had more of the party animal in them than others: there was no doubting that the Jeremy Guscotts, Jason Leonards, Lawrence Dallaglios, Keith Woods and John Bentleys of the parish were a little later to bed on occasion than the near-silent but brilliantly effective Scotland loose-head prop Tom Smith, for instance. But there was an atmosphere of informality than ran right the way through the squad and, as far as the travelling media were concerned, everyone was in it together – not least when it came to time spent in the bars and restaurants of Cape Town, Durban and one or two other seductive corners of the country.

For many of the journalists, the trip was a slow burn in generating interest back home. But certain incidents, good and bad, raised the profile of the tour ahead of the opening Test at Newlands. On the downside, there was the distressingly cynical attitude of some Mpumalanga players during a rough midweek game in Witbank, in which the lovable Scottish lock Doddie Weir had his knee ligaments wrecked in one of the worst incidents of stamping I ever witnessed (made all the worse by the fact that Doddie was actually standing up at the time). On the upside, there was Bentley's extraordinary solo try against Gauteng at Ellis Park – a game that would prove extremely significant in Geech's thinking on selection. And when the Lions absorbed everything the Springboks could throw at them in that first meeting and then trumped them with tries from Matt Dawson and Alan Tait, the first of them one of the great sucker-punch scores in recent rugby history, the whole of Britain and Ireland were alive to the events unfolding down south.

Suddenly, rugby's profile had never been higher: the

travelling support seemed to grow by a factor of hundreds overnight, the back pages of the papers were jammed with Lions news, the airwaves were full of red-shirted blood and thunder. After the great rearguard action in the second Test at King's Park – an almost suicidally brave defensive perform-ance, rewarded by Guscott's late series-winning drop goal – I sensed that the sport had turned another corner, barely two years after Jonah Lomu's world-changing displays in the same neck of the union woods. When I arrived home, I was sure I was heading towards something uncharted. And I was right. Within weeks, Clive Woodward emerged as the new England coach, and a whole new age dawned. For the next eight years, there was a sense not just that anything could happen, but that almost everything *would* happen.

Looking back on events from this distance, it is hard to work out why the lessons of 1993 and 1997 were largely ignored by Graham Henry and his top brass in 2001. I have already made my feelings known in respect of that trip to Australia, but it is worth reiterating that the key to Lions success is unity. Geech understood this when he reflected on the '93 experience and went out of his way not to allow such divisions to undermine his efforts four years later. Yet under Henry, the Lions were split once again. A number of high-profile players felt they were treated unfairly; others lambasted the brutality of the training regime; a few threatened to leave the tour early in the kerfuffle over Matt Dawson's newspaper diary, which was published on the morning of the first Test in Brisbane – a game the Lions won so thrillingly, with memorable tries from Jason Robinson and Brian O'Driscoll, that Matt's rather incendiary account of internal unrest did not appear worth the paper it was written on. There's timing for you. There was a similarly controversial contribution from another England scrum-half, Austin Healey, a few hours ahead of the deciding Test in Sydney. If Henry hadn't been at all amused by the first piece, the second sent him into orbit. One way or another, the tour was a mess. Yet the Lions would have won a high-quality series but for a couple of unforced errors. They became known as 'The Nearly Men' and for good reason. This was an opportunity missed.

Realistically speaking, there was no such opportunity in 2005, when Henry found himself on the other side of the argument in his coaching role with the All Blacks. Again, there was a split in the camp: not an acrimonious one on this occasion, but the product of managerial strategy. Clive Woodward's idea of squad separation, with two distinct coaching teams operating independently of one another, annoyed the traditionalists, and the feeling that there were different squads on different tours under a single Lions umbrella filtered into the bloodstream of the operation. Some players barely spoke to some of their colleagues, let alone got to know them. It was a bold experiment but sadly, it failed.

Would things have been any different had the sensational Brian O'Driscoll, named as tour captain to popular approval, lasted more than a few seconds of the opening Test in

Christchurch? Probably not. But what happened to him left a sour taste and throughout the following week, every rugby journalist under the sun was pressing Henry on the questionable legality of the challenge by two of his senior players, Tana Umaga and Keven Mealamu, that left the Irish centre with a serious shoulder injury, which bordered for an uncomfortable few days on the career-threatening. As they have done so often in the darker moments of their history, the New Zealanders closed ranks. The more they were challenged by reporters who accused the All Blacks of terrible crimes and misdemeanours, the more Henry and his colleagues resisted. At one particularly prickly press conference, Henry effectively told his interrogators: 'Look, I'll make a comment about last Saturday's game and that'll be it. I'll then look forward to this weekend's game. We're extremely sorry and disappointed at Brian's injury and wish him a speedy recovery.' He repeated himself at least four times before I lost count and made it clear that if the next query was the same as all the others, the conference would be over.

I decided to try a different approach. 'Could I ask a question with no specific bearing whatsoever on the O'Driscoll tackle?' I ventured. 'Good, please do,' said the coach. 'Excellent. Yesterday, I did a little research and found out that there are dozens of people with serious neck injuries caused by playing rugby here in NZ, including a worrying number of schoolchildren.' A fold of the arms from the men on the top table. 'Per head of population, it's a far greater percentage than in the United Kingdom. If you are as horrified as I am, would you be prepared to go on television and say that the tip-tackle should be immediately eradicated?' A pause. 'Yep, I'd be prepared to do that,' said Henry. What a result! As the journalists headed out of the room, he turned to me and said: 'You're a clever *?&!.' 'What you've done is very important,' I replied. And I meant it. We always got along after that.

Following the low point of a second Blackwash in three visits to New Zealand, the Lions have made significant progress in performance, on and off the field. The 2009 series in South Africa could easily have gone their way, they were worthy victors against a weak Wallaby team in Australia in 2013 and if they were just a little fortunate to escape with a draw against the All Blacks in 2017, only a hard-hearted sort would begrudge them their share of the spoils. Since when has anyone from the northern hemisphere travelled to the Land of the Long White Cloud in anticipation of an even break? The first two of those tours, I covered in full as a commentator and correspondent. Both can be placed in the 'happy' category. The last of them gave me a very different perspective on life with the Lions.

The BBC had no broadcasting rights in 2017, so I accepted an invitation from my old pal and 'second voice extraordinaire' Gareth Chilcott, who has long been involved in the sports travel business and had put together a group of enthusiastic punters intent on enjoying the trip in all its aspects. It was a tremendous giggle from start to finish. Geech came along for the ride, as did the folk-hero Welsh wing Shane Williams and a try-scorer of rather older vintage, the once-super-fast Bath and England back David Trick, who had played plenty of rugby with Cooch and, thanks to his fleet-footedness, had just about stayed out of range of any Chilcottian front-row shenanigans. David is a wonderfully funny public speaker; Geech and Shane have bags of stories and are naturals in the Q and A department; Cooch could have Ebenezer Scrooge in fits of laughter with any one of a thousand tales of rugby in the raw. I was there in a master of ceremonies role and had the best time. There were 300 paying customers on the trip, so we handled 60 each through the daily activities – a round of golf, a visit to a winery, more golf, more wine, followed by a glass or two of wine – and then came together in the evening for some rugby talk, some of it of the educated variety. If I have the chance to tour South Africa in 2021 with the same people, there'll be no holding me back.

But I have my concerns on the Lions front. Deep concerns. If the fixture list drops from 10 matches to eight, as some influential people insist it should, will it still be a Lions tour in anything but name? I fear not. Under such a programme, matches five, seven and eight would be Tests. This would leave only two further weekend games, the first and the third, and the latter would have to be a dress rehearsal for the putative Test side. It's unworkable. In practical terms, that elite XV would have to be selected in advance of the tour. What price the Lions ethic then? There would be no team-building, no chance for players to force their way into the senior line-up through weight of performance. Form would count for next to nothing. The magic of the Lions? Gone.

Those of us who have had a lifelong love affair with rugby must surely ask whether this makes sense. There is always talk of tens of thousands of supporters crossing the Equator every four years to follow the Lions and while that talk tends to be a shade exaggerated, it is still the case that the numbers are massive by the standards of the union game, despite the weather in New Zealand and the shortage of top-quality opposition in Australia and the continuing security risks in South Africa. Financially, the Lions are negotiating increasingly lucrative deals with their hosts; media-wise, the competition for rights is hotter than it has ever been. The BBC knows that better than anyone.

And the players? A Lions Test is still the ultimate honour, the most potent driver of ambition. No other major sport in existence has an asset quite like the Lions. There is no equivalent in football or cricket or in any of the games that capture the imagination of the North Americans. The people charged with running rugby union should think anew about what the concept means and why it matters. In an age of academies and factory-produced players who do nothing else but train and play together, the Lions rage against the machine. Are they also raging against the dying of the light?

HORSES AND COURSES

HE was in his final year at Fettes, the school in Edinburgh where my brief but enjoyable teaching career was unfolding gently from one term to the next, so he must have been in his mid-teens. He was wearing the proper uniform – grey blazer, grey shirt – and being a sharp eyed sort, I also noticed his blue tie. That meant he was one of mine. The students at Fettes were divided into houses, one of which went by the name of 'Carrington'. Mike Leslie, who taught Latin, was its master. His assistant was a certain Mr Robertson. I wielded a significant degree of authority in this role and was expected to use it, especially if I spotted one of 'my' pupils out of bounds during classroom hours. And if that pupil just happened to be emerging from a bookmaking establishment . . . let's just say all options were open to me, short of hanging, drawing and quartering.

The poor chap noticed me just as I was noticing him and his face turned sheet-white in the time it took for a second to split asunder. He had no excuse, standing there on the doorstep of 'Honest' Ricky Nelson's gambling emporium in the Stockbridge area of the city, but I felt a little sorry for him all the same. He could hardly have expected to walk out of the bookies just as his assistant housemaster was walking in. How could he have known that there was a small-time betting syndicate in the staff common room and that of the four of us, I was the one with the Lambretta scooter and therefore had the ability to whizz over to Stockbridge, lay our money down and whizz back again without anyone noticing?

'Excuse me,' I said, by way of beginning my interrogation. The lad's eyes were out on stalks; the rest of him edged back into 'Honest' Ricky Nelson's and came to rest on the ledge where the race cards and form guides of the morning newspapers were on display. He could barely speak, but he managed to squeeze out the odd word. 'I'm so sorry, sir,' he muttered. 'So sorry. I know I shouldn't be here. It's a library period and I've already done the work, so I thought I'd come down here.' He paused, gathered his second wind and continued. 'It's a special day, sir. It's my birthday and I've received this letter from my grandfather. You can read it.' 'Why would I want to read that?' 'It explains why he's sent me a £10 note.' At this point, I failed to see the relevance. 'What's your name?' I asked. 'Wragg, sir.' 'Look, Wragg,' I continued. 'This is absolutely out of bounds. You shouldn't be leaving the school grounds during lunch interval, let alone during a library period, and you certainly shouldn't be coming half a mile to a . . . just a minute.' At this point, the penny dropped – and along with it, one or two pound signs appeared in my mind's eye. 'How are you spelling Wragg?' 'W–R–A–G–G,' came the reply. 'As in Harry Wragg?' 'Yes, sir. He's my grandfather, sir.' 'Let me see that letter.'

There was lots I didn't know about the sport of kings at that particular point in my life, but I knew about Harry Wragg. The 'head waiter', as he was nicknamed by those who admired his ultra-patient style of riding, had been a natural-born winner on the flat – three victories in the Derby, four in the Oaks, half a dozen others in the remaining classics – and had been crowned Champion Jockey in the 1940s. He had been every bit as productive as a trainer: by the time of my conversation with his grandson Philip, hundreds of high-performing horses had emerged from his Newmarket-based stables.

His communication was therefore of considerable interest to me. It went something along these lines: 'Dear Philip. So sorry not to have sent you your birthday present, but it's a little bulky and you'll get it when you return home at the end of term. In the meantime I enclose a £10 note, which I suggest you put on as a win double. The first horse will be 20–1, but don't worry: it's had three races so far – a couple last year over five furlongs as a two-year-old and one this year over six furlongs when not quite fully fit. We're now trying a two-mile handicap and I expect him to win with plenty to spare, so do not on any account back him each way. The second horse is my best two-year-old. It's his first time out but it should be too good for everything else. It'll be 3–1 or thereabouts. That's £600 for the double.' If there were eyes on stalks now, they belonged to me. I ordered young Wragg back to school: apart from anything else, he'd already made his investment with 'Honest' Ricky. Me? I felt it important to wait for the outcome of the first race, featuring the well-priced horse of which I'd just read. Sure enough, it romped home.

The second race was later in the afternoon, so I was back on my scooter the moment school ended. Once again, the outcome was as predicted by Harry. As I was being paid out, the bookie behind the counter said: 'I heard you shouting at that boy earlier. Wragg, eh? Any relation to Harry?' I came clean. 'Right,' said the bookie. 'You're welcome to pop back in here any time, but I would ask a favour of you: if you have any more interesting information of that kind, just give me half an hour's notice so I can have a bit on for myself else-where in Edinburgh.'

Back at school, a good deal of money stowed safely in my pocket, I sent for Philip. 'Listen very carefully, Wragg,' I told him. 'You're never to be seen in that bookmaker's shop again. If I see you there – even if I see you walking straight past the door without breaking your stride, or standing on the opposite side of the road looking in the opposite direction – it will not be Mr Leslie who deals with the matter. You'll be taken straight to the headmaster.' He nodded. 'That being said, if you come to me at 11am with whatever information

you may have, I'll make sure the bets go on.' Which they did.
Harry rarely, if ever, bet on a race himself. 'If I need money,'
he once told me, 'I go to the bank.' It was a reasonable explanation, given that he was enormously successful in training
horses for the very rich, including the diamond magnate Sir
Philip Oppenheimer, the Aga Khan and the Moller family,
who had made a fabulous fortune in shipping. Happily, he
was prepared to help those who, like me, were interested in
making a modest few bob from the gambling side of the
sport. The tips usually came at a rate of one a month. I think
the strike rate was seven tips, seven winners. Those were the
days: I even enjoyed an overnight stay at Aldington Place,
Harry's Newmarket headquarters, before watching the gallops
in the early morning and spending the afternoon hoovering
up precious information. In the final reckoning, I came out
well ahead!

My interest in the gee-gees had been sparked by accident,
during my days as a post-graduate student at Cambridge
University. Little more than a dozen miles separated Grange
Road, where we played our games, from the paddocks and
stud farms of Newmarket, and it just so happened that another
of the elite local trainers, Ryan Jarvis, was a rugby nut who
enjoyed his time on the touchline, roaring on the bright young
things in light blue during their meetings with the high-and-
mighty teams of grown-ups from London and Wales and the
West Country. After one game, Ryan wondered if a few of
us might fancy a visit to his Phantom House stables. Why

not? It was a day out. He then took us to a race meeting at Newmarket, each of us travelling with a couple of pound notes and a vague plan of risking a small flutter on each race. Ryan had other ideas. 'I think there's a good chance of a Yankee coming up today,' he told us. We were more than a little bemused. A Yankee? What the hell was *that* when it was at home? Was he expecting a Roosevelt or a Kennedy to make an unexpected appearance, secret servicemen in tow? Ryan embarked on an idiots' tutorial and while the explanation was not entirely easy to understand for those of us who could barely tell a horse's head from its backside, it amounted to this: we'd back four horses in a combination bet – six different doubles, four different trebles and a one-off 'roll-up'. I was no mathematician, but it occurred to me that this might be lucrative if we could pull it off. Ryan added that the horses involved were running at various meetings around the country and that it might not be easy to find an on-course Newmarket bookie willing to take the bet. 'Come down to the rails with me, and keep quiet,' he ordered. Happily, he found a compliant bookmaker. Even more happily, our horses won. All four of them. We pulled in the best part of £1,000 – a lot of money in those days. The bookie had to borrow cash from his rivals, just to pay us out. That was me hooked.

From those humble beginnings, it was quite a leap to find myself co-owning a Grand National winner. But strange things happen in all sports and in my experience, there is no predicting what wonders might occur if you find a way of staying connected. When I left Fettes and joined the BBC, I made a point of mentioning my fondness for the racing scene and was only too happy to play whatever role the producers felt might suit me: reading the results, supporting the great correspondent and commentator Peter Bromley at meetings up and down the land, conducting trackside interviews. To me, it was pure fun. I liked the atmosphere and the people involved in the industry. And yes, I loved a bet or two, though I confess to being very cautious in my gambling.

As my knowledge and level of involvement grew, I found myself taking an active interest, as well as a journalistic one. Peter Wragg, son of Harry, was operating as a bloodstock agent and he had a horse he thought might interest me and a few like-minded Scottish souls with a background in rugby. I felt the same way. So in I plunged, along with a handful of others, and Peter told us he'd get Ryan Jarvis to train the horse concerned. What we didn't know at this point was that the Jarvis stables was full of high-end animals worth just a little more than the 200 guineas our creature had fetched at market. Ryan turned it down flat, without bothering to give it so much as a glance. Peter refused to give up. 'If you just let the horse out of its box and take a look at him, you'll find he's small but perfectly muscled. Please cast an eye over him before you tell me to get lost. If you really don't like the idea then, I'll tell myself to get lost.' Ryan did as requested but remained unconvinced. 'Why was it only 200 guineas?' 'The dam never raced and the dam of the dam was no better than moderate,' Peter explained. 'But the sire was El Gallo.' Ryan was listening now. El Gallo had won the Cork and Orrery Stakes – now known as the Diamond Jubilee Stakes – at Ascot. He had been trained by Noel Murless and ridden by Lester Piggott, a jockey of whom you may have heard. That made him good. Better than good. There might even be some remnant of class lurking in the DNA of his unimpressively priced descendant.

Ryan relented and we started racing this apparent nag, under the sleep-inducingly predictable name of Rugby Special, after our BBC television show. He turned out to be a fabulous little horse: he raced 10 times and gave us four firsts, together with three seconds and three thirds. Most importantly of all, we had more than our fair share of fun out of watching him run until an enthusiast in Argentina took him off our hands and gave him a well-earned retirement somewhere on the pampas. My association with Rugby Special – the horse, not the programme – did not always run smoothly, however. On one occasion, Ryan told us he was planning to run him in a race at Windsor. 'The trouble is,' he said, 'we don't have a jockey. Eric Eldin (his go-to man) will be at York, so we'll need a replacement.' I happened to know Willie Carson – no mean jockey, you will surely agree – through my work at the BBC, so I dialled his number and asked him if he might be in the vicinity of Windsor on the day concerned. Willie said he would indeed be riding at the meeting and asked his agent, Ted Leavy, if he was already fixed up for the race in which Rugby Special had been entered. 'Ted tells me I'm free,' he said. 'Excellent. Would you be happy to ride our little chap as a favour? He's won his first race, so he's not completely useless.' Willie agreed. Chuffed, I phoned Ryan to tell him the good news. Big mistake. '*WHAT??? You've done WHAT???*' If that was the start of the diatribe, it was by no means the end. The stream of abuse was as long as it was inventive, and long before the conclusion of the phone call I was in need of a stiff whisky. 'Willie's a good jockey,' I argued, meekly. 'And I'm the bloody trainer,' Ryan roared. 'I know more jockeys than you've had hot dinners and I can tell the good ones from the bad ones. Don't tell me who's good and who isn't. The fact is, you've acted entirely inappropriately. People like you don't choose their own jockeys. Never, ever. Got it?' 'But I was only trying to help. I did it in good faith.' '*Good faith, you lunatic?* Just get off the line.' Slam. Down went the phone. For some reason, I didn't think it a good idea to ring back.

I phoned Willie instead, and it was some time before he stopped laughing. He knew his trainers, and the two Ryans – Ryan Jarvis and his rival Ryan Price – were known to have the shortest tempers in the whole history of racing, stretching all the way back to the 18th century. 'I'm still available if you want me,' he sniggered. Thanks. Thanks a bunch. An hour later, Willie was back on the line. This time, he was paying for the call. 'Ryan has just booked me for the Rugby Special ride,' he said, still chuckling. 'Which is fine. But if you want my advice, I'd leave it to him in future.' On the day of the race at Windsor, I entered the owners' enclosure wondering whether Ryan might have forgotten, or forgiven, or both. Fat chance. 'Ah, Ian: I suppose you've popped in to give Willie his instructions,' he said, with withering sarcasm, before turning away and addressing our jockey. 'Willie, this horse has plenty of speed, so let him see daylight a couple of furlongs from home and give him some hands and heels. That should do it.' Rugby Special won, by several lengths. 'Do you have any more friends who might fancy a ride?' Ryan asked me as we left the ring after unsaddling. There were no niceties, just more scalding sarcasm. The lesson I learned was a painful one, particularly in the area of the eardrum. I also paid a price in lost pride.

For all the discomfort at having the sacrilegious nature of my behaviour described to me in the most colourful way imaginable – and, indeed, at the greatest volume – we at least had a viable horse on our hands. We would soon have another one. His name was Rubstic and he happened to be in training in Scotland under the ownership of John Douglas. John was something more than a keen rugby man: he was a 6ft 3ins, no-nonsense forward who had won international honours in both the second and back rows of the Scotland pack and was selected by the Lions when they toured South Africa in 1962. It seemed perfectly rational that a few of us with similar passions and connections should band together in common purpose. Together with Gareth Edwards, Barry John and Gordon Brown, I was involved with a second horse, going by the name of Twickenham, trained by Ian Balding. In return for a small share in Twickenham – the horse, not the stadium – I received a similar interest in Rubstic and entered into the orbit of that wonderful animal.

Rubstic, far from the biggest racehorse in the land, was trained by John Leadbetter at his place in the border country near Berwick. And he was a star. At least, he became a star. Certain very gifted individuals in the racing world were a little suspicious of him at first, including Lester Piggott. Lester rode Rubstic on the flat, over five furlongs, and trailed in last. 'The trouble with this horse,' he said, making light of the speech problems that had plagued him since childhood, 'is that he needs a bit further than five furlongs. What he needs is five bloody miles, because he's that slow. I might ride him again, but not this year. Or next.' So John tried him over hurdles at a distance of two miles, and discovered that the race still wasn't long enough, or slow enough. From there it was three and a half miles and preferably more, over steeple-chase fences – those big brutes that don't collapse on impact, but stay put and win the collision, as Colin Meads tended to do when he pulled on an All Black shirt. The only realistic option was the Grand National and John spent seven or eight months building Rubstic into a contender. He always raced at the northern courses, so I didn't have too many opportunities to watch him. But I knew he was capable: victories at

Kelso and Sedgefield in the run-up to the big event told me that much.

So it was that in the spring of 1979, Rubstic found himself on the start line at Aintree, with Becher's Brook and Canal Turn and The Chair stretching out before him. Maurice Barnes, a highly talented jump jockey who now trains horses in Cumbria, was the man charged with getting him round, and he set about it with great care and patience. Maurice was well aware of the horse's reputation as a 'genuine animal who always does his best' – a racing euphemism for 'dead slow' – and also knew that despite being vertically challenged, Rubstic was as safe as houses even over the biggest obstacles. If the horse could have spoken, he would have said to the rest of the field: 'This is as fast as I can go. You might be quicker, but can you maintain it over almost four and a half miles?' The answer to the question, on that day of days, was that his opponents could not. There were five still in it a couple of fences from home, but as his main rivals went backwards on the run-in – Zongalero and Rough and Tumble both seemed to be wading through treacle – Rubstic kept flogging his way up the track, winning by a good length or so at the handy price of 25–1. He was the first ever Scottish winner of the great race (there has been only one since) and it was the bravest of runs. Furthermore, it was undoubtedly the most rewarding moment of my racing life. If only I'd been there to witness it! Unfortunately, I was covering a rugby match for the BBC. In those times, there was no easy way of getting away from the day job.

Rubstic gave us no end of fun. He finished second in the Scottish Grand National at Ayr and had another couple of cracks at the Aintree showpiece – a challenge so considerable that a year after his great triumph, even this ultra-reliable jumper fell to earth by taking a tumble at The Chair. In the 1981 race, he stayed upright to finish seventh. That was the most emotional of races: the winner was Aldaniti, but more importantly, the victorious jockey was Bob Champion, who had only just won a desperate battle against cancer. It was quite a tale: in fact, they turned the story into a movie starring John Hurt, no less. One way or another, then, our horse made sure we were at the centre of things. He passed away peacefully at the ripe old age of 26, still under the care of John Leadbetter and still at home in the tranquil fields of Berwickshire.

Throughout this period, I was spending my summer Saturdays on the country's racecourses with my pen in one hand and my microphone in the other. In the eyes of some people, my role was nothing more elevated than 'chief flunky to the great Peter Bromley'. In my own eyes, I was in the thick of a sporting scene I loved and as happy as could be. Peter was a magnificent commentator – among the very best I've encountered, in any field of radio work. Even when I had years of big-occasion broadcasting under my belt, I was in awe of his powers of description and the accuracy of his horse-spotting. It was an education in the art of broadcasting to watch and listen to him operate at Goodwood, where a big field of sprinters would suddenly loom into view and there was a tight finish between half a dozen horses flashing by at the speed of sound. He was not, perhaps, the easiest man to deal with when the microphone was live and there was work to be done, but to hear him rattling off the names without a slip of the tongue was quite something.

If he did not suffer fools gladly – truth be told, he didn't suffer them at all – something persuaded Peter that I was less of a fool than some. I think it was because I took the sport seriously and went out of my way to make that point clear to him. Racing may have been my second-string task as far as the BBC producers were concerned, but I wanted to be involved and was determined to give it my all. Bill McLaren and Cliff Morgan had taught me wonderfully well in terms of rugby broadcasting, but if I wanted to be as word-perfect at Ascot or Epsom or Sandown as I tried to be at Twickenham or Murrayfield or the Arms Park, the method was obvious. Listen to Peter Bromley and learn. So I did my homework, made an effort to look the part by putting on a shirt and tie and generally went the extra furlong in an attempt to come across as something other than the office junior.

In particular, I made it my business to get things right on what we called the 'You Said' front. This was the main task of the day for Peter's sidekicks. The great man would call the 'one, two, three, four' as the leading horses passed the finishing line before going through the rest of the field as they dribbled in at a distance, and it was the flunky's job to write down those initial names in the correct order so Peter could repeat them during the recap immediately following his race commentary. If there was a mistake on that all-important piece of paper – or worse still, if the paper was still blank by the time he reached for it – you were in an ocean of trouble. Don Mosey, hardly a shrinking violet himself when in his comfort zone as a cricket broadcaster, once committed that cardinal sin. 'Just to give you the one, two, three, four again,' said Peter, looking at Don. He had written down precisely nothing. Not a word. There wasn't even a smudge. Suddenly, he was on the wrong end of the sharpest of tongues. Hell had no fury like a Bromley scorned.

There was a second great racing commentator around at that time, of course: Peter O'Sullevan, the voice of the sport on television. For anyone with the slightest feeling for the race game, having two such magical communicators working simultaneously was the very definition of a golden age. I had far fewer dealings with O'Sullevan, but it was obvious that in some ways, if not quite all, the pair were cut from similar cloth. Both had enjoyed the benefits of a high-quality education – Bromley spent his school days at Cheltenham College, O'Sullevan at Charterhouse – and in their highly distinctive ways, both extended and improved the language of sports broadcasting. They also enjoyed a bet. In O'Sullevan's case, those bets could be very substantial indeed, although he tended to refer to them as 'small wagers'. I remember him attempting to place one of these investments during a race meeting somewhere in the home counties and vividly recall his reaction when, rather than accepting the whole sum at the advertised price, the bookmaker insisted on lowering the odds on a sliding scale. 'I do apologise,' said Peter, barely containing his disgust. 'I seem to have dialled the wrong number. I thought I was speaking to a bookmaker.' He then referred to the incident in his commentary, in the most subtle yet lacerating of fashions. That was him all over. As an enthusiastic racehorse owner, he sometimes found himself describing the performance of an animal in which he had a direct interest. No one could have guessed. If his horse won, there was no change in the cadence of his voice. If it lost, likewise. He was a consummate professional.

Peter Bromley, who had been to Sandhurst and served with the King's Hussars, owned gundogs rather than racehorses, but it was not unheard of for him to risk a few shillings on a sure thing. I remember Ryan Price, a trainer with a combustible side to his character, entering a good prospect for the Cesarewitch, a high-profile handicap race at Newmarket. As part of his preparation, the horse ran at a lower level meeting a few weeks beforehand, with Lester Piggott on his back. Ryan gave the legendary jockey precise instructions: Lester should get him home first, but not by such a distance that the Cesarewitch odds would fall off a cliff. 'And don't give him a hard race, Lester,' he added. 'We want him right when it matters.' I had money on the horse, as did Peter, so when we saw from the radio broadcasting position that he was boxed in, and that Lester was in no rush to press the button, we were both alarmed. Pretty much at the last moment, Lester gently pushed the animal past the first three horses in front of him before producing the whip and seeing off the rest of the opposition to win by a short head. What a relief.

Peter finished his wrap-up, mopped his fevered brow and said: 'Right, Ian. Let's get down to the ring and establish what the hell happened out there.' As we arrived, we saw Ryan Price. At least, we would have done had he not been concealed by the smoke emanating from his nostrils. 'Christ!' he shouted as Lester dismounted. 'You've just thrashed the living daylights out of him. How many times did you hit the poor thing?' Lester was calmness personified. 'Look at his bum,' he said. 'That'll tell you all you need to know.' And off he walked. Ryan immediately inspected the horse's hind quarters and found not a hair out of place. The only thing Lester had whipped was fresh air. And on further review, he had been holding the horse back while pretending to 'thrash the living daylights' out of him. The man wasn't just a jockey. He was a genius.

It's fair to say that as far as racing was concerned, I was the opposite of a genius. I had no great expertise, no particular insight. I was an enthusiast, pure and simple. There were many occasions when enthusiasm was enough to carry the day – especially as I was generally able to supplement my keenness with a little bare-faced cheek – but the line between getting away with it and getting caught out was a thin one. Every now and again during my broadcasting dabbles in the equine world, I made a fool of myself. Not least when my acquaintance Willie Carson had a rather challenging mount at Epsom and needed to employ all his tricks to get the thing home in first place. I was in the ring for the obligatory interview, with Peter Bromley listening intently from the commentary box. 'That was a tough one, Willie,' I said, erring on the side of too-clever-by-halfness. 'You were in some trouble out there, yet you made it in the end. It was the same at York last time out. It seems to me that you've just ridden the same race twice!' Willie looked at me, an impish smile on his face. 'Thanks, but I didn't ride him at York,' he replied before turning away from the microphone and laughing out loud. I'm not the tallest of men, but I have an inch or two on most of the flat jockeys. Just then, I felt as though Willie was the giant at the top of the beanstalk . . . and I was Jack.

More often than not, however, I came out ahead. If I hadn't, I'd have been hauled off the racing beat by the scruff of the neck in the mid-1980s, long before I bowed out because of increasing rugby commitments. On one memorable occasion, I even managed to bag myself an exclusive interview with the mighty Piggott, whose impatience with racing journalists was legendary. We were at Doncaster and true to form, Lester left his mark on the big race of the day. Peter Bromley sent me down to the ring in pursuit of him, even though he assumed I'd draw a blank. I could see his point: it was the television boys who expected privileged access to the biggest names in the sport. I adopted my usual hover, microphone in hand, as Lester walked straight past the cameras and towards the weighing room. Then, he spotted me. 'You're the rugby bloke,' he said. 'I don't mind talking to you.' So off we went for our chat. When I returned to the press room, I heard John Oaksey – Old Etonian, graduate of Oxford and Yale, aristocrat, jockey, hugely successful broadcaster and writer, wonderful company – berating me in unusually direct terms. 'That chap Robertson – you know, the rugby chap – has just elbowed me out of the way and spoken to Piggott! And he knows bugger all about racing.' I really couldn't help myself. 'You're quite right – I *don't* know a thing about racing,' I said from behind his back. He turned around, aghast. 'I'm *so* sorry,' he said. 'That was unforgiveable of me.' He could not have been more polite, either then or in our subsequent meetings. That's the thing with racing. It's all down to breeding.

If I never pretended to be a racing expert, I was in even less of a hurry to present myself as an active horseman. Leaving aside an ill-fated adventure in the saddle during Scotland's rugby tour of Argentina in 1969, where my impersonation of a gaucho ended with me dangling from the branch of a tree and was therefore even less accurate than my impression of a hard-tackling Jonny Wilkinson prototype, I made it my business to avoid all forms of four-legged activity. Golf?

That's different. I may have lost control of the odd buggy heading down the 18th, but there are few dangers on the fairways of the world when compared with the perils of the paddock, let alone the racecourse itself.

Golf is the third element in my holy sporting trinity. I've been playing the game for almost as long as I can remember: my father, an excellent golfer, was a member of the local Murrayfield club, situated only a mile and a half from the centre of Edinburgh, and I joined him on the course at a very young age with my little bag of irons and wedges. 'Sawn-off shotguns', we called them. I also had early lessons from the professional there – a chap who had lost an arm in a work accident, yet could smack a ball 230 yards down the middle without appearing to think about it and find his way round in level par. Almost seven decades on, my two arms are no longer capable of matching what the pro did with one. My distance off the tee is diminishing and I don't have much length with my second shot. Back in the day at the Highgate club near my home in North London, I played off 12. More often, I was a 14-handicapper – my true level, I think. I then spent 20 years playing off 16. Now, I'm up to 18. Does that upset me? Not at all. For one thing, no one can accuse me of golfing banditry if I live down to my handicap, as I generally do these days. For another, I'm not playing to win the Masters. I play for fun, which is what golf gives me. The simple fact of the matter is that I always love every single minute of my time on the course, wherever in the world that course may be. Even if I manage only a few good shots in a bad round. That's the clever thing about golf: it always gives you just enough encouragement to carry on.

Rugby has done me proud when it comes to golf: thanks to the union game, I've played many of the finest courses in Australia, New Zealand and South Africa. Closer to home, I've had my moments in Ireland – as seductive a golfing country as it is possible to imagine – and of course in Scotland, where the game was invented. I am a member at Loch Lomond and Gleneagles, wonderful locations both, and I've had the good fortune to play all the courses on the current Open Championship roster, in addition to one or two from the dim and distant past, like Musselburgh, just outside Edinburgh on the Firth of Forth. I never feel anything less than privileged to tee off at Birkdale or St George's, at St Andrews or Muirfield or Troon. If I have a regret concerning my golfing life, it is that I have never broadcast on the game. How I would have loved to commentate in hushed tones at the climax of a Major – to have said: 'Here's Joe Bloggs, with a six-footer to win it, breaking left to right . . . and he's nailed it!' In my dreams, my co-commentator is always Rob Andrew, no mean golfer himself and an acknowledged master of the shrieking interruption at the crucial point in a mass-audience production!

I cannot begin to explain this, but it seems to me that the golfing public are in a class of their own when it comes to venerating their heroes. Footballers have something of a following, of course. So do cricketers, particularly in India and other parts of the sub-continent. And while the overwhelming majority of British and Irish rugby players have always been able to shop in Sainsbury's without being hassled over the frozen peas – with the obvious exceptions of Barry John in the early 1970s and Jonny Wilkinson more recently – the likes of Dan Carter, Richie McCaw and Jonah Lomu knew what it was to live their lives in a goldfish bowl down there in All Black land. But golf is different somehow. Most leading professionals are relatively anonymous, but the crème de la crème – Gary Player, Arnold Palmer, Jack Nicklaus, Seve Ballesteros, Tiger Woods – are held in awe, frequently by people who are wildly successful in their own right. Not just sportsmen, but businessmen and politicians. It seems to me if Jack Nicklaus had run for the White House in his heyday, every rival presidential candidate would have dropped out of the race for fear of being buried by a landslide.

I make a point of attending the Open Championship every year and if I can, I head for Georgia each April to watch the Masters at Augusta. I've never met Tiger Woods, but I've seen him play in the tournament he once threatened to monopolise more completely than any golfer in history and I've witnessed at first hand the effects of his charisma and game-changing talent on the golfing public in America. I've also seen each of the so-called Big Three – Nicklaus, Palmer, Player – in the white heat of major-tournament competition and been lucky enough to hit a few balls with two of them.

Nicklaus may still be considered the greatest golfer of them all, but my dealings with him have been few and far between. That is not the case with the other two and I speak from experience when I say that Arnold Palmer, who died in 2016, and Gary Player were always as friendly towards me as they were inspirational.

Some time ago, I was struck by a rather grand idea. Craig Campbell, a highly regarded artist from Ayrshire who studied at the Glasgow School of Art and frequently turned to sport for his subject matter, had produced a work based on studies and portraits of Palmer, Player and Nicklaus – a striking piece that caught each man both in his golfing pomp and in his later years. 'If I could just persuade all three to sign the painting,' I thought, 'it would be worth its weight in gold at a charity auction.' The problem was how to go about it. Gary Player was living at his home on the South African highveld; the others spent the vast majority of their time in Florida – Arnold Palmer somewhere around Orlando, Jack Nicklaus in Palm Beach. It wouldn't be a case of paying each of them a personal visit in the space of an evening. And anyway, there was no guarantee they would be willing to stick their thumb-prints on a Scottish canvas at the request of a Scottish rugby broadcaster. There was no doubting the fact that all three of them knew and loved Scotland as a country: Arnold had won the Open Championship at Troon; Gary at Carnoustie; Jack at St Andrews. What was more, both Gary and Jack knew what it was to bag an Open title at Muirfield. Even so, I knew I had set myself a challenge, both logistically and persuasively.

I phoned Peter Alliss, another prominent figure in the pantheon of BBC sports broadcasters. 'Nice plan,' he said, 'but do you actually know any of them?' I certainly knew Gary Player. I'd shared speaking duties with him at charity dinners – one of which had, at the last minute, featured the brilliant Ronnie Corbett on the bill, which rather undermined my assumption that I would be the funniest man in the room. I had also stayed at Blair Atholl, the Player family estate and golf complex situated on the Crocodile River, just outside Johannesburg. Indeed, I had played with the winner of nine Majors on his own course! I had always found him an approachable man – devout in the religious sense and a generous spirit when it came to charity. I had no doubt that Gary would pick up a pen if I asked him to do so. 'That's a good start,' Peter acknowledged. 'I know Arnold very well indeed and I'm sure he'll do the necessary. He's a perfect gentleman. If you phone Doc Giffin (Arnold's assistant of 40 years and his closest friend), he'll sort it for you.' And Jack? 'He might prove a little more elusive,' Peter told me. 'He can be just a little wary about this kind of thing.'

As I had anticipated, Gary readily agreed to sign the painting. Arnold also came up trumps, if not quite in the way I had imagined. When I phoned his home number, I heard a man's voice confirm that this was indeed the 'Palmer residence'. 'Would it be possible to speak to Doc Giffin?' I

asked. 'Doc isn't here right now. He's out shopping for crois-
sants. Can I help you?' 'Probably not. I need to speak to Doc
Giffin.' 'May I ask what it's about, sir?' 'You may. I'm very
friendly with Peter Alliss and he suggested I phone Doc to
ask him if Arnold Palmer might be persuaded to sign a golf
painting. It's a painting of Arnold, in actual fact, along with
one or two others he might have stumbled across down the
years – a chap called Player, another by the name of Nicklaus.
It's for charity.' There was barely a pause. 'I might be able to
spare you the effort,' said the man. 'I'm Arnold Palmer.' I was
so bowled over with surprise, I only just stopped myself saying:
'Jesus . . . you mean you answer your own phone?' Arnold
was happy to oblige. 'If you send the painting to me here in
Florida, I'll sign it while the driver waits outside and have it
mailed right back to you. Best of luck with Jack, by the way.'
Then, there *was* a pause. 'Actually, will you be at the seniors'
event at Turnberry this year – the one being held straight
after the Open? I'm playing, so we can do it then. Come to
think of it, Jack should be there too. Now, I can't promise
anything, but I'll try my best to get him to join in.'

When the Turnberry moment came Arnold signed the
painting as promised, and with a little help from George
Mathewson, then the chief executive of the Royal Bank of
Scotland, who were sponsoring the seniors' tournament, we
secured the Nicklaus signature into the bargain. By way of
placing a cherry on the cake, Arnold then asked me if I might
fancy playing half a dozen holes in celebration. It was an

offer impossible to turn down, even though a small part of me was petrified, to the extent that I proceeded to ask one of the world's greatest ever golfers if he'd be offended by the on-course crimes I was certain I'd commit: hooks, slices, air-shots, you name it. 'Don't worry about that,' he replied with a soft smile. 'There'll be no pressure on you.' Easy for him to say, I thought, as I approached the first tee, utterly convinced that if I hit the ball at all, it would be backwards. As it turned out, I made a reasonable contact. The ball veered to the right, but at least it landed in the right postcode. 'Would you like a tip?' Arnold asked. He might as well have asked the world's greediest dog if he'd fancy a sirloin steak, cooked to order. 'I can sort that slice for you. You don't have a bad swing: your leg position is good, your shoulders are good. Your right hand? Just turn it anti-clockwise by an inch. Do that and you'll be dead straight.' A little later, he told me that he'd noticed four issues rather than one. 'Go on,' I said, eager for instruction. 'I'm not telling you about the other three. One thing, you can handle. Four? Too confusing. You'll spend the rest of your golfing life thinking rather than playing.' It made perfect sense: to this day, I concentrate on keeping my right hand in the correct position, and I continue to reap the rewards. I can't thank him enough.

The most recent of my golfing idols was, and remains, the sensational Seve Ballesteros. He was the very definition of a box-office golfer – a player who went for broke with every shot and in so doing, turned fairways and greens around the world into film sets and theatre stages. He could be wild off the tee, yet his short game was so brilliant and his putting so inspirational, it scarcely seemed to matter. In Ryder Cups, perhaps the nearest equivalent we have to a Lions tour in the sense that disparate individuals come together once and once only in common cause, he was a force of nature. At Open Championships, he was my number one priority – the player I wanted to watch over and above everyone else.

It was back at Turnberry in 1986 that the Ballesteros magic made its greatest impact on me. I went to the course early in Open week to watch the top contenders in practice and, to my delight, Seve was among the first to emerge. I followed his progress with a BBC cameraman for company and was treated to one of the best sporting moments of my life. 'How far to the pin?' Seve asked his caddy midway through the round, well within earshot of the small handful of watchers, no more than 15 yards or so away. It was not his regular caddy, for he wouldn't be arriving in Scotland until late that evening. This was a local by the name of Willie, and his answer was immediate. 'For you, it's a six-iron.' Seve furrowed his Spanish brow and his face darkened. 'That's not what I asked,' he said. 'You think I can't choose my own club? How far to the pin? Not to the front of the green, not to the back. I want to know how far it is to the pin.' Brave chap that he was, Willie stuck to his guns. 'I'm telling you: it's a six-iron.'

Seve's response was interesting, to say the least. 'Give me the bag,' he said. On receipt of it, he tipped it so that every club fell to the ground. It was a tantrum. There was nothing especially ferocious about it and there was no risk to life or limb, but it was very definitely a tantrum. It wasn't over, either. 'Okay. Put down 14 balls and space them out. Six inches apart. Now, give me the driver.' Bang. Seve sent the first of the balls sailing onto the green, no more than 10 feet from the pin. 'Right. Give me the three-wood.' Bang. Centre of the green. 'Other wood.' Bang. On the green. Four-iron, five-iron, six-iron . . . he went through them all with similar results. By now he was down to the short stuff. 'Pitching wedge,' he said, his hand outstretched. Down on one knee, with the face of the wedge angled so the bottom of the club was clearly visible, he hit another ball towards the heart of the green. 'Okay. Sand wedge.' At which point, I thought 'this is impossible' and stared at the Spanish maestro, reluctant to blink in case I missed something. The ball soared through the air and trickled onto the front. He then reached for his putter and simply smashed the remaining ball as hard as he could, giving it the full 'seven bells' treatment. Somehow, he got it airborne. Somehow, it too reached the front of the green. 'Right,' he said, with an air of satisfaction. 'I've used every single club and put every ball on the green, so I'll try once more. Tell me: what is the distance from here to the pin?' Willie's answer was a 24-carat classic. 'Aye, it's 160 yards,' he said. 'And I think you'll find that the one nearest the pin is your six-iron.' I wondered then whether my great hero might implode, but Willie wasn't remotely worried. Coming from Glasgow, he'd come across bigger, tougher men than Seve. When he walked past us, he even gave us a friendly wink. A cool customer, all things considered.

Later, the media had a chance to speak to Seve about the forthcoming tournament. Some of the questions were predictable, but instead of restricting himself to stock answers, he gave us a tutorial, beginning with a lesson on grass. 'It's something a player must know,' he said. 'What is the grass doing? If it is facing towards me, I must hit the ball a little harder and play into it.' I'd never once thought about the direction of the grass. Grass was grass, wasn't it? Apparently not. Then he talked about the wind. 'Okay. So I'm 250 yards from the green. Can I get there with a three-wood? No way. What about a hitting driver? Insanity, you say. But I like risks, so I take the driver. If there's a big slice, who cares? I recover. I know I must put things right if I play wild, but I'm lucky. I'm very good at putting things right. People say it is never good to try to be clever: they say you should take your punishment on the course. But I say it is possible to play out of a bad position if you are brave enough. If you are behind a tree, you can stand with your right leg forward and your left leg back, take your club up and across . . . and then, you can hit the ball round the tree. Let me show you.' We went back onto the course and into the woods. Down went the ball, directly behind a tree trunk. 'Most people come out sideways,' Seve said. 'Let me show you a better escape.' Smack. The ball went around the tree, straightened up and ran 180 yards down the fairway. 'Would you do that in a tournament?' someone asked. 'No, never.' He paused. 'Except sometimes.' He did it again, and again. It was simply brilliant. Seve changed the game with his powers of recovery. Some of the old-time greats, Sam Snead and Ben Hogan and Bobby Jones, must have been wonderful retrievers – masters at rescuing seemingly lost causes. But I find it hard to believe they played the way Seve played, or that they performed with his kind of panache.

By comparison, my golfing exploits have been modest in the extreme. There are some good players amongst the rugby fraternity, none of them better than my friend, countryman and frequent broadcasting colleague Gavin Hastings. He's a big bloke, Gavin, and he uses his height and weight to hit the ball 300 yards off the tee with his driver and 150 yards-plus with a pitching wedge. He can spin the ball on landing too, the clever so-and-so. I sometimes think that if he had switched his attention away from rugby at the right age, he might even have made himself a living on the professional circuit. But there are mere mortals, and then there is Ballesteros and his small handful of fellow titans. All of the pro players have virtually all of the shots, and many of them have the winning mentality. What they don't possess is the combination of technique and imagination that Seve brought to the game. It was a privilege to watch him play. Even when he was only practising.

CHARITY BEGINS
AT DINNER

'WHEN it comes to charity, too many people stop at nothing.' It's an old joke, and it may well be that for those who look at the world from a sceptical point of view, it hits the nail on the head. Many a true word spoken in jest, as they say. But there are many different approaches to life – I don't suppose for a moment that there has ever been a rugby dressing room, let alone a whole society, in which everyone agrees with everyone else about everything – so I feel both entitled and proud to take a less cynical, more positive view of fund-raising for good causes. If there is a one-liner that sums up my attitude, it's the one ascribed to perhaps the most celebrated sportsman of them all, Muhammad Ali. 'Service to others is the rent you pay for your room here on earth.'

Over many years – a period almost as long as my stint at the BBC – I've had virtually as much fun, and taken the same kind of enjoyment and satisfaction, from my charity work as from my broadcasting and associated sporting pursuits. I've attended and participated in many hundreds of lunches and dinner events set up specifically to generate financial support for people who need it most, and my roles have been many and varied. Quite often, I've performed the master of ceremonies duties; frequently, I've done a turn as an impromptu auctioneer; every so often, I find myself as one half of a question-and-answer act with a sporting personality of note. On more occasions than I care to remember, I've even been the main speaker. 'Could you pop along and give us half an hour of your drivel, Robbo?' an organiser will ask. 'Of course. Who else is speaking?' 'Er . . . you're on your own.'

Almost always, I've been pleasantly surprised by the generosity of those who make the effort to turn up to these events: not just sportsmen, but administrators and businessmen and high-flying professionals, together with the occasional blue-blooded aristocrat. On occasions, their support has moved me to tears. Many of these people prefer to downplay their involvement and keep a low profile, and I go out of my way to respect their wishes. Every now and again, a well-known individual might go against the grain by flatly refusing to give up a moment of his time or demanding payment despite the fact that everyone else is working for free. I'm happy to grant anonymity to these people too. As far as I'm concerned, their names are not worth recording. I'm sure they know who they are.

I've already mentioned the wonderful Make-A-Wish Foundation, which brings such joy and positivity into the lives of young people suffering from life-threatening medical conditions. It was formed in Phoenix, Arizona, in 1980 and now has a global reach, with active wings in 15 European countries and another couple of dozen in further-flung corners of the world. Almost half a million kids have benefited from the work of the charity since its launch and the people at the heart of the organisation have done a remarkable job in attracting corporate backers on the scale of Disney, CNN and United Airlines.

By comparison with such a broad-based international network of volunteers, it might be argued that the Wooden Spoon Society is a more modest concern when it comes to the numbers. But that depends on your definition of 'modest'. If you believe that the raising of well over £22m over a period of 30-odd years – money used to help more than a million disabled and disadvantaged children – is something worthy of respect and celebration, then 'modest' is perhaps the least appropriate word in the dictionary. Wooden Spoon is one of the charities closest to my heart and it has taken up much of my time and energy. I wasn't involved right at the start in 1983, when five England rugby followers had the germ of an idea while drowning their sorrows after a particularly painful Five Nations defeat at the hands of Ireland in Dublin, but David Roberts, one of the central figures in the charity during the early days, introduced me to its work by taking me to a couple of homes for seriously underprivileged kids that were in dire need of assistance. I'm rather ashamed to admit that at the time, I was reluctant to actually witness the problems with my own eyes. I knew I wasn't made of stern enough stuff. But very quickly, I found myself visiting a home for young children born blind and deaf. I decided that I had to help. This was an important concern, and I wanted to be a part of it.

That 1983 season had been a calamitous one for England. Only three years previously, Bill Beaumont had led the national team to a first Grand Slam since 1957 and only their second since World War Two. Now, they were all over the place: most of the forwards who had dominated the 1980 tournament had packed it in – there was no Bill or Fran Cotton, no Roger Uttley or Tony Neary – and the selectors were back in panic mode, where they had spent so much of the previous decade. They chopped and changed at half-back, they diddled around with the tight five and they changed captains in mid-course. France outscored them three tries to nil at Twickenham, and while England did manage to cross the opposition whitewash in a drawn game with Wales in Cardiff, there were no home comforts when the Scots ran them ragged on the Old Cabbage Patch a month later. The finale in Dublin had trouble written all over it, not least for a young and eye-blurringly rapid attacking runner from Bath with whom I would share the stage at many a charity dinner in the future. David Trick was a natural right wing, picked by England on . . . the left wing. It would have been difficult enough for him had Ireland chosen any old outside-half with a boot sufficiently educated to expose the muddle-headedness of the decision. As the green-shirted No.10 that day was Ollie Campbell, whose boot was of PhD standard, poor David was really up against it. And on his debut, too.

Ireland won 25–15 and would have smashed England clean out of sight but for the magnificent goal-kicking of Dusty Hare. Not that the popular full-back from Leicester could spare his country the indignity of finishing at the foot of the tournament table. Afterwards, in one of the many watering holes situated within staggering distance of Lansdowne Road, those five travelling supporters were numbing their pain in time-honoured fashion when a local wag presented them with a wooden spoon, ceremonially wrapped in an Irish scarf and served on a silver platter. There followed a long discussion over who should take ownership of this 'prize'. What better way to decide the matter than over a round of golf? The Farnham club in Surrey was the preferred location and it caught the imagination of the quintet and their friends to such an extent that £8,500 was raised on the day. So now there was another question: what to do with the money? There was a school in the area that did valuable work in supporting children with special needs – a school that would be able to do a whole lot more with a reliable means of transport. Within days, the head teacher took possession of a new minibus and the charity sector was bolstered by the formal creation of a new rugby-based fundraising organisation. Since when, many hundreds of projects have been launched and completed by the Wooden Spoon Society.

I'm proud of my association with this most generous-spirited and open-hearted of groups. Not being one of life's natural administrators, I'm happy to leave the committee work to those better equipped to organise their way out of a wet paper bag. But when it comes to making sure that our events go with a swing – literally, in the case of the many golf days staged by branches up and down the country – I'm always keen to help. I do my bit on the literary front too: thanks in no small part to the efforts of my friend, the publisher Adrian Stephenson, there have been more than 20 editions of our rugby yearbook – a well-produced hardback volume that appears on charity lunch and dinner tables all over the country. Many of the best writers on the sport have shown a great willingness to support the Wooden Spoon, as have the top players. The most dedicated of these include such significant figures as Phil Vickery, Jason Robinson and Maggie Alphonsi, all three of them World Cup winners with England; a pair of Lions captains in Gavin Hastings and Gareth Thomas; and a sprinkling of current Red Rose performers, including Chris Robshaw and Danny Cipriani. One more thing: as of 2015, the society can legitimately claim that it goes to the ends of the earth in pursuit of its aims. It was then that Tim Stimpson, an England full-back under both Jack Rowell and Clive Woodward, and Ollie Phillips, a World Sevens Player of the Year in his heyday, led a fundraising trek to the North Pole. That was some effort in anyone's language. When I

It's up … It's over … He's done it … Jonny Wilkinson did his best to confuse me by dropping his World Cup-winning goal off the wrong foot, but it was still the commentating moment of a lifetime

Ben Cohen, the Northampton wing, has possession of the Webb Ellis Trophy during the London street parade in 2003. Later, the squad were given the full red carpet treatment

The smile of global success: Clive Woodward celebrates a job well done

All aboard the Fun Bus: Jason Leonard prepares for another World Cup scrum

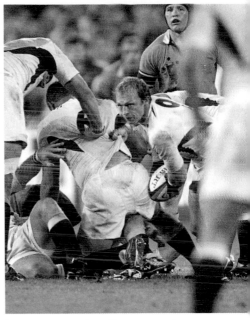

No stopping him: Lawrence Dallaglio played every minute of the 2003 campaign

Hitting the spot: Matt Dawson was the crucial link between forwards and backs

Four rugby wits: clockwise from top left – Jim Renwick, Fergus Slattery, Moss Keane and Gareth Chilcott

Four rugby titans: clockwise from top left – Gavin Hastings, Brian O'Driscoll,
Ian McLauchlan, Martin Johnson

Eddie Jones, the first overseas coach to take control of England

Daniel Carter, a small-town boy with the whole world at his feet

Our names are Robertson and O'Reilly. Ian Robertson and Tony O'Reilly. And you are … ?

Pitchside at Murrayfield during my final
Calcutta Cup commentary, after being led up
the garden path by Gavin Hastings

Severiano Ballesteros was, and remains,
very high on my list of sporting heroes.
What skill. What charisma. What a player!

The winning post is in sight for Rubstic, left, as the 1979 Grand National reaches its climax.
If only I'd been there to see it!

We all love a party but for some reason, my invaluable PA Joanna Carolan, left, and my daughter Clare have dispensed with their fashionable headwear

Charlie Wigglesworth, my great canine friend, is known as the Highgate Rottweiler. He's the one on the right

Graduation days are special moments. My children Clare and Duncan, have good reason to be proud of their achievements

have a spare moment, I'll give them a ring to see if they've made it back.

If much of my charity work has been, and continues to be, conducted in the public space, there is also a deeply private and personal dimension to it. I participate because I'm moved. Which brings me to Alastair Hignell, whom I've known for more than 40 years. Whenever we share a glass of red wine or two, as we try to do as often as possible, I rarely fail to point out that I was the making of him during those early days at Cambridge University: that without my priceless guidance as to his best position on a rugby field, he would have found himself watching four consecutive Varsity Matches at Twickenham rather than playing in them and would certainly not have enjoyed an international career as England's number one full-back. (In truth, he would have made it anyway, for he was almost as good a scrum-half as he claimed to be when, during his fresher's year, he first bent my ear about selection.) On the flipside, he has been nothing short of an inspiration to me. Multiple sclerosis is a cruel disease and it must be fought with every weapon we can muster. In my experience, no sufferer has fought harder, more honourably, or with greater energy and determination and distinction than Higgy.

When he was diagnosed in the early weeks of 1999, he was in his early 40s. He had enjoyed a wonderful sporting career, combining top-end rugby with a dozen summer sojourns as a professional cricketer with Gloucestershire – a feat that made him one of the last of our great all-rounders. He knew what it was to be the last line of rugby defence against the Wales team of Phil Bennett and Gareth Edwards and the Pontypool front row in Cardiff, and against a blood-thirsty band of Wallabies at the 'Battle of Ballymore' in Brisbane. He had also reached the heights with the bat, once taking a century off a West Indies pace attack spearheaded by Vanburn Holder, Bernard Julien and Collis King in a tour match at Bristol. (The supremely elegant Pakistani batsman Zaheer Abbas, one of Higgy's idols as well as a teammate, scored precisely nought in the same innings!) And now he was stricken with the secondary progressive form of MS, which, as he subsequently put it, meant he was 'on the slope' and would 'gradually go downhill'.

It was not until the following year that he let on about his condition to those outside his close family circle. By that time, we'd been working closely together at the sharp end of BBC Radio's rugby union coverage for some time. Higgy had joined the corporation in the mid-1980s, left to try his luck in tele-vision, and then put himself back on the side of the angels ahead of the 1997 Lions tour of South Africa. Quite soon, Ed Marriage joined the team as rugby producer and we would stick together as a trio for the best part of a decade, as thick as thieves. I could not conceivably have been luckier in having two such professional, dedicated, eternally patient and glori-ously good-humoured colleagues. They were the easiest company imaginable: even when Ed, on whose shoulders the organisational side of the operation naturally fell, was completely at his wit's end, his gentle character shone through. So when we went to Paris in mid-February 2000 for the first England–France game of the Six Nations era, I felt justified in thinking that with the three of us complementing each other so well, these were the best of times. But for Higgy, it was among the worst of times. What was it Charles Dickens had written in *A Tale of Two Cities*?

As I remember it, we were heading for a pre-match press conference when I noticed that Higgy was walking awkwardly. 'What's going on?' I asked, vaguely aware that he had retired from professional cricket because of increasing problems with his ankles. He was quiet for a second. 'Let's do the press conference and get the interviews tied up, then have a coffee in our library,' he eventually replied, referring to our regular café stop-off on the Rue St-Honoré. 'It's not good news,' he said later as we sat at the table, sipping our milky drinks. 'I have MS. It's progressive.' What was there to do, except cry together? So we shared some tears. What was there for me to say except: 'I'll do everything I can.' So that's what I said.

Later that year, I organised a fund-raising dinner for my great friend and colleague at the Café Royal in London. By that point, Higgy was aware of the potential benefits of a new range of drugs called beta interferons. He was also aware of two other things: that they were expensive, and that they were not available through the National Health Service. I drummed up as much interest in the charity bash as I could

– and believe me, there was a lot of interest. A good number of Higgy's fellow Cambridge graduates threw themselves behind the event, as did a lot of movers and shakers on the professional club rugby scene: players, coaches and incredibly generous club owners like Nigel Wray of Saracens, who was the first to offer crucial help in accessing the required drugs and has continued to support the cause. What was more, virtually every member of the England set-up was fully on board, even though the dinner would be held at a crucial stage of the autumn international series at Twickenham. The problem? Those England players were also smack in the middle of what amounted to an industrial dispute with the Rugby Football Union over match fees, image rights and other commercial matters. The talks were going nowhere fast, the mood was darkening, both sides were digging in. On the Monday before the meeting with Argentina that weekend, the players' representatives – the captain Martin Johnson; his predecessor as skipper, Lawrence Dallaglio; the scrum-half Matt Dawson – talked through the various options and their likely consequences at a team meeting and then called for a secret ballot. Two squad members abstained. The rest voted to go on strike. Unless the union moved, they would not take the field against the Pumas.

Our Café Royal dinner was scheduled for the following evening. On the Tuesday morning, the players were told to leave their team base at the Pennyhill Park hotel, just outside Bagshot. According to Martin Johnson, who wrote in detail about these events in his autobiography, home phone numbers were exchanged by members of the squad, some of whom feared that the RFU would order their 'company' mobiles to be cut off. There was a press conference with the governing body and another with the senior players. All hell was breaking loose. I could not help wondering if any of the big names in the English game would attend our event; in fact, I set about preparing myself for the worst. There would be a lot of very disappointed guests, just when poor Higgy needed them to be in the best of spirits. As it turned out, Lawrence and Jason Leonard took the lead in drumming up support. 'We've agreed to back Higgy at tonight's do,' they said to their colleagues, 'and we're definitely going. You guys are all free agents and you may want to go home, but we hope you'll join us at the dinner.' Which they did, to a man. As master of ceremonies, I was able to have a little fun with the audience, all of whom were aware of the whiff of the picket line around the England camp. 'Ladies and gentlemen,' I began. 'I know you were expecting the whole England team to turn up.' The diners were so deflated by my opening words, it was almost as if the air had been sucked from the room. 'They don't actually have anywhere to stay in London tonight, having been kicked out of their hotel. But . . . they're here anyway.' And in they came, to a standing ovation.

Something in the region of £170,000 was raised that night, which provided Higgy with his safety net and also set him free to launch his own charitable work in the fight against

MS. I recall asking one of the major businessmen at the dinner, the British Airways chief executive Rod Eddington, whether he might stump up a couple of good flight tickets for the auction. 'Tickets to where?' he asked. 'Anywhere really,' I said before thinking of a location a good distance away. 'Buenos Aires would be nice.' 'Funnily enough, we're the only ones who fly there direct, so let's do it,' Rod said. 'Business class?' I replied, now pushing my luck quite a long way. 'Certainly.' When the bidding started, I told the guests: 'These tickets can be used at any time, apart from over Christmas and New Year. You could, of course, choose to go in April. They're holding the World Cup Sevens in Mar del Plata, which happens to be a one-hour flight from the capital.' There was a distinct thud as Rod's head hit the table. Andrew Brownsword, then the owner of the Bath club, bought the trip for a handsome five-figure sum. 'So you stitched me up well and truly,' Rod said with a grin when he caught up with me later in the evening. 'Only a little,' I replied. It was that kind of night.

I still put on dinners and charity quizzes for Higgy when the opportunity offers itself: since that first event, there have been more than 20 of them. But I'm proud to say that when it comes to raising money and, just as importantly, awareness, a lot of the drive and momentum comes from the sufferer rather than the supporter. Given his condition, Higgy is incredibly active in working for the cause, especially around the southern counties of England. He became a patron of the MS-UK organisation in 2002; he set up the Higgy's Heroes group, in which runners both serious and non-serious participate in distance events, including the London Marathon; he was heavily involved in financing the building of the new West of England Therapy Centre just outside Bristol and in equipping a similar service up the road in Gloucester; he is a life member of Mutual Support, the armed forces' MS charity; he is an active supporter of the Wooden Spoon Society; he is a Lord's Taverner; he is a trustee of the Leonard Cheshire Disability organisation, which works wonders in helping to maximise the independence of those affected by life changing conditions. That is quite a record of service. I was devastated when he felt obliged to leave full-time broadcasting after the 2007 World Cup in France, but I just about pulled myself together when asked to say a few words about him at the BBC's Sports Personality of the Year awards a few months later. In fact, it was one of the greatest pleasures of my life.

Higgy was receiving the Helen Rollason Award for achievement in the face of adversity (the first female presenter of the flagship *Grandstand* programme, Helen had helped raise £5m for a new cancer wing at North Middlesex Hospital after falling terminally ill with the disease) and would be joining a very select group of winners: the racehorse trainer Jenny Pitman, the Paralympian Tanni Grey-Thompson, the sailor Ellen MacArthur, the boxer Michael Watson. Initially, I was not expecting to speak: the powers that be at the corporation rather sprung it on me. 'Don't do more than five minutes, Robbo,' came the order. I don't think I managed much more than five seconds, such was the emotional charge I felt as I took the stage in front of a television audience of millions. To this day, I'm not sure what words I managed to squeeze out. What I do know is this: I had never been prouder of Higgy, nor more in awe of him.

Very few people knew it, but the rather substantial chap who wore the All Blacks' No.11 shirt for a while and scored the odd try when the mood took him – a chap by the name of Jonah Lomu, if memory serves – was struggling with a very serious illness of his own when he first came to the attention of the wider rugby community. Two things happened to Jonah in 1995: he reinvented rugby – or at least, gave the age-old game a fresh sense of what it might have to offer to a modern audience – with his performances at the World Cup in South Africa; and he was diagnosed as suffering from nephrotic syndrome, a condition linked to kidney failure. It remains the most extraordinary thing that he should have performed as he did on his sport's grandest stage while dealing with a medical problem on such a daunting scale. He even managed to win games for New Zealand virtually single-handedly at the following global get-together in 1999, by which time his illness had taken several turns for the worse. Come the 2003 tournament, Jonah's playing career was on hold, for the very good reason that he was having dialysis treatment three times a week. The following year, he underwent kidney transplant surgery. It is doubly extraordinary that two years later, he was back on the field in a serious way and pushing for a Super Rugby contract.

It was a privilege to have dealings of the after-dinner variety with the great man in the years leading up to his distressingly premature death at the age of 40. To many people, including the massed ranks of journalists who met him only occasionally in formal media settings, he was painfully shy, to the point of being uncommunicative. This was only partly true. Jonah was certainly reserved – rather like Jonny Wilkinson, he was not naturally suited to the extreme demands placed upon him by worldwide sporting fame – and as he had seen a tougher side of life as a boy growing up in the meanest of mean streets in South Auckland, you could argue that he had plenty to be reserved about. But I quickly found that he could communicate enthusiastically and entertainingly in an environment he considered comfortable. Together, we put on a few 'shows' as part of various charity drives, often in pop-up theatres at big hotels in Test match cities around the world. It was a simple formula: I would spout comic nonsense for 15 minutes, hold a Q and A session with Jonah for half an hour, then he would take questions from the paying guests for the rest of the evening. He had a story or two to tell, and if you teased the details from him in the right way, those stories went down a storm. Sadly, he was never completely on top of things when it came to money management and when he died in 2015 after a long-haul flight to New Zealand from Dubai, he had very little in the way of savings, despite the millions upon millions of dollars he had generated for the game of rugby union. It was so sad. To this day, the sport misses him.

On the more positive side, many of those at the heart of the New Zealand rugby community have worked hard to ensure that Jonah's family can face the future with a degree of financial security. That's what rugby does – what sport does. The sporting charity movement and its associated corporate support is far more of a big-money concern nowadays than it was when I first committed myself to raising cash for the Wooden Spoon Society, and I'm so happy to have played a tiny part in whatever growth has taken place. But it is not, and never has been, a one-way street. Whatever time and effort I've put into this side of my life, I've always had something back. How else would I have experienced the thrill of speaking to hundreds of guests at the Savoy or the Hilton Park Lane; at Twickenham or Murrayfield or, perhaps most evocative of all, the Long Room at Lord's? These are fabulous venues, full of fun and laughter. On a good night, there is not a dry eye in the house. Which is as it should be.

TREADING THE
BOARDS

AFTER my memorable afternoon in the company of
Oliver Reed at Rosslyn Park, which stands very high
in the list of the most disconcerting episodes in my time on
the airwaves, there was little in the way of further contact
with that unusually larger-than-life character. What contact
there was could be painful. Oliver's brother Simon had joined
the BBC Radio sports team in the late 1960s – he is now a
seasoned television commentator, specialising in tennis – and
on occasion, there would be a noisy sibling reunion at
Broadcasting House, our base in Oxford Circus. On one of
these occasions, Oliver spotted me at my desk, strode towards
me with a glint of devilish intent in his eye and gave me the
biggest, lung-crushing bearhug of my life. It would be an
exaggeration to say that all of my ribs were damaged, but not
much of one.

Yet there was no escaping the lure of the acting community
– and in particular, those members of it who loved everything
about the sport of rugby union and felt the best place to
analyse and celebrate the game was at the bar. I'm talking

about Richard Burton, Richard Harris and Peter O'Toole, three of the finest screen actors of their time ... and three of the most fascinating, uproarious and downright exhausting people I can remember meeting in any walk of life. Like Oliver Reed, they went at things full-tilt; like Oliver, they made a habit of setting light to the middle of the candle while simultaneously burning it at both ends. Rack my brains as I may, I simply cannot remember seeing Peter O'Toole without a glass in his hand. There again, he was the longest-lived of them, making it all the way into his 80s. I hesitate to suggest that there's a lesson to be learned, but facts are facts.

I'm not sure if O'Toole had been any kind of union player while growing up: there was always some confusion as to whether he was born in the wild west of Ireland or deep in the heart of Yorkshire, and it seems that rugby league was a sporting priority at one point in his upbringing. But Harris was a dyed-in-the-wool 15-a-sider whose exploits with age-group teams in his native Limerick suggested he might have made something of himself as a union player had he not been laid low by tuberculosis in his late teens. For the rest of his life, he followed the fortunes of the Munster provincial side with a rare passion, and even though his friend O'Toole's family roots were up the coast in Galway, there was a meeting of minds – not to mention a clinking of glasses – when it came to the important matter of supporting the men in the red shirts. Needless to say, their common cause was strengthened when it came to international rugby. The Ireland team meant the world to them, to the extent that they routinely secured bespoke get-out clauses in their Hollywood contracts. (By which I mean, they obtained the producer's permission, in advance, to get the hell out of the United States whenever Ireland were playing a serious game at Lansdowne Road or Twickenham or just about anywhere else in the world. The story goes that one of them had gone AWOL from a movie shoot to watch a match in Dublin and that his passport had been confiscated by the studio as a consequence. Rather than risk it again, the two of them decided on joint pre-emptive action.)

As in so many other things, the inspirational Cliff Morgan was a crucial figure in providing access to this circle. It was through Cliff that I met Richard Harris, and through Richard that I met Peter O'Toole. Initially, I was keen to speak with them because I was writing a book about Richard Burton, whom they knew better than almost anyone outside his family and his most intimate group of friends. Richard Harris lived in a ramshackle house in south-west London – somewhere in the Barnes area, close to the Thames – and I spent time with him there. Peter O'Toole? We first met in the lounge of the Grosvenor House Hotel, where they served afternoon tea and cucumber sandwiches. Just his kind of thing! Thereafter, the three of us would meet up in the pub: far more like it as far as they were concerned; far more perilous from the point of view of a lightweight drinker like myself.

They were phenomenally bright men and the most brilliant company, full of eyebrow-raising stories about the biggest, most familiar names in the movie world. There were times, I must confess, when I struggled to believe what I was hearing – a very good reason, if not the only one, for keeping certain tales to myself. As for rugby, they really knew their stuff. Their attachment to the Ireland side was every bit as strong as Richard Burton's was to the Wales team, which made it unbreakable. I'm not putting it too strongly when I say that for all three of these great actors, rugby was among the most important aspects of their existence.

For Richard Burton, the game was one of the foundation stones on which his extraordinary life was constructed: a fixed point, I suppose, in a world of flux and upheaval. He once said, famously, that he would rather have won a full cap for his country at the Arms Park than play Hamlet at the Old Vic in London, and while it is often wise to take the off-the-cuff musings of actors with an ocean-full of salt, I have no reason to think that he was being in any way whimsical or disingenuous in this instance. I met him only four times – he died, at the heartbreakingly early age of 58, just as we were in discussions over a schedule of interviews for his book – but I was left in no doubt as to his passion for the game. Not everyone blessed with a rare gift for performance would trade the dark battlements of Elsinore for a green field in the middle of Cardiff, but here was a man who would. For many years, he would not leave his house without something red upon his person. A tie, a handkerchief, socks, underpants – he didn't much care about the item itself, just so long as it was the right colour.

To people of my generation – people who knew about him as a stage actor, performing some of the great Shakespearean roles while storming his way down Broadway; who revelled in his screen portrayals in *The Spy Who Came In From The Cold* and *Who's Afraid Of Virginia Woolf* and watched him pick up BAFTAs and Golden Globes and Oscar nominations by the dozen; who read the newspaper coverage of his long, close and combustible relationship with Elizabeth Taylor – there was no bigger name than Richard Burton. To today's generation, he might not mean much more than Willie John McBride or Phil Bennett or any of the other Lions greats of the 1970s. It is therefore worth reminding ourselves briefly of the Burton history – of where he had come from and where he had reached by the time of his death in the summer of 1984. (Strange to relate, his final screen performance was as the frightening O'Brien in Michael Radford's film of *Nineteen Eighty-Four*, the George Orwell classic. It makes you wonder, doesn't it?)

He was born Richard Jenkins in Pontrhydyfen, a small mining village in the Afan Valley, not far from the local rugby hotbed of Neath. His father, another Richard, worked down the pit; his mother Edith was a barmaid, and he was the 12th of 13 children. The 13th, Graham, was only a few days old when Edith died. Richard, just two at that point, was raised by his married sister Cecilia in the steel town of Port Talbot, while one of his much older brothers, Ifor, introduced him to the rough and tumble of rugby. Other sports registered strongly with Richard – cricket, boxing – but rugby was the game for him and he showed a good deal of promise as a young player. Yet there were other forces at work: he had a feel for literature, for singing, for public speaking. He also had the support of a wonderful schoolteacher in Philip Burton, who not only sparked an interest in performance but fanned the flames until they became a conflagration. Philip, a frustrated actor, dedicated himself to driving Richard forward and eventually, he made him his legal ward – a process that ended with Richard taking the 'Burton' name by deed poll. Over the following decades, during which the two men remained for the most part the closest of friends, that intensive one-on-one training underpinned a series of triumphs on stage, screen and television. It is said that Philip, then working at the BBC, was the man who persuaded the poet Dylan Thomas to commit himself to reworking an existing piece that would eventually emerge as *Under Milk Wood*. When it was first produced as a radio play, Richard Burton took the role of First Voice, with Philip Burton as the Reverend Eli Jenkins. It may well be the most celebrated piece of radio drama ever recorded.

It was in the early '80s, with a good deal of broadcasting and three years of newspaper journalism behind me, that I was approached to 'ghost' Richard on a book project based on his sporting passions. It was quite an opportunity, especially as I'd negotiated a percentage deal on sales rather than a flat fee: I was sure the book would sell extremely well in America as well as in the United Kingdom, and if my hunch was correct, I'd be handsomely rewarded for my efforts. We met twice on this project: once at the Dorchester Hotel, once down in Wales. He was a phenomenally powerful personality and the task was a daunting one, but we struck up a rapport and started making detailed plans, sketching out the shape of the book and putting together a schedule that would give us at least half a chance of hitting the publisher's deadline. He had just bought himself a house in Switzerland – in Céligny, just outside Geneva – and I was looking forward to my first visit. Then he died, very suddenly, of a brain haemorrhage. His health had been in decline for some time, but the news still came out of the wide blue yonder. His funeral was held in Céligny, and for the burial he was dressed in a red suit. The works of Dylan Thomas were placed in his grave.

As it happened, Richard's younger brother Graham was then working as an 'organiser' in the BBC's sports department. He had sometimes acted as Richard's double in stage and screen productions and even had the famous Burton voice off to a tee. Keener than ever to put some kind of book on the shelves, the publishers decided on a more formal biography of the great actor, constructed around Graham's intimate reminiscences. After discussions with other family members, Graham asked me to do the writing. So it was that I found myself in California, spending a week with Elizabeth Taylor, who had twice been married to Richard and stood front and centre as the key character in his story.

Together with Graham and his sister Hilda, I flew to Los Angeles to meet her. We were collected at the airport by a driver in a stretch limo. Elizabeth had personally arranged our accommodation in the Beverley Hills Hotel and when we arrived, she was there to meet us. There was also a bottle or two of Dom Pérignon chilling by the side of the swimming pool. I'd been lucky all my life – raised and educated in a nice part of Edinburgh, blessed with sufficient rugby talent to win a Blue at Cambridge University and a bunch of caps for Scotland, fortunate enough to make the acquaintance of such broadcasting giants as Bill McLaren and Cliff Morgan and to join the BBC in a golden age of radio commentary – but this was a different world. When we went to the Taylor house for dinner, there were Goyas and Van Goghs and Monets on the wall. Originals, not prints. They must have been worth millions upon millions. And to top it all, our hostess was as generous as could be. She was a goldmine of anecdotes – funny, touching, joyous, sad – and she was perfectly willing to enter into the spirit of things. She agreed to write the foreword to the book, something of a triumph in publishing terms, and even offered to fly me back out to the States for another week of story-telling. 'I don't think the BBC will agree to a whole week,' I replied, only half in jest. For some reason, that comment reduced her to tears of laughter.

We *did* meet a second time, as it turned out – at a place in London, just around the corner from the Dorchester. Over lunch, she handed me a long list of Hollywood powerbrokers who would provide plenty of material on Richard – directors and producers, mostly. All of them were massive names and I couldn't help wondering if these people would really fall over themselves to meet me, even with someone as stellar as Elizabeth Taylor pleading my case. It wasn't a world I knew. True, I had the support of Richard Harris and Peter O'Toole. 'Burton?' they would say. 'Oh yes. We have stories about Burton. Where would you like us to start?' But this was to be a book about a film star, not a sportsman, and while I did as much research as I could and got the best part of 90,000 words down on paper, I felt there were sides to Richard that would be best brought to life by a real authority on the acting business. It would have been different had Richard been alive to tell his own tale, but that was not the case, tragically. Under the new circumstances, I took things as far as I felt I could before Barry Turner, already a prolific author, came in to see the project through to completion. As for Elizabeth, she sent me a Christmas card, invariably smothered in kisses, every year for the next decade. She was a dog lover and once included a picture of her latest pets. By return, I gave her a photograph of me with my rottweiler. 'What a handsome beast,' she responded. To which I could have replied: 'What about the dog?' But I didn't.

To my great regret, I never saw Richard Burton perform

on stage. Or Richard Harris, come to that, largely because his appearances in the theatre were few and far between once his film career took off. I was, however, lucky enough to see Peter O'Toole in *Jeffrey Bernard is Unwell* – a spellbinding tour de force. The play was written by a journalist, Keith Waterhouse, about a journalist, the Jeffrey Bernard of the title, and first produced at the Apollo Theatre in Shaftesbury Avenue while the subject was still alive. A number of very fine actors have played the lead role down the years, but Peter made it his own. No one else quite achieved the right balance of hilarity, melancholy and bitterness that characterised this booze-addled hack at the end of his tether. By way of an additional challenge, the play called for the perfect delivery of an old pub trick involving an egg, a matchbox and one or two other everyday items. Peter mastered it effortlessly. He was quite a craftsman.

In the years before Richard Harris passed away in 2002, the two rugby fanatics were often to be seen at Twickenham for England–Ireland matches and we would meet up for a glass or a bottle – often in one of the hospitality areas run by Will Carling, the former Red Rose captain. And when the annual game was played on the far side of the Irish Sea, I was able to take advantage of the fact that Richard's brother was the manager of a very good hotel close to Lansdowne Road. The advertised price for a common-or-garden room was £450 a night, even back in the Five Nations era. For the BBC, the rate for a very good room was £100 a night. Contacts are everything in the world of journalism! One of the last times I saw Peter, some time after the death of his great friend, was in Australia. The rugby media had congregated in Sydney for the 2003 World Cup and were about to enjoy a rare free afternoon on the water. Suddenly, I heard a familiar voice from the harbourside. 'Is that boat licensed?' shouted Peter, glass already in hand. On assuring him that there might be a chance of a drink, he said: 'May I come aboard?' There was no stopping him. I don't think I'm speaking purely for myself when I say that he made the trip go with a swing. Everyone who met him and listened to his stories that day would agree with the sentiment.

In much the same way as I was introduced to golf at an impressionable age, my initial exposure to the theatre came early and grew into a lifelong passion. More than anything, I loved the funny guys: as a kid, I saw Stanley Baxter in pantomime at the King's Theatre in Edinburgh, and Jimmy Logan at the Princes Street Gardens – an open-air venue in the centre of the city, situated beneath the castle. Jimmy was an absolute natural as an entertainer: his parents were music hall performers, his aunt had a career on Broadway, and the family genes certainly worked their magic when he took to the stage. I remember going to watch him at the Gardens with my cousin Peter. We couldn't have been much more than eight years old. As we were sitting in the front row, we were in prime position to join Jimmy on stage when he asked for some singing accompanists. Both of us were profoundly tone deaf and made a terrible hash of the traditional Scottish song 'A Gordon For Me', so Jimmy bellowed out the words as loudly as he could to deflect attention from the racket we were making. At the end of the show, he came down to see us. 'Are you really tone deaf, or were you just pretending to be totally out of key?' he asked with a grin. 'That was so bad, it was brilliant.'

Thanks to my working life at the BBC, I made the acquaintance of a good number of great performers. Not all of them were rugby followers, far from it, but that didn't mean it wasn't a thrill to meet them. Eric Morecambe, one of the funniest men who ever lived, would often pop into the sports department at Broadcasting House to talk about his football interests, which included a directorship at Luton Town. 'Peculiar game, rugby,' he said to me once. 'All that jumping on top of each other. Can they really be fun, all those rucks and mauls?' 'Don't know,' I replied. 'I played rugby for years without ever going near one.' Tony Hancock would also make the odd appearance and could be seen chewing the football fat with Peter Jones and Bryon Butler, those star chroniclers of 11-a-side affairs. And then there was Sean Connery. Yes, *the* Sean Connery. I'm not sure how much rugby means to him, but it was the union game that brought me into the orbit of my fellow Scot and golf nut (perhaps the only things we have in common!).

He was filming in New Zealand in 2011 when the rugby media pack pitched up for the World Cup, not that I was aware of this fact on arrival. During a stay in Auckland, I agreed to host a charity lunch for 800 people in one of the city's casinos. As my daughter Clare was also in town – she'd secured a job there after leaving university – she joined me at the event. Just as we were about to get things underway, she came running up. 'Dad! Dad! Do you think I can grab a photograph with him?' She nodded towards the top table, where, following her gaze, I saw Tony O'Reilly – businessman, newspaper proprietor and legendary Lions wing of the 1950s. I knew Tony well enough: our paths had crossed on many occasions. 'Of course you can,' I said to Clare. 'He's a friend of very long standing and as good as gold. Just wait until I welcome everybody to the lunch and tell them to enjoy their first course, and I'll sort it.' At which point Tony leaned back in his seat and revealed the identity of the guest sitting beside him, who had been wholly hidden until that point. 'Ah,' I said to myself. 'It's just possible that she meant Sean Connery, not Tony O'Reilly. And I can't say I know Sean Connery.' I sidled over, rather hesitantly, and with an earnest expression on my face, explained the situation to Tony in the quietest of whispers. 'Sean, let me introduce you to Ian Robertson,' Tony said in his most beguiling tone. 'He's the BBC's rugby man, but he's Scottish and terribly biased in your direction. Us Celts have to stick together!' It was cringeworthy stuff, but it had to be done. 'Now. Ian's daughter would love a photograph with you. Would that be alright?' There was a momentary pause. 'Yes,' said the actor. 'That'll be fine. But we can't do it here. If there's one photo, there'll be a thousand. Let's go somewhere discreet.'

As luck would have it, there was a fire escape door a few yards from the table. I reached for my phone just as Sean was preparing to leave the table and rang Dave Rogers, the long-serving, good-humoured and eternally helpful rugby photographer from the Getty Images agency – the best rugby photographer anywhere in the world for decades. 'Where are you?' I asked. 'Are you near the casino?' 'I'm in the hotel opposite,' came the reply. 'That's a relief. Drop everything and get yourself over here *now*. And bring your camera. I have Sean Connery waiting.' Dave materialised within seconds, box brownie at the ready, and did the necessary with a minimum of fuss and bother. Clare could not have been more delighted, until she discovered that in using the picture for one of my regular World Cup books, we managed to crop her out of the frame. I was in shot. More importantly, Sean Connery was in shot, along with Tony O'Reilly. My daughter? Nowhere to be seen. And no, there isn't a copy of the original anywhere.

Talking of originals, has there ever been a performer quite like Barry Humphries? I've lost count of the times I've spent an evening at the theatre in the uniquely entertaining company of Dame Edna Everage, with his/her wisteria hue hair and weapons-grade gladioli. Only once, however, have I shared the stage with him/her. The venue? Harrow School, alma mater of several Prime Ministers, from Sir Robert Peel to

Winston Churchill, none of whom, as far as we know, spent much of their time in drag. The occasion was a grand 'thank you' dinner for parents. Guest of honour and top-of-the-bill speaker? Dame Edna. Master of ceremonies? That would be me. It was always going to be a late-night event, owing to the fact that Dame Edna was performing in the West End and was being transported up the North Circular by taxi as soon as the show ended. It was my job to keep things ticking along until his/her arrival. The headmaster just happened to be Ian Beer, who had won caps for England during the 1950s and would go on to serve as president of the Rugby Football Union. Initially, I assumed I'd be speaking for five minutes maximum. When it became clear that no one, not even Dame Edna, could cover the distance from the West End to Harrow at the speed of sound, those five minutes became 10, then 15, then 20. All I could see as I ran out of relevant material was Ian making signs with his right hand that could only be translated as 'keep going, you fool'. Eventually, Dame Edna arrived – and the moment he/she walked into the room in full costume, it was obvious that few, if any of the guests, knew who the hell he/she might be. The poor possums were certainly bemused by the outrageousness of his/her outfit: understandable, I suppose, given the traditional Harrow get-up of top hats, morning suits and canes. It took Barry, a comic genius if ever there was one, some considerable time to break the ice, but he got there in the end. When he sat down next to me for coffee he was on top conversational form, but it had been a far more difficult gig than the one he'd just completed in town. Perhaps if he'd arrived in time to listen to my speech, he might have picked up a tip or two. Only joking.

When it comes to the funny stuff, I have a soft spot for what used to be called 'regional' comedians. Of course, the best of them transcend 'regionalism' and become truly national. The best of the best, like Billy Connolly, go further still by bordering on the universal. I may be a rugby man from Edinburgh, but like any good Scot, I can instantly relate to a football man from Glasgow when he tells stories the way Billy tells them. He's an unbelievable performer: from strumming his acoustic guitar in the pubs and clubs around his home town, he has received standing ovations in the heartland of establishment England, sold out sports stadiums in the United States, starred in television specials, fronted highly acclaimed documentaries and made appearances in dozens of movies, sometimes in extremely prominent roles. Years ago, I watched a show of his in Edinburgh and stumbled into him during the interval in the nearby Greyfriars Bobby pub. (That pub is known the world over. The name relates to a famous Skye Terrier that spent 14 years guarding his owner's grave before finally passing away.) 'Do we have time for a drink?' I asked Billy. 'Absolutely.' 'Are you sure?' 'It's my show. We'll go back when we've finished.' When we saw each other again at the end of the evening, he said: 'Let's go and have another one.' Which we did. Since then, I've followed his career with enormous interest and seen him perform on many occasions. He's just the funniest man. And the miracle of his comedy is that it's all in the moment. You can laugh solidly for hours on end, yet wake up the next morning and remember barely a line of it. And when you repeat to others the small snippets you *do* recall, it's nowhere near as amusing. Why? Because no one tells a story like Billy Connolly.

One of his fellow 'regionalists' is very definitely a rugby nut. Max Boyce was born near Neath, worked in a colliery and, in his spare time, composed songs and constructed good-hearted tales about rugby union and the people involved in it. One concert at Treorchy Rugby Club was so wildly successful, it sent him on his way to fame and fortune. Our paths have crossed on many occasions and one trip in particular stands out in my mind. We were travelling to Hong Kong for the annual HSBC World Sevens – one of the great weekends in the rugby calendar – and fell into conversation on the plane. 'I don't know the place at all,' he said to me. 'What's the set-up?' I told him there were two major theatres and that he would be performing in one of them. 'Who's in the other?' 'As it happens, Elton John.' Come the evening of the performance, Max had it all worked out. 'Hello, everyone: good to see you,' he began. 'There are two shows on in town tonight. I'm here – and over there, in the inferior venue, is Elton John. But we all know the truth, don't we? In *that* family, all the talent went to Barry.'

Max may generate his fair share of laughs, but he also has

the ability to laugh at himself. I remember him appearing at a charity golf day in Wales featuring some showbiz celebrities and well-known professionals, even though he was some way short of being a lion of the links himself. 'Who am I playing with?' he asked. 'I hope I won't be embarrassed.' When the foursomes list was published, Max was drawn with two unknowns . . . and a chap by the name of Severiano Ballesteros. Seve was in high good humour. 'You like golf, Mac?' the Spanish maestro asked on the first tee. 'It's Max,' came the trembling reply. 'What's your handicap, Mac?' As Max told it later, he was in one hell of a state. 'For the first time in my life,' he said, 'I couldn't remember if I was right-handed or left-handed. It was the caddy who saved me. "If you just take a club out of the bag, it might jog your memory," he said. Brilliant!!! At least I knew which way round to stand.' This from a man who had sung 'Sospan Fach' and 'Hymns and Arias' in front of 80,000 rugby fans without missing a beat. 'I felt as though I was standing on a volcano,' he said. 'That's how much my legs were wobbling.' A powerful thing, sport. Even when you're playing for fun.

SENDING THEM
HOMEWARD

I T'S February 2018 and I'm on my way to Murrayfield to commentate on my last ever Calcutta Cup match. My plan, as usual on my visits to Edinburgh, is to pay an after-match visit to Gleneagles, where I have a golf membership and a place to lay my head. I'll be in town in good time for the pre-match press conferences; on the day after the game, I'll enjoy a round of golf with my son Duncan. We won't attempt to tame the PGA Centenary Course, for the very good reason that it is almost 7,000 yards long and I don't have the luxury of a fortnight's holiday, 13 days of which I'd need to get round the thing after traipsing the Grampians in search of my sliced drive off the first. We'll try the Queen's Course instead. It's half the length and has played host to any number of distinctly average golfers, from Lee Trevino and Tom Watson to Greg Norman and Seve Ballesteros. If they were able to complete the 18 holes before nightfall, how difficult can it be? I'll be back in London in time for lunch, with a deeply satisfying 63 on my scorecard.

But first, it's the match. There has not been so much as a

whisper of anything out of the ordinary being planned to mark my last working day at the stadium where I won the first of my international caps, almost exactly 50 years ago. All I know is that Chris Jones, my ultra-keen and extremely talented young colleague, will be sharing the commentary duties, with Gavin Hastings performing his customary role of analyst – or 'second voice', as the broadcasting jargon has it. Gavin is as reassuring a presence to me as he was to Scotland and the Lions over a 10-year stretch as one of the world's finest full-backs (61 caps, 53 more than I managed; 667 points, 658 more than I can claim; six Lions Test appearances, which, by a peculiar quirk of arithmetic, beats my own tally by precisely half a dozen), and he has a wonderful sense of rugby's dynamics. I've worked with him for years, secure in the knowledge that he has the most reliable of eyes when it comes to spotting specks of fine detail amid the overwhelming carnage of a big game.

An example. When Scotland played the Wallabies at Twickenham in the quarter-final of the 2015 World Cup – which turned out to be a very close game, far tighter than either of us had expected in light of the Australians' comprehensive demolition of England on the same patch of grass the previous weekend – the closing few minutes were chaotic in the extreme. The man largely responsible for the pandemonium was the South African referee Craig Joubert, who entangled himself in his own underwear when confronted with a marginal offside call following a Scottish line-out malfunction. His decision to award Australia a match-winning penalty was crucial . . . and wholly incorrect. After blowing the final whistle, he then compounded his error by sprinting from the field at the speed of light and leaving a stunned full-house crowd with the distinct impression that he would not be stopping until he was safely back home in Durban. For broadcasters commentating live, especially to a BBC audience counted in the millions, this was as close to a nightmare scenario as it was possible to get. So many things to misread. So many things to miss altogether. Yet with Gavin's invaluable help, the Radio 5 Live team found themselves on the right side of the ledger. I had already spotted Drew Mitchell, the Wallaby wing, hitting the Scotland full-back Stuart Hogg with a late, illegal shoulder charge – not so much late as posthumous, frankly – and thumping him into the advertising hoardings. It should have been a penalty to the Scots and at least a yellow card for Mitchell, with play restarting deep in the Wallaby half. Instead, we ended up with a line-out 30 metres from the Scotland line, which went wonky and bamboozled everyone on the field, Mr Joubert included. Gavin was razor-sharp with his assessment of the situation and it was he who spotted the referee heading for the tunnel like greased lightning. 'It's a disgrace,' he said, flatly. 'It's an insult to the game of rugby.' All things considered, it was a pretty decent piece of radio, delivered in the moment with force and clarity and something close to precision. It's what we're paid to do, of course, but that doesn't make it easy.

Backs tend to have a different approach than most forwards when it comes to analysis. More often than not, they complete an English sentence with verbs and nouns in the correct formation, perhaps because during their playing days, they suffered fewer bangs on the head. Before Gavin, like me a product of George Watson's College who went on to play club rugby for Watsonians, claimed his seat in the BBC commentary box, the corporation relied on another magnificent Scottish full-back in Andy Irvine, who was every bit as accomplished despite being a Heriot's man and therefore a slightly inferior species. (There has always been a mighty sporting rivalry between the two establishments, even if it doesn't run quite as deep as the Celtic–Rangers version.)

But there is an exception to virtually every rule, and this particular exception goes by the name of Gareth Chilcott – also known, to friend and foe alike, as Coochie. An England prop of the spherical variety who knew how to look after himself whenever the fur was flying – and, if the situation demanded it, protect all 14 of his teammates into the bargain – he brought a certain West Country style to his analytical work, shining a light on the dark work afoot in scrum and maul for the benefit of bewildered listeners and perfecting the art of describing the indescribable in tones of deepest Bristolian, complete with errant 'Ls' on the end of words ending in vowels. One of the funniest men I've had the good fortune to encounter, he was also crafty enough to avoid mentioning a player's surname if he found it a little too challenging. Not that he always got away with it. Once, during a Test in New Zealand featuring the great All Black centre Tana Umaga, he questioned my pronunciation. 'You keep on referring to "Umanga" when there's no 'n' in his name,' he told me. 'I think you'll find I'm right on this one, Cooch,' I replied, fairly sure of my bearings. 'No, Robbo, you're wrong. Believe me.' As it happened, another All Black maestro, the No.8 Zinzan Brooke, was in the commentary booth next door. 'Let's check with Zinzan at half-time,' I suggested. 'Perhaps you'll believe him.' When Zinzan confirmed my version as correct, we returned to our own box and started our second-half commentary. Within seconds, Tana made a stunning burst upfield, splintering the England defence and steaming towards the line. 'What a break!' Cooch yelled into the mic. 'What a player! They don't come better than Tangle Umangle!' I told this story at a recent Bath annual dinner, where Cooch was among the guests. 'Cheap laugh, Robbo,' he said, with a friendly snarl.

Arriving at Murrayfield for the Calcutta Cup shindig, there is plenty going on between my ears. First and foremost, I am genuinely excited by the prospect of a proper contest between the oldest international rivals in the whole of rugby. (The first meeting, back in 1871, had been played at Raeburn Place, very close to the grounds of Fettes College, which had opened the previous year.) Agreed, the Scots have not won one of these matches since 2008, when England travelled north in disarray – at the last minute, their coach Brian Ashton had dropped a bright young thing by the name of Danny Cipriani after learning of an ill-advised nocturnal adventure in the build-up to the game – and failed to survive a bombardment of penalties from the unfailingly accurate Chris Paterson. Yet as things stand, Scotland are up to fifth in the world rankings – as high as we have ever been – after scoring well over 100 points in the 2017 autumn series, more than 50 of them against those damned Wallabies. We'd even finished within five points of the All Blacks themselves and might have won had Stuart Hogg's brilliant last-gasp attack not ended with a foot in touch. There is now no end to our talent, it seems. How can the lugubrious England hope to live with our quick-witted, fleet-footed brilliance? As I head for the media entrance, I draw the happy conclusion that victory is written in the stars.

I have also decided that no reference should be made to my Murrayfield farewell as we preview the game live on air. 'Please don't ask me any personal questions,' I say to the people back in the studio. 'The very last thing I need to be when the game kicks off is overly emotional, and if I've just spent 20 minutes reminiscing about great Calcutta Cup occasions of yore, I might be in a bit of a state. Let's just talk about the game and leave me out of it.' Which is what we do. Chris Jones takes the first 20 minutes of commentary, with Gavin contributing his pearls of wisdom, and by the time I take over, Scotland are 10–6 up and playing the house down. Huw Jones, one of the most instinctive attacking outside centres to break into the side since the days of the Hawick maestro Jim Renwick, had reacted quickest to a bobbling ball and outstripped the England defenders, who were all over the place, to score the game's opening try. Greig Laidlaw, such a consistent marksman off the kicking tee, had added the extras to go with an early penalty and with the Scottish back-rowers scavenging on the floor as though their lives depend on it – our grand old sport may adopt new airs and graces with each new generation, but some things never change – there is already a feeling in the stadium that this might be something to remember. And sure enough, something truly memorable happens a dozen minutes into my first live stint of the afternoon.

It seems strange to describe something as 'merely' wonderful, but the second pass thrown by the Glasgow outside-half Finn Russell in the build-up to Sean Maitland's try down the left, high class as it may be, is as nothing compared with his first intervention, some 70 metres away at the other end of the pitch. I was a No.10 myself and rather fancied myself as a distributor, but I cannot claim in good faith to have ever floated such an exquisite ball, or anything close to it. Particularly not off my left hand, under pressure so deep in my own half. If Russell had plotted the journey of the ball in advance, using several sheets of graph paper and the most advanced range of geometric equipment, he could not have been more accurate in terms of pace, flight, weight and direction. It seems to me, watching from behind the mic as events unfold, that the pass is certain to be intercepted, if not by one opponent, the centre Jonathan Joseph, then by his colleague, the wing Jonny May. As it turns out, both Englishmen are gloriously wrong-footed by Russell's genius, and the rapid Jones is suddenly free to wreak his havoc. A couple of phases later, the ball is switched across field through Russell's hands to Maitland and the try of the tournament is duly registered.

I don't want this to end, and it doesn't. Jones scores again six minutes later, this time taking advantage of a defensive disconnect between the England No.8 Nathan Hughes and the inside centre Owen Farrell before dragging two white-shirted stragglers, Anthony Watson and Mike Brown, over the line to the left of the sticks. Scotland are 22–6 up at the interval and well on course to score 80, if not more.

It is at this point, just as the players are heading for their dressing-room breathers, that Gavin says to me: 'Robbo, just pop downstairs with me for a moment. There's someone we need to see.' I may not be the quickest when it comes to spotting the cunning plans of friends and colleagues, but I'm alive to this. 'I'm going nowhere, Gavin,' I say. 'I'm staying right here.' It is only when my producer, Steve Jones, virtually orders me to do as I'm told that I follow Gavin into the lift and head in the direction of sea level. 'This is crazy,' I say, as the last of the players brushes past me in the tunnel. 'We're back on in no time.' 'Don't panic,' Gavin replies. 'We just want to give you a "going away" present. There'll be nobody watching. Just a cameraman. And if we're really fortunate, he'll have his camera with him.' I'm still not completely on board with this project, so Gavin gives me a little more information. 'It's nothing much: just a Scotland shirt, signed by the players.' I am deeply moved and honoured, but I still feel the need to hurry Gavin along. 'Let's get it over and done with and head back upstairs. And by the way, I can tell you that if the score stays the same, the shirt will fetch four grand, maybe five, at a charity auction.' Gavin looks at me in utter disbelief. 'That's a terrible thing to say, Robertson,' he says. 'I'm truly appalled.' 'Only joking,' I reply. 'Just stop it,' he says. 'Stop it immediately.'

And it is then that he gets even by leading me onto the field, taking hold of a microphone and introducing me to the vast throng. 'Ladies and gentlemen,' he begins, giving it the full dramatic treatment. I don't know where to put myself. I'm no stranger to introductions: at hundreds upon hundreds of sporting lunches and dinners down the years, I must have introduced half the rugby population of these islands to the other half, maybe twice over. But when you're the one being introduced; when you're the 'star turn', so to speak . . . well, that's different.

Carrying my shirt, I scurry back to my commentary position just in time for the resumption and as a consequence have a perfect view of Farrell, that fiercest of competitors, scoring an unnervingly simple try to drag England back into the argument. The Saracens player then thinks he has crossed the line a second time, but a slight knock-on in the tackle by the flanker Courtney Lawes wipes those threatening points from the board and gives Scotland an opportunity to recalibrate. They use it well. A Russell penalty brings a little more stability to proceedings and even though England lay siege in the last 10 minutes, there is no further scoring. It is our biggest Calcutta Cup win of the professional era. Not since 1986, when some of the genuine greats of Scottish rugby – Gavin and his brother Scott, John Rutherford, Colin Deans, Iain Milne, John Jeffrey, Finlay Calder – put 33 points past the enemy while granting them only half a dozen in return, have we recorded a winning margin in double figures.

Happily for me, my colleague Chris Jones shoulders what I like to call the digital burden: all the internet stuff – the podcasting and uploading and whatever else it is the younger generation does in the name of broadcast journalism these days. I don't have a clue about this side of the job. I wasn't much interested at the start and I'm even less interested at this late stage of my professional life. I struggle to read my text messages and answer my emails, let alone connect with the online community on Twaddle or Snapdragon or Instagranny. All I have on my to-do list is a wrap-up for 5 Live and a posh piece for Radio 4. I know I can't afford to crow on either station – particularly on R4, the BBC's flagship spoken-voice offering. I suppose I could gamble on saying something about hammering the Auld Enemy, this being my Calcutta Cup farewell, but I think better of it. Hell hath no fury like an R4 audience scorned, and I don't want important people on my back.

So that is that. My last remaining commitment is to put on a tie and attend the after-match banquet in the President's Suite – a function I have not attended, or even been invited to attend, in all my time as a broadcaster. In fact, I have not been through the door of the suite where dinner is being served since 1970, when I played outside-half for Scotland against . . . England, in the Calcutta Cup – and somehow created one of the tries that earned us a 14–5 victory. Alastair Biggar, a hefty wing from the London Scottish club, was the beneficiary of my largesse that day, and from memory he capitalised on his moment of fame by drinking all the free booze that came his way. Speaking for myself, I'm wondering if, after an absence of 40-odd years, the Scottish Rugby Union might stand me a pint this evening. Then I think better of it. 'They'll allow me a half,' I say to myself, 'on the grounds that I drank the other half in 1970.'

You think I'm joking? I well remember arriving in Edinburgh by train on the Wednesday before a Five Nations Championship match and grabbing a taxi from Waverley Station to the Braid Hills Hotel in Morningside to meet up with the team. Braid Hills is situated on land originally owned by Sir Henry de Brade, the sheriff of Edinburgh from 1165 to 1200, and it seemed to me as I fought to reclaim my taxi fare that it would have been easier to deal with him than with the SRU secretary of the time, John Law – who, at a rough guess, would probably have considered himself the most frugal member of the city's active Presbyterian community, few of whom were among the most cavalier of spirits when it came to throwing money around. 'Robertson, there are two buses you could have caught from Waverley, so I'll repay you the price of the ticket you didn't buy,' he said. That was the way of it then, as Peter Stagg, a giant lock forward of the time, would readily confirm. Before one of the internationals we played together, Peter asked for a new pair of 'stockings', as socks were then routinely called, because his existing pair were in tatters. On being told that he was asking for the moon and should not, on any account, make such a ridiculous suggestion in future, he applied black shoe polish to his legs to hide the holes and took to the field. After the game, he was given a dressing down for not using blue shoe polish.

As it turns out, the banquet is a hoot – not least because several members of the England hierarchy are among the 400 guests. The first person I see is Jason Leonard, the great Red Rose prop and now one of the Rugby Football Union's more presidential figures. He shakes my hand in hearty congratulation. 'I'd love to say you were hard done by today, Jason, but you weren't,' I tell him. 'I'm relishing every moment of this.' 'Actually, I don't mind if you win just one Calcutta Cup every 10 years,' he retorts. To which I respond: '*I'm* perfectly happy for us to win one every 10 years. And today's the day, thank you very much.' Steve Brown, an excellent choice as the RFU's latest chief executive, is seated on the same table. I am tempted to say: 'Steve, I know you've only just started the job, but the buck stops with the CEO.' But as he is giving me a welcoming smile, I decide not to rock the boat. Instead, I turn my attention to the chairman of World Rugby. 'Bad luck Bill – great game, wasn't it?' I say to my old friend Bill Beaumont, who, during his garlanded playing days, won a Five Nations Grand Slam at Murrayfield. He's not so joyous now and it shows. Smiling, I rush off to my own table.

It's a perfect end to a perfect day.

TWO
TEAMS

S ELECTION. It's the biggest thing. We all have our views
on the fundamental nature of rugby: for every union follower
who clings to the idea of the sport as an art form and therefore
regards it as essentially unmeasurable, there is another who
prefers to take the scientific approach, arguing that there are
sound statistical reasons why this team won and that team lost.
I do not expect either side to be proved right or wrong in my
lifetime. All I know for sure is that the team sheet matters more
than anything else. If you choose the correct players, you at
least have a shot at success. If you opt for the wrong ones,
you're wasting everyone's time. Rob Andrew – two-tour Lions
outside-half, Grand Slam winner, Premiership-winning director
of rugby and Twickenham bigwig, not forgetting his role as
BBC Radio's chief shrieker on World Cup final night in 2003
– had it absolutely right when he said: 'Selection is the measure
by which coaches must be judged. I wouldn't go quite so far
as to say that everything else is just wallpaper, but the ability
to pick the right side at the right moment is overwhelmingly
the most important part of the job.'

I'm happy to say that since calling time on my tracksuited role with Cambridge University in the mid-1980s, I've been able to give a very wide berth to the crushing responsibility of writing down 15 names on a sheet of A4 and pinning it to a clubhouse noticeboard. But time has a nasty habit of catching up with those of us who have made a good living out of reporting on, and analysing, the decisions of other people. After a lifetime spent watching, playing, coaching and chronicling this wonderful game of ours – after almost half a century of reporting on it, commentating on it, writing about it and making wisecracks about it – I feel it is my duty to make some very grave decisions by selecting my ultimate team. Not just a team of greats. That won't do. I'm talking about the greatest of the great. No pressure, then.

It is a complicated business, for there are so many factors to consider: raw talent is a key component, but far from the only one. There have been brilliant individuals who were simply ill-suited, temperamentally and emotionally, to the collective nature of team sport – who undermined and weakened the group of which they were a part. Either it never occurred to them that there is no 'I' in the word 'team', or they didn't care. Others soared skywards early in their careers but then came crashing to earth, like a rugby-playing Icarus, because of injury or loss of confidence or untrammelled ambition. To be a true rugby great, resilience and long service at the very top level are key attributes, as is the ability to keep playing, and winning, in the face of adversity. To my mind, size and speed are hugely desirable, but not non-negotiable. There are players I cherish who were somewhat disadvantaged in terms of pounds, ounces, feet and inches, but still left an indelible mark on international rugby through a combination of bravery, intelligence, craftsmanship and game understanding. In their cases, knowledge was everything.

But to my mind, there is something else to be considered. Rugby has changed almost out of recognition since I stunned Jim Telfer into near silence by making the one try-saving tackle of my career in Buenos Aires a million years ago: the game is infinitely more physical, more punishing, more relentless and a greater risk to life and limb than it was even at the end of the amateur era, and as professionalism has evolved, so too has the coverage of the sport in the media. I'm not at all sure that it is common, or even possible, for wordsmiths and broadcasters to develop the close friendships with players and coaches that were almost routine in the decades before the great upheavals of the mid-1990s. Yet at heart, rugby union remains the most convivial of team sports. It is a game of generous spirits, of fun and laughter, of long nights and bleary mornings. So I think I can be forgiven for picking two teams rather than one: a team of the very best players, and a team of players who would go very close to beating all-comers on the field while winning their games of après-rugby hands down. You will see that in many cases, the individuals selected are interchangeable: indeed, I would back my 'fun team' to win 99 per cent of their matches, irrespective of the opposition. But they must be drawn from the four home nations alone (to choose the best company for a night in the bar, you have to know them extremely well). As for the players picked on the basis of their rugby achievements alone, they are a truly international body of men. The best of the best, from all corners of the rugby landscape.

MY TEAM OF CHARACTERS

15 ANDY IRVINE (SCOTLAND)

Those who came to rugby after the great days of the British and Irish Lions, who ruled the world in the first half of the 1970s by beating both the All Blacks and the Springboks, will know Andy as much through his achievements in rugby management and governance as through his brilliance as one of the world's great attacking full-backs. He served the maximum period of time as president of the Scottish Rugby Union and during his stewardship of the national game, there was a rare Six Nations victory over England to savour. He also headed up the Lions operation in Australia in 2013 – a 2–1 series victory over the Wallabies accomplished with a minimum of fuss and bother, thanks in no small part to Andy's approach to his duties: warm and inclusive, yet deeply determined and single-minded. He has always managed the way he played. You don't win a half-century of caps for your country and make nine Lions Test appearances across three tours without having some steel in your spine, but there is a lightness of touch about Andy – something that allows him to cope in hostile environments with a knowing smile on his face, whether it be sidestepping his way out of trouble on his own line with half of South Africa bearing down with the scent of blood in its nostrils, or treading delicately through the minefields of rugby officialdom. He'll laugh at your jokes, then tell you a funnier one. He's also a golf partner of long standing, so I can even forgive him for being a Heriot's man rather than a Watsonian.

14 TONY O'REILLY (IRELAND)

Tony had it all: the talent, the looks, the drive, the ambition ... and the wit. Was there ever a top-level player with a greater mastery of the quick-as-a-flash one-liner? I doubt it. And he could laugh at himself, too. He proved that after being recalled, seven years after his previous international appearance, for Ireland's meeting with England at Twickenham in 1970. Already a highly successful businessman, he arrived for training in a chauffeur-driven car, to the complete bemusement of his countrymen, one of whom mentioned that his opposite number, the lightning-paced Keith Fielding, might give him the runaround on match day. Tony looked down at his own waistline, a trifle thicker than it had been in his Lions pomp, and said: 'He might have the speed to go round me, but will he have the stamina?' During the game, as he was being trampled at the bottom of a ruck, he heard an

Irish voice in the crowd imploring the English forwards to 'give him one for the chauffeur too!' He found that hilarious. In fact, his unfortunate experiences in that game formed the basis of many an O'Reilly after-dinner speech. To him, rugby was serious without being a matter of life and death – a philosophy that allowed him to be devastatingly funny, whatever the circumstances.

13 JIM RENWICK (SCOTLAND)

When it comes to my outside centre from the Borders, I must bow to the superior knowledge of my friend Andy Irvine, who played alongside Jim in the Scottish back division on so many occasions – indeed, they arrived at their half-century of caps at virtually the same time. As I could never get to grips with Jim's accent and therefore struggled to understand a word he said, it is difficult for me to argue with Andy when he describes him as the funniest guy in the world. I know this much, though: throughout my early years of rugby commentary, I always admired Jim's combination of low-slung strength and super-sharp attacking gifts. He was also one of those priceless individuals blessed with the happy knack of generating humour when a long way from home. On a trip to New Zealand, he was approached at an official function by an unknown local who attempted to engage him in small talk. Jim couldn't think of much to say, so he simply asked the man what he did for a living. 'I'm Robert Muldoon,' came the reply. 'The Prime Minister of New Zealand.' 'Aye,' said

Jim. 'And I'm the Provost of Gala.' When it came to the formal speeches – yes, you guessed it.

12 RAY GRAVELL (WALES)

Rugby is good at hero worship, so it follows that the sport must be equally adept at hero creation. Ray was a hero to thousands upon thousands of Welsh rugby folk and had achieved that status long before his death in 2007, at the age of 56. He embodied the spirit of the game in his country, celebrated and honoured it as though it were his life's work and helped redefine it for new generations of players and followers who had not been around to witness the glory days of Gareth and Barry and JPR and Grand Slams aplenty. If he was a good enough centre to play all four Tests for the Lions in South Africa in 1980, Grav also excelled in a wide range of other fields: as an actor, a broadcaster, a populariser of the Welsh language, a cultural ambassador. At the bar, he could tell you what it was like to be the youngest player in the Llanelli side that beat the All Blacks at Stradey Park in 1972 – the 'day the pubs ran dry' – and then explain in fine detail the challenge of appearing on a movie set alongside Peter O'Toole or Jeremy Irons. Fabulous company.

11 JOHN BENTLEY (ENGLAND)

'I come from Cleckheaton, where the pigeons fly on their backs because there's nothing worth shitting on down there.' So said John Bentley at the start of his speech at the Rugby

Union Writers' Dinner in 2009, a dozen or so years after his career-defining performances for the British and Irish Lions in South Africa. As opening lines go, it was a beauty: cheeky, irreverent, self-deprecating. Just like John, as it happens. He would never claim a place for himself amongst the most naturally gifted wings of the last half-century, but he was powerful and aggressive enough to make a name for himself in both codes of rugby and when it comes to the scoring of tries that live long in the memory, he made his mark with an absolute blinder for the Lions against Gauteng in Johannesburg – a pivotal midweek match in the build-up to the first Test against the Springboks. That solo effort was more than a match winner on the night. It was a momentum-generator for the rest of the tour. John has been known to mention it every day since, and it gets better with each telling.

10 CLIFF MORGAN (WALES)

The romance of rugby personified. A child of the tight-knit Rhondda community – his father was a miner – Cliff eventually commanded all the broad horizons he surveyed. He mastered the arts of his position on the field and is automatically included among the most prized products of that fabled No.10 factory hidden somewhere beneath the valleys of his homeland. As a very young man, he was part of a Five Nations Grand Slam-winning side and tasted victory over the All Blacks with both his club, Cardiff, and his country. When he took on the formidable Springboks with the Lions in 1955, he was the number one attraction for the South African public, who labelled it 'Cliff Morgan's tour'. When he made the move into broadcasting, he became a big hitter in the current affairs department as well as in sport. He had the voice of an angel (every sentence he uttered was a poem) and could thump out virtually any tune on the piano without thinking twice. He was kind and generous, funny and gregarious. He was also a perfectionist who demanded the best from those around him, at work as he did in play. He was an inspiration to me and I never came close to repaying the debt I owed him.

9 ALASTAIR HIGNELL (ENGLAND)

Forty years late, my great friend and colleague gets a run at scrum-half. I must be going soft in my old age! In fairness to Higgy, this is no act of charity: I may have felt there were better options at No.9 when he first arrived at Cambridge University all those decades ago and set his sights on a Blue, but had he been my only option, I wouldn't have lost much sleep. He was among the most outstanding all-round sportsmen of his generation and the skills he displayed on the rugby field helped make a professional cricketer of him. I remember talking to the mighty South African fast bowler and middle-order batsman Mike Procter about Higgy, alongside whom he played for Gloucestershire. 'He's one of the best fielders I've ever seen,' he said, unhesitatingly. 'So what are you saying?' I asked, alert to the possibility of a wind-up at Higgy's expense. 'That he can't bat and can't bowl, but he can catch?' Mike was having none of it. 'Believe me, Higgy can bat,' he said. 'It's just that as a fielder, he's something else. Never underestimate the importance of it.' That was me told. I still try to twist the story to my advantage, but I'm rarely successful. Higgy just rolls his eyes and drinks his beer. A brilliant, brave, generous-hearted bloke.

1 JASON LEONARD (ENGLAND)

Talking of brilliant blokes, how about the Fun Bus, aka Jase the Ace the carpenter from the East End who played his heart out for England for ever and a day, finished most international matches on his knees, yet was always as quick to the bar as the great All Black flanker Michael Jones was to the loose ball? Just ahead of the 1995 World Cup, when the England players had agreed a self-imposed alcohol ban, Jason was singled out by the coach Jack Rowell during training and accused of returning to the hotel at 2am. 'I denied it,' he recalled. 'As I told Martin Bayfield, who was standing next to me: "It couldn't have been me, Bayf. I didn't get in until four." He once picked a Drinkers XV, dropping himself for being too much of a lightweight but selecting the teetotal Test wing Rory Underwood as 'designated driver'! He also said this after the 1997 Lions tour of South Africa, where he failed to win a starting spot for the big games against the Springboks: 'I am as competitive as the next person, but Lions tours are different. I knew I wasn't going to make the Test side, so I decided to try and help the other front-row players as much as possible. Lions tours aren't about Test caps. They're about big groups of players going away together and, between them, doing what is necessary to win.' I couldn't have put it better myself.

2 KEITH WOOD (IRELAND)

The ultimate heart-and-soul hooker with a human side: a front-row warrior with twinkling eyes and a heaven-sent ability to charm the birds from the trees. To my way of thinking, the man from County Clare is as much a symbol of rugby's romantic past as Cliff Morgan, even though their playing careers were separated by more than 40 years. There is an incredibly touching moment, captured by the men behind the original fly-on-the-wall documentary *Living with Lions*, when Keith pulls a callow Matt Dawson to one side in the dressing room before a midweek game with Mpumalanga in Witbank – a match the '97 vintage knew would be rough. You can barely hear him as he says: 'I'd rather I be kicked than you be kicked. It's the way we have to have it. We have to look after you because you're our eyes and you look after us. If there's a chance of you being knocked, give me the ball. I'll be there.' I don't remember any forwards saying that to me during my Scotland days, but I'm sure they would have done so had they thought of it.

3 GARETH CHILCOTT (ENGLAND)

When 'Cooch' retired, he told everyone within earshot that he was 'heading off for a quiet beer . . . and about 19 noisy ones.' He is a tough man from a tough background, but if there is a better, funnier companion on a night out anywhere on this sporting planet, the name escapes me. I've heard his great story about thumping Nick Farr-Jones, the World Cup-winning Wallaby scrum-half and captain, a thousand times, but it still brings tears of laughter to my eyes. 'It was my England debut,' he says. 'I was at Twickenham, living my dream. I cried during the national anthem. And after a couple of minutes, here's this Farr-Jones bloke running past me, saying: "Come on, Fatty, catch up." Well, it took me a while . . . but I caught up with him in the end.' He also prides himself on his quick thinking in the broadcasting box. Aware that he might have some trouble pronouncing the tongue-twisting names of the Georgian players during a World Cup match in 2003, he talked his way through the entire commentary without mentioning a single one of them except by number. And no one noticed! Genius.

4 MOSS KEANE (IRELAND)

Sadly, I did not travel to New Zealand with the Lions in 1977. Had I done so, I would have seen County Kerry's finest at close quarters. But I came across him later and now see him almost as a forerunner of Keith Wood: a very clever man

– Mossy earned himself a Master's degree in dairy science – who somehow represented the best of Irish rugby in all its many dimensions, both on the field and off, with his own unique brand of humour, shot through with a passion for the green shirt. He was a big bruiser of a fellow – '18 and a half stone of prime Irish beef,' as my mentor Bill McLaren once said of him – and he had quite a reputation as a good time sort. But it was the wit that marked him out as different. The story goes that as a youngster, he was sent to the local butcher's shop to buy a pig's head. Asked where it should be cut, he replied: 'As close to its arse as you can.' How good is that? Almost as good, I suppose, as the tribute paid after his death by the journalist Con Houlihan. 'He was a man of few airs and many graces.'

5 GORDON BROWN (SCOTLAND)

An automatic choice. If I was the one responsible for introducing 'Broon frae Troon' to the highways and byways of the after-dinner speaking circuit, he was the one who raced past me on the first lap and promptly disappeared into the distance. Keeping up with him was not an option, for he seemed to bring exactly the same levels of zest and zeal to the stage as he did to the rugby field. The thing with Gordon was veracity: the more ridiculous the story he told about his rough-and-tumbles on the pitch, the more accurate it turned out to be. Yes, he really did engage in a bout of fisticuffs with Johan de Bruyn, the 'Cyclops' of the Springbok pack, in Port

Elizabeth in 1974; yes, the formidable De Bruyn's glass eye did fly out of its socket as a result; yes, Gordon and the rest of the Lions forwards did drop to their hands and knees in search of the missing article; and yes, De Bruyn did arrive at the ensuing line-out with the eye back in place, together with a clump of turf hanging from its corner. Following his retirement from rugby after the Lions tour of New Zealand in 1977 – his third tour of duty in the red shirt – he happily appeared at five dinners a week, every week, and had them laughing all night, every night. Bobby Windsor, that teak-hard hooker from one of the less forgiving parts of Wales, described Gordon as a 'lovable rogue'. Coming from the 'Duke', that is praise indeed.

6 CLEM THOMAS (WALES)

Dear old Clem. If variety is the spice of life, there was nothing like an afternoon's sport and an evening's drinking with the long-serving rugby correspondent of the *Observer* to pep you up. Clem was far more than a journalist. He was a Cambridge graduate and a magnificently abrasive back-row forward – Swansea, Wales, the Barbarians and the Lions, among others. He was a butcher by trade before turning to the public prints; he stood twice as a parliamentary candidate for the Liberal Party and also had a dart in the European election of 1970. He was a Francophile, a bon viveur and the proud owner of the deepest growl of a laugh known to man. Tony O'Reilly, with whom he toured South Africa in 1955, penned a brief obituary of Clem following his death in 1996. 'It was the laugh that distinguished Clem,' Tony wrote. 'Part upper class; part working class; a cross between a real chuckle and just the hint of a tease. It was the sort of laugh that made you think he didn't give a damn, but there again he just might.' Quite.

7 FERGUS SLATTERY (IRELAND)

I dimly remember Fergus tackling an opponent who was still in possession of the ball, but it's possible that my recall is no longer completely reliable. If it happened, it may even have been against Scotland while I was on the field. Fergus was a fresh face in the Irish back row when we played a Five Nations match in Dublin in 1970 – a game in which I achieved a rare feat by dropping a goal. Much good it did me. We were outscored four tries to two and lost 16–11. I came to know him better while covering the second half of the Lions tour of South Africa four years later. He could talk the talk with the best of the Irish contingent and to the best of my knowledge, he hasn't stopped talking since. He is also an independent spirit. During that trip to Springbok country, highly controversial for political reasons, he took it upon himself to make late-night trips by train to the townships, to see things with his own eyes. On one occasion, the station master discovered that a Lion was on board the train and ordered his staff to form a guard of honour. Fergus always had the knack of commanding attention.

8 JIM TELFER (SCOTLAND)

Someone has to keep this lot in order, so there will always be a place in this team for a sergeant-majorish type like 'Creamy'. But people shouldn't get the wrong idea about Jim: beneath that stern façade lies something far more intimidating! We played a good deal of rugby together and I consider him to be one of the key figures in the development of Scottish rugby over the last 50 years. On the field, he was the very last person to ask something of a player above and beyond what he was willing to do himself. As a coach, he has admitted in print to possessing a dictatorial streak. There again, so did Brian Clough. And like that most fascinating of football managers, Jim could lay it on the line with humour. He was absolutely in his prime with the Lions in South Africa in 1997, where some of his behind-closed-doors team talks have passed into legend. During a meeting with the senior players early in the trip, he said: 'I haven't coached all that much for a while, so we have to decide on a way we're going to work. And once that's decided . . . I'm in charge.' Brilliant. Every team needs a Jim Telfer. The man is a diamond.

MY TEAM OF TEAMS

15 GAVIN HASTINGS (SCOTLAND)

Who would be a selector? If my good-time team was picked on purely personal criteria ranging far beyond mere rugby-playing talent, choosing a team capable of winning the game that saves your life is a different, more challenging matter still. Fifteen magnificent individuals lavishly equipped with the ability to make you laugh all night long in the bar are of limited use if you don't actually get to the bar! So this is where the hard choices must be made, and the full-back position is no easier than any of the others. How can I leave out Andy Irvine and his long-range attacks? Or Serge Blanco, the very epitome of French *joie de vivre*? Or JPR Williams, that implacable gun-slinger of a No.15 who touched the hearts of Wales supporters in places other full-backs failed to reach? My choice of Gavin rests on his ability to do many of the things his rivals did at a high level, with added extras – most notably, the power and reliability of his kicking game. He was also an outstanding captain, although it is a moot point whether he would beat half a dozen other contenders in the race to lead this particular side!

14 DAVID CAMPESE (AUSTRALIA)

It hurts me to leave out Gerald Davies, whose place in the pantheon of Wales and Lions greats was secured long before his retirement in 1978. But if any right wing in history set tongues wagging and jaws dropping way beyond the confines of traditional rugby circles, it was the Wallaby maestro from New South Wales. Campo was a box-office character right from the start: those of us privileged to see the game-changing Australian tourists of 1984 at first hand still remember the new things he brought to the sport: the timing, the trickery, the sheer effrontery of his attacking style. He was also spectacularly good at getting on the nerves of his opponents – especially the English, for whom he saved his most waspishly provocative comments. Fourteen years in the green and gold, more than 100 caps at a time when international matches were rarer beasts than they are now? That's some record. And if you never saw a rugby ball passed again, you would die happy with the memory of his blind flick to Tim Horan in the World Cup semi-final against the All Blacks in 1991. Someone once called him the Pele of rugby. They may well have had a point.

13 BRIAN O'DRISCOLL (IRELAND)

Some coaches consider the outside centre position to be the most difficult on the field in modern-day rugby and I understand their thinking. Defensively, you are massively exposed; in the attacking sense, there is enormous onus on your decision-making capacities and your distributive skills. The list of those who really mastered the role may be short, but it is also of stunning quality. Danie Gerber of South Africa may have proved beyond all doubt that he was the best ever, had the Springboks not been in sporting isolation for much of his career. Philippe Sella of France was as effective as he was stylish; Jeremy Guscott of England always lived up to the 'prince of centres' label bestowed upon him by his coach Jack Rowell; Conrad Smith of New Zealand was perhaps the most intelligent of all the supremely clever players who won back-to-back World Cups in 2011 and 2015. But I must go for O'Driscoll as a warrior midfielder, a player who changed his style when his extreme pace began to fade and found new ways to win games single-handedly. Has any centre in history been more effective in the darkened recesses traditionally inhabited by back-row forwards? The answer is no.

12 IAN MCGEECHAN (SCOTLAND)

I've spoken a good deal about Geech in the course of this book, but I make no apology for adding a few lines of explanation as to why he merits a place among my best of the best. All great teams need their thinkers and Geech spent a glorious few weeks of his life playing for one of the two or three greatest teams I've ever seen. What was more, the 1974 Lions achieved what they did not through years of careful team-building and trial-and-error strategy development, but through an ability to identify the kind of rugby needed to beat their Springbok hosts and put things in place in the blink of an eye. Geech understood the game in ways many outstanding players never even begin to understand it. He may not have been the quickest centre of all time, and he was a long way short of the biggest, but if you're sharper than everyone else in the top four inches, you can happily surrender a yard of pace and a stone or two in weight. Tim Horan of Australia, my other contender, was similarly blessed in the brain department. The Wallabies won two world titles with him in the No.12 shirt.

11 JONAH LOMU (NEW ZEALAND)

My choice here is hardly a shock to the system. In so far as these things are measurable, no individual player ever affected rugby's present and future in the way Lomu did during the 1995 World Cup in South Africa. His achievements on the international stage over the course of his career would have been remarkable had he been in rude health, yet he was in long-term physical decline from a very early stage. Astonishing. To a certain extent, you can narrow down the Lomu Effect to his performance in one game – perhaps to one half of one game, and even to the opening minutes of one half of one game. Bill McLaren and I shared the commentary on that New Zealand–England semi-final in Cape Town and I can unhesitatingly say that Jonah's impact from the kick-off was way above and miles beyond anything I'd previously seen or have witnessed since. The men in suits were already wrestling with the idea of a relaxation of the amateur laws when the Big Man from Auckland ran over everyone to score the most startling try in rugby history, but this was the accelerator. Jonah changed the union game that day, for ever.

10 BARRY JOHN (WALES)

Where to begin? Outside-half being my position and allegedly my area of expertise, I would hate to get this wrong. But there are so many contenders from every decade of my rugby life and all deserve a hearing. None more so, perhaps, than Hugo Porta, the architect from Buenos Aires who might also be described as the architect of Argentine rugby. He spent almost 20 years playing international union for the Pumas and when he was in his pomp as a goal-kicking game manager with all the talents, a number of good judges put him at the very top of the No.10 tree. It is one thing to leave a deep mark on the union game if you're surrounded by fellow All Blacks or Springboks. It is quite another to do it with a second-tier nation, as Argentina were during the Porta years. I could choose one or two all-time goal-kicking greats – Grant Fox of New Zealand, who had rather more to his game than a Master's in marksmanship, or Naas Botha of South Africa, who was probably more limited but won tight game after tight game with a swing of the boot. More persuasively, I could go for one of two stellar Wallabies – the magically inventive Mark Ella, who helped reinvent back play in the 1980s, or the supremely intelligent Michael Lynagh, who could be relied upon to do the right thing at the right moment, pretty much all the time. And then there are the modern giants, Daniel Carter and Jonny Wilkinson. The New Zealander had the sharper attacking game and there were spikes of genuine greatness in his career, notably during the

Lions tour of 2005 and the World Cup of 2015. As for the Englishman, there were parts of his game – tackling, kicking from hand and from tee – that set new standards for the No.10 fraternity, and by staring down injury to extend a broken career by a decade and win major titles into the bargain, he proved that through tenacity and resilience and dedication to the cause, a true sportsman can prevail over the worst of setbacks.

But in the end, I struggle to move past the two most treasured No.10s in the annals of Welsh rugby: Barry John and Phil Bennett. How do you separate them? How do you place one above the other? For the most part, they cancelled each other out, achievement for achievement. Both tasted victory over the All Blacks – indeed, both were largely responsible for those rarest of triumphs – and both spearheaded series victories by the Lions after the barren years of the not-so-swinging '60s. Both were great kickers, both could open up the field with their running games, both could distribute, both understood more about rugby's dynamics and the management of a game than most of their peers put together. If I were to make this choice on national television with 100 million people watching worldwide, I'd take the soft option and toss a coin. But in the end – and Phil knows my view on this – it has to be Barry. Why? Because there was something other-worldly about him. Someone once said he could materialise in a crowded room without appearing to have used the door. That summed him up. So did Cliff

Morgan's line, borrowed from the war poet Wilfred Owen: the one about being blessed with both mystery and mastery. There. I've said it. Let's move on.

9 GARETH EDWARDS (WALES)

This is easier, thank the lord. I have my favourite scrum-halves, including England's own Matt Dawson, who did not always receive the credit he deserved after finally prevailing in his individual battle with the gifted but slightly less resilient Kyran Bracken – one of the most fascinating one-on-one individual selection battles I can recall. I would place Nick Farr-Jones of Australia high on the list of No.9s, along with at least one All Black in Dave Loveridge, whose influence in the 1983 series against the Lions was close to decisive, and the ferociously competitive Joost van der Westhuizen of South Africa. We Scots have always produced half-backs of high quality: you would go a long way to see a better operator than Gary Armstrong at his best. As for the French, the names trip off the tongue: Fouroux, Gallion, Berbizier, Galthié. But Gareth may well have been the best player in post-war rugby history, in any position. So strong, so explosive from the base of the scrum, so cunning, so predatory. So everything.

1 IAN MCLAUCHLAN (SCOTLAND)

There have been times in recent Lions history – too many times for my liking – when the Test pack has been a Scottish-free zone. Leaving aside the very occasional appearance off the bench by a Gordon Bulloch or a Richie Gray, there has been precious little to write home about since the admirable Tom Smith ended his long run in the loose-head prop's role. But it wasn't always like this. Back in the 1970s – the glory years, lest we forget – we could depend on Gordon Brown to force his way into the fray. The same goes for Ian 'Mighty Mouse' McLauchlan (so called because at 5ft 9ins and a long way short of 15st, he was no one's idea of a giant). The Mouse was as tough as old boots: you didn't square up to All Blacks and Springboks of the size, scale and calibre of Jazz Muller and Hannes Marais and look them straight in the eye before popping them clean out of the scrum without having an awful lot of what it takes. I played a good number of games with the Mouse and while my knowledge of the precise details of his style was necessarily scratchy, I knew one thing for sure: I was glad to see him on my side. To put it bluntly, we needed someone like him if we were to stay afloat.

2 SEAN FITZPATRICK (NEW ZEALAND)

There would often come a time in after-match press conferences when Fitzy, as captain of the All Blacks, found himself on the uncomfortable end of a difficult question. He would always react in the same way, by answering politely and then continuing to stare at his interlocutor while he scribbled away in his notebook. When said interlocutor looked up, it was *his* turn to feel uncomfortable. Imagine how it must have been for opposition hookers in the heat of battle! I was friendly

with his predecessor in the New Zealand front row, Andy
Dalton, and knew how fiercely the Test-hardened campaigner
from the Counties provincial side fought to see off the young
pretender from Auckland. Andy had been one of the most
successful skippers in All Black history, winning 15 of his 17
internationals in charge, but Fitzy forced his way past him,
played a major role in his country's victory at the inaugural
World Cup in 1987 and then developed into one of the truly
great players of this or any other age. There was so much to
admire about his rugby: above all, a competitive streak the
width of the Tasman. He must have been a hell of a player
if a hooker as magnificent as Peter Wheeler of England comes
up short.

3 ROBERT PAPAREMBORDE (FRANCE)

I am deeply thankful for many of the things rugby has given
me – and equally grateful for one of the things it denied me:
that is to say, the opportunity to share a pitch with the most
ferocious, downright scary French pack ever pieced together
in pursuit of the sport's glittering prizes. There was nothing
very glittery about Gérard Cholley, nicknamed the 'Master
of Menace' – or, as the Hawick lock Ian Barnes famously
described him, 'Moby Dick in a goldfish bowl'. The same
went for Alain Paco and Jean-François Imbernon and the
terrifying Michel Palmié. These people made the back-row
trio of Jean-Pierre Rives, Jean-Claude Skrela and Jean-Pierre
Bastiat look like horizontal pacifists, even though they alone

had normal people heading for the hills. Rives, in particular, was a sensational player, but it may well be that Robert Paparemborde, the tight-head prop from the Basque country, was the pick of the bunch. Fran Cotton, no mean prop himself, described him as 'not excitable like some of his colleagues, just incredibly hard.' That makes it worse somehow, as does the fact that Paparemborde was a judo black belt. I missed facing him by about five years. Which was far too close for comfort.

4 MARTIN JOHNSON (ENGLAND)

England's captain supreme was no namby-pamby pushover either, but top grade rugby was slightly less of a Wild West barroom brawl in the 1990s than it had been 20 years earlier. Not that Johnno steered clear of trouble all the time: there were controversies and disciplinary hearings and suspensions aplenty. But he was also an engine-room lock for the professional era before the professional era began – a genuine tight forward, rather than a multi-tasking skills machine like John Eales of Australia, but completely on top of his brief. Andy Robinson, the forwards coach when England won the world title in 2003 under Johnno's leadership, did not always find it easy to praise Leicester forwards to the high heavens: after all, he had played his rugby for Bath, the Tigers' arch-rivals. But Andy placed the great skipper in a category of his own, commenting: 'With most players, you hope and pray they'll perform at 90 per cent capacity minimum on the big occasion. With Martin, 90 per cent is the guaranteed starting point.' He was a mighty scrummager, ultra-reliable at the line-out, extremely fit and utterly ruthless. The tougher the going, the better he played. It takes someone special to keep Willie John McBride out of this line-up, but I believe I have the right man.

5 VICTOR MATFIELD (SOUTH AFRICA)

I have already mentioned the eye-wateringly gifted Eales, whose mastery of the second-row skills was only half the story. (Among other things, he could pass and make cover tackles and kick goals.) I must also include my old friend Gordon Brown in the list of contenders, not to mention the undeniably great Colin Meads of New Zealand: a lock who bestrode the rugby world in the 1960s. But Victor Matfield was probably the finest line-out forward I ever clapped eyes on – his performance in this department against England on World Cup final night in Paris in 2007 was perfection itself – and when you consider his length of service in the Springbok cause, it is hard to imagine matching him. He played for a decade in the white heat of the South African pack, making his debut in 2001 and announcing his retirement after the 2011 World Cup campaign in New Zealand. Three years later, he was back for another tilt at the big prizes. In all, he won 127 caps – more than any Springbok, forward or back. If New Zealand has a rich history in the open-side flanker position. France once cornered the market in great centres and Wales reaped the benefit of that No.10 factory buried deep in the earth, South Africans have always prided themselves on producing world-class locks, from Salty du Rand and Frik du Preez back in the day to Bakkies Botha and Eben Etzebeth in the 21st century. Matfield stood taller than anyone in that grand tradition.

6 LAWRENCE DALLAGLIO (ENGLAND)

One of the two or three most influential English players in the history of the professional game – I have no hesitation in making that claim – 'Lol' did it all. He was a World Cup winner, a Lions series winner, a Heineken Cup winner, a Premiership winner, a World Sevens winner. At various points in his garlanded career, he was among the best performers in all three back-row positions. Indeed, I would argue that in his pomp, he seemed to be playing all three roles simultaneously. Had he been a New Zealander, he would have won scores of All Black caps. Had he been an Australian in Sydney on that night of nights in 2003, it is perfectly possible that the Webb Ellis Cup would have stayed in the southern hemisphere. Along with Jonny Wilkinson, he spent years as the most visible presence in British rugby. He survived chronic injury setbacks, tabloid newspaper stings and family tragedy. As a young man – he was little more than a kid in sporting terms – he rescued Wasps from the worst ravages of the club rugby revolution in the mid-1990s and stayed with them for the duration. He was a world-beater and a one-club man, a spirit as generous and gregarious as he was driven. Old-time romantics like Tony O'Reilly, Cliff Morgan and Clem Thomas would have recognised him as one of their own. There is more – so much more – to say about Lawrence Dallaglio, but you get the picture. A remarkable human being, in every respect.

7 RICHIE MCCAW (NEW ZEALAND)

Here's a question for anyone picking the best of the best in the All Black open-side flanker department (which basically means the best of the best whatever the nation). Are you a Michael Jones man, or a Graham Mourie man? A Josh Kronfeld man or a Waka Nathan man? It depends on your age, as much as anything, so the only solution is to choose a breakaway for all the ages: a player with two world titles to his name, who led his country on both of those occasions; a captain who, like Sean Fitzpatrick before him, understood how to referee a game while playing it. No player on the field stands more chance of being penalised than the No.7, given the central nature of his role at the tackle area, which just happens to be the most spectacularly over-legislated area of the sport. Richie McCaw saw half a dozen changes to the breakdown laws, at the very least, over the course of a 14-year Test career and was quicker than anyone in reacting to each and every one of them. If you're keen on statistics, feast your eyes on the following numbers: he played 148 Tests, losing just 15 and drawing two, and led his country in 110 of them.

On three occasions, he was voted World Rugby Player of the Year. In Tri-Nations and Rugby Championship tournaments, he won 10 titles in 13 attempts. With Canterbury, his provincial side, he won six domestic titles; with Crusaders, his Super Rugby franchise, he triumphed on four occasions. One other thing: he was, and remains, the most humble of great sportsmen. End of argument, I think.

8 SERGIO PARISSE (ITALY)

There is a back-row forward out there who wins next to nothing, despite being every bit as passionate and driven and extravagantly gifted as those who hoover up titles and honours with McCaw-like regularity. It is for this reason, among others, that I include Sergio Parisse in my ultimate team. If Lawrence Dallaglio would have won fistfuls of caps for any rugby nation under the sun, the same goes for a No.8 who has now, through an accident of nationality (he was born in Argentina to Italian parents and elected to play his rugby for the Azzurri), finished on the losing side in more than 100 Tests. How painful a milestone is that? How brutally unfair is it on one of the genuinely great forwards of our era? Under normal circumstances, I would probably have selected Mervyn Davies of Wales or Brian Lochore of New Zealand in the middle of my back row. I could have gone for Dallaglio and chosen someone else on the blind-side flank. I could have considered another All Black in Kieran Read, or the politically astute Morne du Plessis of South Africa. But Parisse was blessed with skills not even dreamed of by the common herd, and there can be no questioning his resilience – physical, mental, emotional. To stand out as he has done in defeat after defeat, in a game as exhausting and debilitating as international union, is indescribably difficult. It's such a hard, hard thing to do. In a perfect world, rugby would have given him his just reward. He'll just have to make do with being picked in the perfect side.

So there we have it: two teams packed with everything any rugby follower could wish to see, on the field and off it. If only I could have watched them play – and joined them in the bar at 'no side'. There are no regrets, though. It's only a game. A good game. The best of games.

DEBTS OF
GRATITUDE

TOP of my list of people to thank is Bill McLaren, who was, and remains still, the greatest rugby commentator of all time. I was privileged to worship at the altar of his genius. He helped me cross the threshold of Broadcasting House to join the BBC in 1971 and kept an eye on me for the next 30 years. I shared three World Cup Final commentaries with Bill in 1991, 1995 and 1999. He had a wonderful, natural way with words and was a joy to work alongside. Cliff Morgan was another supreme rugby commentator on both radio and television and was a tremendous mentor to me in my fledgling days.

In the 1970s I started doing commentaries with my great friend and fellow Scotland international Chris Rea. We had eight great years together before Chris moved to print journalism. Peter West, accomplished as a commentator on both rugby and cricket, also contributed regularly in those early days. I then enjoyed eight memorable years of co-commentating with Alastair Hignell, covering all the big matches at home and Lions tours and World Cups abroad. Three others made very significant contributions at this time: Miles Harrison, David Parry-Jones and Ian Carter. Alastair Eykyn became my penultimate co-commentator and we shared eight thoroughly enjoyable years together, covering every Six Nations Championship, two World Cups and a Lions tour. Since January 2016, Chris Jones has filled the role. I formed a really good partnership with Chris very quickly and he has become a really top broadcaster. And one curious footnote from the old days: for 20 years, whenever Ireland played England in Dublin, I shared a tiny commentary box with Radio Ulster commentator Jim Neilly – great company over a wild weekend in Dublin.

Over the years I have enjoyed the luxury of sharing the commentary box with many ex-internationals, who added pertinent comments as summarisers. These former players know the game inside out and make a massive contribution to the commentary. They include, for England: Gareth Chilcott, Rob Andrew, Matt Dawson, Paul Grayson, Brian Moore and Jeremy Guscott; for Ireland: Fergus Slattery, Hugo MacNeill and Denis Hickie; for Scotland: Andy Irvine, Gavin Hastings and Andy Nicol; for Wales: Barry John, Phil Bennett and Robert Jones.

Good rugby producers are like gold dust and I have been truly blessed with a long list of quite outstanding colleagues in this role. Already in the book I have waxed lyrical about Ed Marriage: his 17 years as my producer up to 2015 were very special. But I have been very privileged throughout my career. Early on, I was very fortunate to have Peter Baxter (the *Test Match Special* mastermind) as my producer – like Ed he was calm, well organised, in complete control and full of good ideas. The next incumbent was Gordon Turnbull, who was out of the very top drawer of producers. I loved every minute of working with him. My good fortune continued with Charles Runcie taking over and we had a really good working relationship. Following the World Cup in 1987 he not only meticulously organised the next four Five Nations Championships in a row, he produced a real rabbit out of the hat when he took the credit for arranging a dramatic Scotland try by Tony Stanger against England at Murrayfield in 1990, to give Scotland a second Grand Slam in six years and only the third Slam in Scotland's history. Well done, Charles! Nick Mullins and Sonja McLaughlan looked after me in the mid-1990s before changing tack completely to become broadcasters, where both are thriving. To all these producers and also to the five or six producers who did only one or two years with me, I thank you.

I would also like to pay tribute to two long-serving and long-suffering colleagues: Shilpa Patel (PA extraordinaire) and Brian Mack (outside broadcast supremo). Rugby on 5 Live now has a new producer in charge: Louise Gwilliam (grand-daughter of the former Welsh Grand Slam-winning captain John Gwilliam). With her and Chris Jones, the future of the sport on 5 Live is gold-plated.

I would like to finish my BBC acknowledgements by

profusely thanking two people of extra importance – the BBC rugby editors. Alison Rusted was brilliant to work with because all she wanted was for the 'Rugby Team' to be the very best it could ever be. The exact same tribute also applies to Mike Carr, who has always been completely behind the team and fighting our corner every day. If a cloud ever appeared, Mike has always been a very reassuring presence.

And finally I come to Chris Hewett, top rugby journalist and colleague, who has given me such invaluable help with this book. Almost immediately after the announcement of my retirement I had a phone call from old friend and veteran publisher Roddy Bloomfield, for whom I had happily written several books over the years. Roddy asked if I would write up the story of my career for publication in the autumn of 2018, i.e. in nine months from that time. He cannily and rather cheekily suggested that I might see if Chris Hewett would act as a co-author to get the best result and ensure that I kept to what would have to be a tight schedule! Subsequently Chris combed through 47 massive transcripts, persisted relentlessly in keeping me focused, and produced a book that I hope will prove to be good fun for its readers. I really do owe him a huge debt of gratitude.

The game of rugby is 100 per cent a team game. So too, is the world of rugby commentary at the BBC. I have enjoyed a great rapport with every commentator and every expert summariser and every producer I've had the good fortune of working with throughout my career. We have formed and reformed over nearly half a century of very special broad-casting teams. I shall without doubt miss the BBC rugby team enormously as I look to the future. But as I look back, I have relished every minute of being a part of it.

PHOTOGRAPHIC ACKNOWLEDGEMENTS

The author and publisher would like to thank the following for permission to reproduce photographs:

Colorsport, David Munden/Popperfoto/Getty Images, Colorsport/Kieran Galvin, Colorsport/Colin Elsey, Allsport UK /Allsport, Central Press/Hulton Archive/Getty Images, Russell Cheyne/Allsport, JEAN-PIERRE MULLER/AFP/ Getty Images, Simon Bruty/Getty Images, Colorsport/ Andrew Cowie, Chris Ware/Keystone/Getty Images, JIM WATSON/AFP/Getty Images, KIRSTY WIGGLES-WORTH/AFP/Getty Images, Colorsport / Matthew Lewis, Jonathon Wood/Getty Images, David Rogers/Getty Images, John Ireland/LennardAssociates, KAZUHIRO NOGI/AFP/ Getty Images, Ben Radford/Corbis via Getty Images, David Rogers – RFU/The RFU Collection via Getty Images.

Other photographs from private collections.

Every reasonable effort has been made to trace the copyright holders, but if there are any errors or omissions, Hodder & Stoughton will be pleased to insert the appropriate acknowledgement in any subsequent printings or editions.

INDEX

'IR' in the index indicates Ian Robertson